Buildings for Mission

This immensely practical, clear and thorough guide, written by acknowledged experts, will be an invaluable aid to anyone who cares about church buildings, realizes their potential for mission and wants to release it. Church buildings can be an enormous asset for the gospel: this book will help anyone who reads it ensure that they are.
The Rt Revd Dr John Inge
Bishop of Worcester, Lead Bishop for Cathedrals and Church Buildings

Any priest or parish stumped by the enormity and complexity of the task of making the most of our inherited buildings need look no further. This book is a superb tool for helping us see with fresh eyes the gift of landmark buildings in key locations, and enabling us to realise their full potential. It supplies the detailed know-how on every aspect of the buildings agenda to inform and direct our energies to maximum effect for the mission of the kingdom of God.
The Very Revd Richard Giles
Author of *Re-Pitching the Tent* and former Dean of Philadelphia Cathedral

With admirable lightness of touch, the authors provide guidance on the procedural and technical issues of church care. This book is a must-have for all involved in caring for churches.
Henry Russell OBE
Member of the Church Buildings Council

It is comprehensive, so encouraging and full of practical advice. A copy should be given to all vicars, churchwardens and PCC members.
Kristina Williamson
Church Buildings Officer and Secretary to Lichfield DAC

Buildings for Mission

Nigel Walter and Andrew Mottram

CANTERBURY PRESS

Norwich

© Nigel Walter and Andrew Mottram

First published in 2015 by the Canterbury Press Norwich
Editorial office
3rd Floor, Invicta House,
108–114 Golden Lane,
London EC1Y 0TG, UK

Canterbury Press is an imprint of Hymns Ancient & Modern Ltd
(a registered charity)
13A Hellesdon Park Road, Norwich,
Norfolk NR6 5DR, UK
www.canterburypress.co.uk

Scripture quotations are from the New Revised Standard Version of
the Bible, Anglicized Edition, copyright © 1989, 1995 by the Division
of Christian Education of the National Council of the Churches of
Christ in the USA. Used by permission. All rights reserved.

British Library Cataloguing in Publication data

A catalogue record for this book is available
from the British Library

978 1 84825 760 3

Typeset by Regent Typesetting
Printed and bound in Great Britain by
Ashford Colour Press

Contents

Acknowledgements   ix

List of abbreviations   x

Welcome!   xi

Section A   Context

A1   Here We Stand   3

A2   Church Buildings – the Essentials   7

A3   Whose Building is it Anyway?   12

A4   Specially for Clergy   15

A5   Buildings at Risk   21

A6   'Buildings, Blooming Buildings'   26

A7   Viable and Sustainable Churches   31

A8   The Church in Numbers   36

A9   ABC of Church Structures   40

A10 What Can We Do About It?   45

Section B   Practicalities

B1   What Sort of Old?   51

B2   Rubble Sandwiches – Traditional Wall Construction   55

B3   Dry Hat and Boots   60

B4   Damp and Moisture Control   66

B5   The Wonderful World of Seating   69

B6   Fonts and Baptistries   76

B7   Multimedia   80

CONTENTS

B8 Heating Basics   85
B9 Energy Efficiency   92
B10 New Heating Systems   97
B11 Lighting – Strategies and Issues   103
B12 Routes for Services   111
B13 Kitchens and WCs – the Essentials   117
B14 Bats   123
B15 Timber Decay   128
B16 Maintenance   132
B17 Asset Management Plans   137
B18 The Church-Carer's Calendar   143
B19 Accessibility   149
B20 Health and Safety – General   152
B21 Health and Safety for Building Projects   159
B22 Mr FixIt or Mr Bodgelt   165

Section C   Principles

C1 Future Survival   171
C2 Sacred Place, Holy Ground   174
C3 Working with Places of Worship   178
C4 The Moment of Truth   183
C5 Serving People – Four Modes of Operation   186
C6 Conservation   193
C7 Open, Welcoming and Accepting   199
C8 Interpretation   206
C9 God and Community   211

Section D   Process

D1	Making Changes	217
D2	How to Write a Statement of Significance	223
D3	Public Engagement	230
D4	Consensus Building – Some Resources	237
D5	Needs Analysis	243
D6	How to Write a Statement of Needs	246
D7	How to Organize Yourselves	250
D8	Ecclesiastical Exemption	253
D9	They Think It's All Over …	261
D10	Friends' Groups	265
D11	Fundraising	270

Section E   Projects

E1	Practical Examples	279
E2	Re-orderings	281
E3	Extensions	286
E4	Community Use	291
E5	Kitchens and WCs	295
E6	New Churches	299

Section F   And Finally …

F1	Afterword – Our Heritage	307
F2	Organizations and Contacts	309
F3	Bibliography	310

Section G   Appendix

G1	Healthcheck	315
G2	Pizzamat	320
G3	Church Buildings Audit	322
Index		330

Acknowledgements

This handbook is the result of conversations with many individuals and congregations; we gratefully acknowledge your input, without which this would not have happened. It is possible that you will recognize aspects of the handbook or think you have come across some of this elsewhere. Neither of us can claim this is all new and completely original. What the handbook aims to do is bring the knowledge, experience and advice of people who have been working with church buildings into one volume where hopefully you can find what you need.

This book would not have come to fruition without the help of our wives and wider families; we are profoundly grateful to you for having travelled with us on what has proved to be an exciting but lengthy journey.

If you find there are aspects of running church buildings that are not answered in the handbook or it fails to point you in the right direction to get the help you need, please email us or join the discussion blog at www.churchbuildingprojects.co.uk.

Nigel Walter and Andrew Mottram
nw@archangelic.co.uk
andrew.mottram@btinternet.com

List of Abbreviations

AABC	(Register of) Architects Accredited in Building Conservation
APCM	Annual Parochial Church Meeting
CA	Conservation Architect
CBC	Church Buildings Council
DAC	Diocesan Advisory Committee
DCC	District Church Council
DBF	Diocesan Board of Finance
EASA	Ecclesiastical Architects and Surveyors Association
EH	English Heritage
FiM	Faith in Maintenance
FG	Friends' Group
HE	Historic England
HLF	Heritage Lottery Fund
IHBC	Institute of Historic Building Conservation
NCT	National Churches Trust
OPC	Ordinary Portland Cement
PCC	Parochial Church Council
QIR	Quinquennial Inspection Report
RIAS	Royal Incorporation of Architects in Scotland
RIBA	Royal Institute of British Architects
RICS	Royal Institution of Chartered Surveyors
SCA	Specialist Conservation Architect
SPAB	Society for the Protection of Ancient Buildings

Welcome!

Where we are

In our church life there is a constant tension between buildings and mission. It is sometimes said that we have too many buildings: in the Church of England we spend some £160 million annually on repairs, maintenance and improving old buildings, plus providing some new ones.[1] Closing churches is considered a sign of failure, whereas a more pragmatic response may be to recognize the need for retrenchment. Meanwhile many church communities are faced with a choice of whether to fix the building or to pay the Parish Share. We can all joke about the need for a diocesan arsonist but nobody wants to close their own church.

Our aim with this handbook is to offer hope, encouragement and support in the everyday practicalities of running a church building, as well as advice on how to get through the tensions and difficulties that often arise. A vicar recently confided, 'Five years ago I was determined not to get sidetracked by buildings, but I have discovered in this rural group of parishes that if you don't get this bit right, you can't do anything.'

Where to begin?

This handbook grew in large part from the daily problems congregations face with their buildings. In our experience of talking with them, the same issues come up again and again and are often easily addressed with some basic information and guidance. Our purpose therefore is to make your life easier by providing a first point of reference for pretty much anything related to the use, care and change of church buildings. The aim is to make this information available to the broadest audience possible, and we have therefore tried to be informal and non-technical in the language used.

This book should equip all Christian churches to make their buildings better serve their mission. Many of the examples relate to the Church of England, as this forms the bulk of our professional experience, but the information and principles will work in many other settings. A great number of church buildings in the UK, and particularly historical ones, are Anglican. Consequently it is the Church of England that has the bulk of the buildings-related problems (and also opportunities, but more of that later). For these reasons alone this handbook follows the Anglican terminology of vicars, Parochial Church Councils (PCCs), Diocesan Advisory Committees (DACs) and so on, in the interests of keeping the text readable. However, most of the same issues are faced across the spectrum of churches in the UK, and we hope that churches of other traditions will find this material worthwhile; we would ask you to bear with us and to translate for your own situation where relevant.

We see this handbook as a companion to *Re-Pitching the Tent* by Richard Giles.[2] First published in 1996, this is still – it is now in its third edition – the definitive guide to re-ordering church buildings, and contains a wealth of thought-provoking material and useful information to help churches shape their buildings for worship.

'C' is for Church

Confusingly, the English word 'church' has more than one meaning – it can equally well be used to refer to the people of God, or to the building where we meet. Some denominations deal with this by using another word than 'church' when referring to the building, e.g. 'chapel' or 'meeting house'. We use 'church' for buildings or individual congregations, and keep the word 'Church' to refer to the title of a denomination or to the whole people of God gathered across time and space.

Frustrating as this double usage may be, it is not a defect of the English language, but more a signal of the relevance and importance that buildings have for the life of the gathered people of God; it speaks of a deep-rooted connection with place, which we often fail to see, to our detriment and peril.

Structure

The handbook is divided into five main sections. Each section (and indeed each chapter) is intended to stand on its own, allowing you to jump into the book at any point in response to a specific query. We hope in this way that the book will be an ongoing reference and source of information.

What you will not find in this book is a specific section on the theology of buildings. This is deliberate, since it is our view that theology belongs in every-day life, and so we have tried to weave it through the whole. The same goes for our approach to mission. Together they are the leaven worked through the whole, though if either of these is your particular interest then you may like to start with Section C.

The sections are:

Section A: Context Aims to give you a map of the overall landscape, by covering some of the historical, political and church background to our buildings; after browsing the book for an answer to a specific problem, come back here for the overview.

Section B: Practicalities How historic buildings are put together, and therefore some pointers as to how to look after them.

Section C: Principles How buildings might fit with your theology, and therefore become a partner rather than an obstacle to your ministry.

Section D: Process An introduction to what you need to know about building projects, including how to organize yourself as a client, some resources for community engagement, what permissions you need and so on.

Section E: Projects Some practical examples of completed projects, some of which we have been involved with directly, others not at all, but which have been chosen to illustrate particular points; more on these examples, plus some others, can be found at www.churchbuildingprojects.co.uk/publications.

Section F: And Finally Some concluding thoughts, and some other sources of relevant information.

Health warning

A resource such as this cannot hope to provide the last word on the subject; all church buildings vary, and there is no substitute for an informed discussion with your church architect or other advisor. It is the 'informed' bit that this handbook seeks to address – we see its usefulness to lie in equipping non-professional clergy and laity with sufficient information to understand the buildings-related issues they face. In this way you will be able to engage on a more equal basis with buildings professionals and others, make better decisions and therefore be freed to make better use of your building to further your ministry.

This handbook also does not attempt to address building a new church – this is an important area, but one with specific issues that are not encountered by the great majority of churches. If you are building a new church then we hope you will find lots that is of relevance – and we have included some examples in Chapter E6 – but you should know this is not our primary focus.

Notes

1 See www.churchofengland.org/about-us/funding.aspx#how.
2 Richard Giles, *Re-Pitching the Tent: The Definitive Guide to Re-Ordering Your Church*, 3rd edn, Norwich: Canterbury Press, 2004.

Section A   Context

A1

Here We Stand

With a physical presence in (almost) every settlement across the length and breadth of the country, the Church is in an extraordinarily privileged position. There are of course many other organizations that have a national 'network' of buildings, such as banks, large supermarket chains and the Post Office (which, interestingly, sees value in boasting that 'every one of our branches is at the heart of its community'). English Heritage looks after 400 historic sites, Historic Scotland over 300 and Cadw (Wales) 125; meanwhile the National Trust protects over 350 historic houses, not forgetting 28 castles and 60 pubs.

Yet local churches far outnumber all these national networks. The Church of England alone has more than 16,000 buildings, and there are of course many other churches and church buildings. Following the retail analogy, the Church can be said to have 'a shop on every corner'. Looking at this 'network' through the eyes of a retailer, one would conclude that for 'market penetration' we are unbeatable.

The Church, of course, is not a retail organization, and (for both better or worse) it does not think like one. The Normans modified the previous 'minster-parish' system and made the parish the organizing unit of an administrative mechanism that was principally about the rule of the king and his ability to raise taxes (the bishops only gaining authority over church buildings with the first faculties in the 1120s). The planning and co-ordination that such a system implies is now almost entirely absent, the individual parish now enjoying a huge degree of autonomy from diocesan and national structures. This makes it almost impossible to 'shape the network', as any commercial organization would seek to do. Recent years have seen the long-term viability of the parish system called into question, but even if we were to implement substantial changes in our structures (the chances of which seem, to say the least, remote), the physical footprint of the Church of England would be largely unchanged, since three-quarters of the 16,000 Anglican churches are listed and cannot easily be demolished or sold off. Not only will they remain standing there, they will unavoidably remain our responsibility.

Reimagining

One of our chief purposes in writing this book is to encourage churches (and particularly the Church of England) to rethink their approach to their buildings, to see them as more an opportunity than a threat, more a springboard than a millstone. Our basic conviction is that this geographic spread represents a huge opportunity for mission. With this physical presence in every community, the Church is woven into the cultural fabric of the country. This is a unique privilege, and offers us a wide range of opportunities for hospitality and mission. Those opportunities are there, but it is down to us to take them.

Essential to seeing our church buildings more positively is a cultural reimagining on the part of the Church – What do we think a church building is, whose is it and, crucially, what activities are appropriate to take place in it? Put another way, *What is it good for?* Given that the Anglican Church is tasked with the care/cure of the whole of our communities, our Church is fundamentally outward-looking in its structure (discuss!). This comes with the implication that the wider communities within which our buildings stand have a legitimate sense of ownership over these buildings, which are just as much 'theirs' as 'ours'.

A tale of two cities

In medieval times the parish church was in most cases the only community building in a settlement, which had a number of consequences. There was a much broader range of activity taking place within these buildings than we would now imagine appropriate, and as a result a much broader sense of ownership of the building and in particular the nave. This of course was in an age in which the Church was central to culture in a way that, following the Enlightenment, it can never be again. Perhaps the most profound difference, however, is in the integration of the worshipping community and the wider community within a single space.

Following the Reformation a formal division developed between these two forms of community. The physical manifestation of this was the progressive emptying out of the 'untidiness' of the wider community activity from the churches into separate village/church halls, with the

aim of making the churches more 'sacred' – most notably in the nineteenth century. While, in our opinion, this was never a good idea theologically, it was for a time sustainable on the basis that enough of the population considered church attendance to be important. Now, however, Victorian chickens are coming home to roost. The implication of the expulsion of the wider community activity was also to remove the human energy from our church buildings. What was once the community hub has become the 'private members' religious club'. In the minds of the wider community

Danger of Falling

the church building has 'migrated' from the centre of the community to its periphery, and the energy in the community is now to be found at the village hall, the school gate or wherever. Of course, the longer a 'split community' model is maintained the further the building is pushed to the periphery. If pushed far enough, in the end it falls off the edge – the worshipping community will die out and the church will close.

What can possibly go wrong?

In an age in which the dominant cultural understanding is that church attendance is a leisure choice (something you do on a Sunday morning instead of football or the car boot sale), the public perception of the local church is often of a few elderly people managing decline in the hope that the building will still be open when it comes to the time for their funeral. While this may perhaps be true in some cases, we also know that the picture is much more nuanced, with plenty of signs of hope amid the despair. Where churches do close, it often follows a familiar pattern of being presented with a large repair bill for the building (following many years of lack of maintenance), and after the church community has ceased to face outwards and instead has turned in on itself. This will often be accompanied by a strong sense of belonging, but in the form of an embattled exclusivity. Both parts of this pattern are forms of withdrawal – the first from the building/the physical; the second from the communal/relational – and both flow directly from the split view of community discussed above. It is therefore in our view of community, with questions of who we as the Church are, what we're for or what business we're in, that a brighter future can be imagined.

At root this is a question of our 'horizon of expectation'. The best that modernity can offer is an idea of mechanical progress, for which the slogan would be 'Things can only get better'. Progress, at least in the West, now has a lot less credibility than it did in the nineteenth and most of the twentieth centuries. There is a good argument to say that entertainment has become such a dominant part of Western culture precisely because we cannot face the future. One reaction is to seek solace in the past, but then 'Nostalgia ain't what it used to be'. Communities die when they 'back into' the future rather than face it assertively. This is a loss of hope; that is, a loss of any positive sense of what the future might be – 'We're all doomed, doomed', to quote Private Fraser of *Dad's Army*. The irony of course is that it is precisely a sense of hope that the Church should be able to offer the wider community. Our role in an age of disenchantment is to have the confidence to stand outside the wider culture and articulate that hope – a hope of flourishing individuals in healthy communities in communion with our triune God.

We have written this book because we are profoundly optimistic about the future of the Church. Furthermore we are convinced that our church buildings, and particularly our historic ones, are part of the solution and not part of the problem. But for this brighter future to become a reality it is essential that we rethink our model of community, replacing a 'split community' view with an interwoven or intermingled view that would be more recognizable to a medieval mind. Whatever the age of your church building, this is an invitation to explore a 'new medievalism'.

A2

Church Buildings – the Essentials

Church buildings are rarely easy. More typically they require constant management, and if you let them get out of hand they can make life very difficult for you. This chapter provides a brief guide of the key administrative things you need to look out for.

Church building, churchyard and other property records

- **Terrier and Inventory** Now often called the Church Property Register, this is an essential document to keep up to date. Make sure there is an accurate record, in both text and plans, of the various land, property and buildings together with their boundaries that are held by the church. Seriously, these items are really important in helping you and your successors look after the property assets for which the vicar, churchwardens and PCC are responsible. Ignore them at your peril!
- **Ownership** Clarify which part of the church body holds which parts of the property (e.g. PCC, Diocesan Board of Finance, a separate church-affiliated trust etc.).
- **Log Book** This is the record of maintenance, repairs, new works and improvements that have been undertaken. It needs to be kept up to date. Entries are best made when the work is done rather than when someone remembers.
- **Filing** File the records in a place, known to the incumbent, churchwardens and PCC, where they cannot get mislaid, lost or disposed of.
- **Records** Keep the records up to date and make sure they are available for inspection at the Annual Parochial Church Meeting (APCM).

Neighbours and access

- Know who your neighbours are – identify the type of properties that have boundaries with the church property.
- Make sure the neighbours are not using church property without proper consent.
- Keep an eye out for planning notices relevant to either the church property or that of your neighbours. If an immediate neighbour makes a planning application, a notice should be sent to the church. However, often the document will be posted to the church building (which often has no letter box) and may not get seen or considered by the church community within the 21-day consultation period.
- If there are any gates from the public highway to any of the church properties, lock them shut for at least 24 hours once a year – otherwise it could be claimed that a public right of way has been established. Although diocesan Chancellors have made a clear ruling that a new right of way cannot be established over a consecrated churchyard, this will have passed most people by and it is sensible to avoid any dispute.

Leases, hirers and users

- **Leases** involve an agreement between a tenant and a landlord. A lease comes with rights and responsibilities on both sides – for example, it should define who is to maintain the building, when the rent is reviewed, whether there are break clauses for either party and so on. So if the church is either a landlord or a tenant, make sure you know the terms of the lease – it can have significant financial implications. Be prepared to pay for legal advice. Under the PCC Powers Measure, no PCC can enter into a rental agreement with a term longer than 12 months and so it is unlikely the incumbent, churchwardens or PCC will hold any leases without the involvement of the diocesan authorities. So if you have a tenant who is on any kind of lease or agreement it is essential that you consult the Diocesan Secretary and all parties are confident that there are proper arrangements in place that are approved by the Diocesan Trustees.
- **Hirers** pay a fee to use a building or property. The fee provides the basis of a contract for which, again, there are obligations on both parties. It is important to have a contract that spells out clearly and comprehensively the terms and conditions of hire. The church community need to know their obligations to their hirers, which might include ensuring the premises are safe and fit for purpose, as well as being warm, clean and tidy, and that hirers can enjoy use of the building or room without disturbance by others.

- **Users** make use of a space by consent, sometimes with, sometimes without payment. There are no formal obligations on either party and neither is there a formal contract, but if it came to a dispute it could be argued there is an implied contract. Allowing individuals or organizations to use property on a regular basis without a written agreement is irresponsible.

Surplus and profit

Like it or not, a church is a financial organization, and needs to think like one. In particular, churches need to understand that surplus and profit are not the same thing. A **surplus** is achieved when the revenue has exceeded expenditure in a given accounting period. By contrast, a **profit** is the remaining sum that is available for dispersal in a given accounting period once all the maintenance, repairs and improvements have been completed and paid for and all other debts and liabilities have been settled.

Given the condition of our church property it is very unlikely that any of it operates at a profit. Some churches may operate with a small surplus but often this is only because they are not attending to the maintenance of their buildings.

The surplus should be set aside and used to pay for future maintenance, repair and improvement of the property. It is irresponsible to use the surplus generated by a building to pay the Parish Share or other church operational costs; these require separate provision.

Church buildings need people to survive

Regular worshippers, volunteers, supporters and visitors are essential to the life (and therefore the future) of any church building; without people animating the building it is nothing more than a pile of brick or stone, however elegant or historic it may be.

People walking past or passing through the building are more of a benefit than a risk. It is the isolated and hidden build-

st rubble's

ings that suffer more problems of vandalism and theft. People are like oxygen – to lock up a church building is like asking it to hold its breath. So do your best to get people around, through, past and into your church site and building.

Understand how old buildings work

Old buildings are different from modern ones. The methods and the materials used in their construction are different from modern buildings, and understanding that principle is essential to discharging your responsibilities to care for the building.

We deal with some of these distinctions in Section C. The Society for the Protection of Ancient Buildings (SPAB) website has good technical information, some of it aimed specifically at churches.[1] The Church Buildings Council, part of the Church of England's central administration and support base at Church House in Westminster, has a huge and extensive (if sometimes labyrinthine) website full of helpful advice specifically for churches, together with examples of good practice. It is called ChurchCare, and is well worth exploring.[2]

Church architects

Different denominations work in different ways, but all Anglican churches should have a church architect or surveyor appointed from a Diocesan Advisory Committee approved list. Your church architect carries out the five-yearly Quinquennial Inspection (QI) of the building; you are not obliged to use the same architect for project work, though it is only fair at least to include them in the selection process.

If your church is listed your architect/surveyor should also be conservation accredited. There are now two schemes of conservation accreditation for architects in England and Wales, one organized by the Register of Architects Accredited in Building Conservation (AABC), the other by the Royal Institute of British Architects (RIBA). This latter scheme has two levels of accreditation: Specialist Conservation Architect (SCA) for those deemed able to work on Grade 1 and 2* listed buildings, and Conservation Architect (CA) for those able to work on buildings listed Grade 2 (see Chapter A8 for an explanation of the listing grades). From a church's point of view there is nothing to choose between someone with AABC after their name and someone with SCA.

The Royal Institute of Chartered Surveyors (RICS) is the professional accreditation body for surveyors, and runs its own conservation accreditation scheme for its members, as does the Royal Incorporation of Architects in Scotland. It should be noted that conservation registration is a requirement for your lead consultant if you plan to bid for Heritage Lottery funds and that, for projects in England, AABC, SCA and CA registrants all satisfy this criterion. Many architects and surveyors involved with churches belong to the Ecclesiastical Architects and Surveyors Association (EASA).

Notes

1 SPAB has some excellent technical information and advice about church buildings, though they can be a bit puritanical about change. Explore www.spabfim.org.uk. Two places to start are the advice notes about understanding the building and its elements. See www.spabfim.org. uk/pages/understanding_buildings.html and www.spabfim.org.uk/pages/building_elements. html.

2 See www.churchcare.co.uk.

A3
Whose Building is it Anyway?

This could get complicated! At the risk of being challenged by ecclesiastical lawyers we are going to keep things simple and provide an overview – if you have specific queries you will need to take detailed advice, and we would suggest you start by talking to your Diocesan Registrar (the ecclesiastical solicitor appointed for the diocese). Nevertheless we hope you will find this simplified introduction helpful.

The key thing to remember is that in English law, property ownership is a big deal. So you need to know who owns the church building, the churchyard and any other property associated with your parish church. The other thing to remember is that the local church is subject to Charity Law, so it is sensible for the trustees to be properly informed.

A complicating factor is that, unlike most property bought and sold over the last few centuries, there are few deeds, conveyances or registration documents for most parish churches and churchyards. This is property that hasn't been bought or sold very often and, prior to the extensive church-building programme of the nineteenth century, most of it came into the 'possession' of the Church of England long before the Land Registry existed.

So when it comes to deciding whose building it is, there is no cut and dried response; nevertheless there are some fundamentals to get right.

The short answer

In a parish, the church building and the churchyard are 'vested' with the incumbent, who holds them on behalf of the parishioners, who are the residents of the ecclesiastical parish.

The incumbent, churchwardens and PCC, acting as charitable trustees on behalf of the parishioners, have the responsibility to look after the property assets and to protect them from loss, depreciation or degradation. The parishioners, meanwhile, have rights of access to the church and the churchyard and to benefit from the services the church provides.

In short it could be said, in terms of moral ownership, that the church building and churchyard 'belong' to the residents of the parish, whether or not they ever darken the doors of your building; the PCC has the job of looking after the property, and it is all held in trust by the incumbent on behalf of the parishioners.

What this means – the long answer

The parish is the base unit of the Church of England. Geographical parishes were introduced to this country following the Norman Conquest in a partnership between the Crown and the Church to 'run' the country.

The concept of the parish came originally from the Roman Empire as a means to administer territory, which was divided up into geographical areas. Each area had a representative of the emperor and a forum for administration and the collecting of taxes, plus the necessary military muscle to impose order and keep the peace.

Ecclesiastical parishes are geographical areas under one pastor. In medieval England, permission to construct a church building and appoint a priest was granted to the local baron or lord by the Crown and the Church. Who owned the church property and benefited from the assets was a long-running and often distracting sideshow in the mission of the Church.

After a series of complex machinations and the passing of much time a working situation has been reached whereby the core property of each parish (i.e. the church building and the churchyard) is not owned by any one individual, institution or corporate body. No person can therefore claim 'this church building is my property' in the way many of us could point to our house and claim it as 'ours'.

The church and churchyard are temporarily, but without any sort of legal conveyance, given to the incumbent while he or she is the vicar or rector of the parish. This temporary holding of the core property is called 'vesting' and the vicar or rector is 'vested' with the property at the service of induction. By contrast, a 'priest in charge' is excluded from being given the property.

But – and it is a big 'but' – this vesting does not mean that the incumbent can claim that the church or churchyard is his or her personal property. Vesting means that the property is held by an individual *on behalf of* others – thus the vicar holds the church and churchyard *on behalf of* the parishioners, and for their benefit.

A local church is a charity whose trustees are the churchwardens (who are elected representatives of the parishioners) and the members of the PCC (who are the elected representatives of the church). With the incumbent they have a duty to look after the property assets, which includes keeping the church insured, maintained and repaired. The trustees carry out these duties and responsibilities on behalf of the parishioners.

The church buildings of the Church of England are therefore most definitely not the private premises of a 'private members' club'. The parish churches of England are a precious communal inheritance. They are markers and makers of sacred space in the townscapes and landscape witnessing to the Christian faith that has shaped and formed us as a nation. The churches hold the stories of the communities they have served through the ages; it is in this sense of being community narratives that our church buildings are 'common property'. This has huge implications for how we relate both to our buildings, and to our communities.

A4
Specially for Clergy

'You can only redeem what you understand'

Buildings and property are integral to the history and development of the Church of England, but also to its ongoing ministry. If you think your ministry as a priest has nothing to do with buildings then you may be in the wrong denomination.

Yet we also know that buildings can be unbearably frustrating, often consuming great quantities of money, time and missional energy. The quote above is from Anthony Russell, a former Bishop of Ely, and has plenty of application to the frustrations of church life in general and the perennial question of buildings in particular – you can only deal well with your building if you have taken the trouble to understand it.

How well do you remember your induction? The following is an extract from a service of induction in the contemporary liturgy for the new rector or vicar of a parish:

This part of the service is only used if the minister is to be made incumbent/team rector/rector/vicar) of the parish/benefice.

The people remain standing while the bishop delivers the Mandate of Induction to the archdeacon, saying

Archdeacon, I have instituted/collated *NN* to ministry in this parish/benefice. I ask you to induct her/him, in the presence of this congregation, and to support her/him in her/his ministry here.

The churchwardens lead the archdeacon and the minister to the door of the church, and the people turn to face the door. The archdeacon lays the hand of the minister on the key or handle of the door, saying

---

By virtue of the authority given me, I induct you into the real, actual and corporeal possession of the parish church[es] of *X*, [*Y and Z*] with all the rights and responsibilities belonging to it/them.

The churchwardens present the key(s) of the church to the minister saying

N, receive these keys in token of the responsibility which we share; and may the Lord preserve your going out and your coming in, now and always.
All   **Amen.**

The Installation

The archdeacon leads the minister to her/his stall in the church, and places her/him in, saying

N, I install you as … of this parish/benefice. Pray for your people, lead them in worship and service, and encourage them in their witness to the Gospel of Jesus

Christ in the power of the Holy Spirit.
The church bell may be rung by the minister.

The 'rights and responsibilities' entailed in your 'real, actual and corporeal possession' of your church are significant. If you are a stipendiary priest serving in a parish with one or more churches, churchyards, halls and other property, this chapter is especially for you – we feel it only fair that we spell out some of those responsibilities. Other readers who wish to understand the 'church property landscape' should also find this chapter informative.

It hasn't always been like this

Before some significant reforms in the early 1970s, it wasn't just the church building and churchyard in which the parish priest had an interest and responsibility. Clergy also had responsibility for:

- **Parsonages**   The residences of rectors and vicars were owned by the rector or vicar as 'benefice property'.

- **Glebe**   The glebe (land, houses or other buildings) were vested in the incumbent for the time being and he was entitled to the rents and profits and liable for the outgoings in respect thereof.[1]
- **Dilapidations**   The buildings of the benefice included all such houses of residence, glebe buildings, walls, fences and other buildings and things as the incumbent was by law or custom bound to maintain in repair.

However, all of this changed in 1972. The glebe land of each parish is now vested with the Diocesan Board of Finance (DBF) and managed by a Glebe Committee. Similarly the rectories and vicarages are vested with the Diocesan Board of Finance and managed by a Parsonages Committee.

Currently the property with which clergy most obviously have a direct connection is the parsonage house in which they live. There is an obligation to keep it in good order but clergy are not expected to repair or improve it. The other property with which clergy have a direct connection are the churches and churchyards of the benefice to which they are licensed. This is vested with the rector or vicar as 'church property' (as opposed to the parsonage, which is 'benefice property') and is maintained by the PCC.

Legal stuff – ignore this at your peril!

The Church of England is, of course, the established Church in England. Like any Church there are certain rules and regulations, agreed by the democratic process of Synod, which govern how we do things. This is known as Canon Law.

Some aspects of Canon Law have legal status as Statute Law (i.e. the same authority and effect as an Act of Parliament). This is the 'Primary' legislation, which is drafted into what is known as a 'Measure', passed by Synod and then approved by Parliament with Royal Assent.

'Secondary' legislation is made under the terms of the Measure and then laid before Parliament as a 'Statutory Instrument', becoming a rule, regulation or order. There is also another form of subordinate internal legislation made by General Synod, which doesn't go before Parliament.

Ecclesiastical courts have jurisdiction over church-related matters, including clergy discipline and alteration of property and churchyards. A faculty is your permission to make alterations to church buildings or their contents, and it is this process that gives the Church of England exemption from normal listed building legislation – see Chapter D8 for more on faculties.[2]

Clergy behaving badly

So as an ordained priest you need to be aware that the rules governing church buildings are a mix of ecclesiastical and civil law, including Listed Building laws, Charity Law, Planning Law and Building Regulations, and the Wildlife Act. Break the ecclesiastical law and you might be deprived of your living or instructed to put things back as they were; break the civil law and you might be fined or go to prison.

But what, you may ask, could possibly go wrong? Well, here are a couple of examples:

- One church moved a font without permission, which resulted in the ecclesiastical court ordering the vicar and churchwarden to put it back at their own expense.
- Another church started building works without the necessary consent in a building known to have bats. This resulted in the vicar and a churchwarden being arrested.

Not bothering to find out about or to follow the rules is irresponsible behaviour. And as we all know, ignorance of the law is no excuse in court. So if you haven't looked at the Canon Law of the Church of England, it might be sensible to make some time to do so!

Canon Law on buildings

> Knowledge of the Canons by the clergy is essential for the right ordering and teaching of the Church of England
>
> *Eric Kemp, former Bishop of Chichester*[3]

Some of the buildings-related highlights within the Canon Law are:

Section C of the Canon law deals with clergy/ministers:

- C11 is all about being given the key and taking possession of property at induction.
- C24.7 requires that the minister and PCC 'shall consult together on matters of general concern and importance to the parish'.

Section F of the Canon law relates to church buildings and the task of the PCC to work with the minister:

- F13 covers repairs and keeping the building in seemly order.
- F17 covers keeping terrier and records (e.g. church Log Book) in accordance with guidance from Synod.

Looking after the church and churchyard is a shared responsibility – shared, that is, between clergy and laity. In practice this means the vicar and churchwardens working together with the PCC; for more on this see Chapter A2 above.

The vicar as 'clerk in holy orders' is expected to know the rules. So Canon Law, The Inspection of Churches Measure (1955) and The Parochial Church Council (Powers) Measure 1956 are the places to start. We bet they didn't teach you this during your theological training!

Legal stuff in summary

- The church building is vested with the incumbent but in another sense it is the property of the residents of the parish.
- The PCC are managing trustees; the custodian trustees are the Diocesan Trustees (often the DBF).
- The PCC (Powers) Measure 1956 limits what a PCC can do regarding owning, leasing and selling property – this includes major repairs, alterations and changes.
- If in doubt, keep the Diocesan Trustees informed, and ask for their consent.

Your key responsibilities:

- Keep the building in seemly order – maintenance, repair and tidiness.
- Keep a record of all property owned or vested with the PCC.
- Keep a record of maintenance and repairs.
- Make proper preparation for the Annual Parochial Church Meeting. At the meeting present annual accounts and reports of all PCC activities and any trusts, subcommittees or associated organizations with which the PCC has a formal relationship.

Look before you leap

When you are applying for a new post as a parish priest, it pays to have a good look round. As well as looking at the vicarage and the community, don't forget to consider buildings; your ministry in that place will at least be framed if not shaped by them. Ask to see:

- **Annual Accounts** for the previous three years.
- **Quinquennial Inspection Reports** for the current period and, if at all possible, the previous QIR. Of the items listed needing work, what have been done, what are outstanding?
- **Log Book** should be current, up to date and accurate.
- **Terrier and Inventory**   (now called the Church Property Register). There is no need to tick the items off against the record but a quick read through should indicate whether or not the PCC know what they have and for what they are responsible.

Don't be frightened to ask for these documents; all are in the public domain and should be presented for inspection at each APCM. Once you have looked at them, what messages do they leave you with? How do they compare with all the other stuff you have seen or have been told about the post? If you can do this exercise before you have any interviews, it will give you plenty of material for well-informed questions.

Notes

1 The slightly quaint language here and in the next bullet point is derived from the *Clergyman's Legal Handbook*, published in 1898.

2 For more on Faculty Jurisdiction, see chapter 7 of Mark Hill, *Ecclesiastical Law*, Oxford: Oxford University Press, 2007, and G. H. Newsom and G. L. Newsom, *Faculty Jurisdiction of the Church of England: The Care of Churches and Churchyards*, 2nd edn, Andover: Sweet & Maxwell, 1993. Neither of these, of course, will include details of more recent changes to the system.

3 The Canons of the Church of England – see www.churchofengland.org/about-us/structure/churchlawlegis/canons.aspx.

A5
Buildings at Risk

'We're all doomed' – or are we?

It's not difficult to find people who are negative about the future of our church buildings; some fear that if we carry on with the way things are, within a couple of generations half of our church buildings will have closed, been converted for other uses or disappeared completely.

Clergy can feel especially exasperated about the buildings because they can seem such a distraction from their vocation, the priestly ministry to which they were ordained. PCC members lament the fact that building issues dominate the agendas of their meetings. Many treasurers feel despondent as there never seems to be enough money to fix the building's issues. Church members complain that getting anything done to the building takes far too long and that there are all kinds of obstacles put in the way of making changes and improvements.

The net result is a negative or at best ambivalent attitude among the majority of congregations to their church buildings – they are viewed as a necessary evil and are ignored as much as possible. Sometimes the building is even blamed for the failure of church life – it is the building that is the problem and it would be better to knock the church down and start again. Consequently many of our church buildings are decaying as a result of both natural forces and the neglect of simple basic preventative maintenance by the people who use or are responsible for them. This is a statement of fact rather than a criticism.

At the same time it is important to acknowledge that there are also church buildings that are loved, cherished and treasured; they are

we're all doomed...

well maintained and consequently dry, safe and spotlessly clean. As a result they are tidy, well-ordered and affirming places that make a positive contribution to the ongo-ing life of the church. Sadly these exemplary buildings are not in the majority, but they offer a positive alternative to the vulnerable position of many church buildings that are steadily moving towards being classified as 'at risk'.

In order to move churches from one category to the other it is essential to under-stand the problem, both in general (part of the point of this book) and in its specific expression in a particular building. Why is this situation happening? What are the factors that put buildings at risk? We need to identify and understand the factors in order to find the solutions. The three core issues to consider are:

1 Decay.
2 Inherent defects, inappropriate repairs and neglect.
3 People.

1   Decay is part of the natural order

Church buildings, particularly historic buildings, are constructed of natural materials that have a finite lifespan. All building materials decay – they will at some point fail and need to be repaired or replaced. Brick and stone decay very slowly but other materials decay at a faster rate and therefore will need replacing more often. Generally most of the structural items of a traditionally constructed church building should last for about 150 years before the natural processes of decay cause either their failure or sufficient problems that some repair work is required. Decorative items might not last as long and some materials, used because of their local abundance or lack of a better alterna-tives (e.g. thatch for roofs), have a much more limited life and will require replacement more often.

Decay is generally slow and gentle, is part of the natural order and rarely results in sudden collapse or failure. If we accept the reality of decay then it makes sense to try to ensure the fabric of the church building survives as long as possible by looking after it. Carrying out regular maintenance and minor repairs without delay, and not doing anything to the building that will put at risk the materials of which it is constructed, slows down the rate of decay and prolongs the life of a church building.

Or alternatively, if you really want to, you can speed up the rate of decay very signifi-cantly, for example by allowing your gutters to block …

2   Inherent defects, inappropriate repairs and neglect

In addition to the gentle process of decay, sudden or accelerated causes of failure of building materials are linked to one or a combination of three basic causes – inherent defects, inappropriate repairs or neglect:

- **Inherent defects** include poor construction, design defects and structural defects, all of which were there in the building from the beginning, generating continual ongoing problems.
- **Inappropriate repairs** cause lots of problems for historic buildings. Done with the best of intentions, mistakes in both the materials and methods used for repairs have often done more harm than good to historic building fabric. For example, the fashion for stripping away the sacrificial external coat of lime plaster and limewash from the external walls in the nineteenth and twentieth centuries has left many congregations with huge bills for unnecessary repointing.
- **Neglect**, however, notwithstanding all the inherent defects or inappropriate repairs, is the major cause of accelerated and premature decay to the fabric of church buildings. Neglect is caused by people.

3   People

'There are no problem buildings, just problem owners' is a much-repeated line quoted by people in the conservation sector. Whether it is a church or a secular building, the future of any building is all down to the people who own, use and look after it. The most significant factor that can put a building at risk is the people associated with it – their understanding and their attitudes.

The situation of church buildings can be more complicated than, for example, a private house, because there are a wide range of people associated with the church, all of whom may have slightly different understandings and attitudes towards it, but none with sole responsibility as with their own home. It can then be dangerous when someone does step forward to take care of the building, and the rest of the congregation are only too pleased to be relieved of their burden by this 'Fabric Officer'. If the individual lacks adequate training in looking after a historic building it can lead to very expensive mistakes.

While this may be an extreme version of the scenario, it can at times go something like this:

On the one hand the vicar and congregation, frustrated by a building they consider not fit for purpose in the twenty-first century and hampered by lack of funds, view the church as a problem. On the other hand local residents and the conservation sector consider the church as a historic asset in the locality and want it to continue unchanged while all around things change at an ever-increasing rate. At the same time the quinquennial inspectors, place of worship support officers and even some archdeacons look at the church building and wonder why the congregation are willing to neglect the maintenance on this historic treasure and are prepared to put up with worshipping in such a mess and muddle! Then, if the PCC is in a position to fund changes to the building that will make it more fit for purpose, they can find their objectives frustrated by both people and a process they perceive as obstructive, complex and negative. The result is that the church congregations consider the conservation sector and Diocesan Advisory Committees (DACs) as the enemy because they are against change.

Fortunately it is not like this for every parish, but everyone involved with church buildings needs to be aware of the potential for differences of opinion and lack of common ground to cause all manner of headaches when it comes to both the looking after and the conservation (i.e. the management of change) of church buildings.

Bite-sized chunks

Solving big problems is like eating an elephant – best done mouthful by mouthful. The advice therefore is to break down the problem into bite-sized pieces and tackle them one step at a time.

The place to begin is to stop the neglect and get the situation under control. Stopping the neglect is usually quite cheap because it is about a change of attitude rather than a load of expenditure. So as a church you have to take responsibility and put together a strategy that ensures the church building is not neglected. There is more information about this in Section C.

Putting right the consequences of neglect is more expensive because repair works cost money. It is at this point that church communities come into contact with a range of people who have an interest in the historic church building and who will want to see the repairs done properly and carefully. Our friend Mr Bodgelt from Chapter B22 is not their preferred contractor.

You will quickly discover that success in this aspect of church building management is all down to people and the relationships they are able to build and sustain. This is why the statement 'There are no problem buildings, just problem owners' has a validity in the conservation sector.

However, it needs to be acknowledged that some of the people who work within the conservation sector can be just as much part of the problem. Purist conservationist attitudes holding a rigid line of 'No change is good' or official responses that are unappreciative of the challenges and needs of the owners can cause just as much trouble in the relationship, resulting in stalemate and a stand-off where nothing gets done. Understanding the issues, committed consultation, effective communications, being prepared to compromise and building consensus are the approaches required by everyone involved. Misunderstanding and being unable to achieve specific objectives has unfortunately led to a troubled relationship between some churches and the conservation sector. This is further discussed in Chapter C6.

If you are to improve the condition of your historic church building it is essential to build and sustain good relationships with those who have an interest in it. These are the stakeholders who represent constituencies of people far wider than the congregation or resident parishioners. While conservation might be the management of change, achieving any change is done by the effective management of people.

So we are not all doomed, but it needs to be acknowledged that it requires a strategy to get from a building that is at risk, or which is feeling a bit fragile, to one with a secure future. Throwing money at the problem is only part of the solution. Enabling people to understand the issues, to appreciate the small things they can do to help, and therefore to engage thoroughly with the building, is ultimately more important.

A6

'Buildings, Blooming Buildings'

Managing buildings and property

The argument is often made that 'Church is all about the people, so we shouldn't invest in our buildings.' Some would go further and say it is positively wrong to lavish money on buildings because our focus should be out in the community, and that one can make Church anywhere 'where two or three are gathered together in my name' (Matthew 18.20).

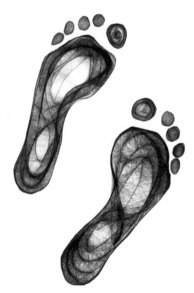

We would agree that Church *is* all about the people, and for that very reason buildings are hugely important. Why? Because of what it means to be human – the way God has made us. A building gives a church a visible footprint on the ground, a base from which to work and a place to offer welcome. Those around us know where to find us when they need us. So buildings are also about identity, the church literally 'having a place' in your local community.

Just as a person's face can speak volumes about their state of mind and character, so a church building as the church's public face speaks volumes about the life within. Sadly many church buildings are overly serious, drab and uninviting or even abandoned, while others affirm you and draw you into the joyful celebration within. God invites everyone to his party, and our buildings are a visible part of that invitation (or then again perhaps not …).

Of course buildings can never do this on their own – the test of the invitation is the love and care of the people within. But nor are these buildings ever neutral and passive. Just as someone's face may conflict with the words coming out of their mouth, so a building that conflicts with what you stand for as a church community is profoundly unsettling when viewed from the outside. When we meet someone we don't know we decide whether to trust them by looking for consistency; that is why, in the commercial world, successful businesses put such effort into trying to align all aspects of their branding with their 'core values'.

Whether we like it or not, buildings and property are a fact of life in the Church. Reluctant as we may be (after all, very few of us joined the Church for its buildings), if we fail to engage with those buildings then (to change metaphor) they are likely to eat us for breakfast – not because they are vicious or predatory but because they will suck the energy and life out of our ministry and congregation.

But a failure to engage with the joys and sorrows of church buildings and their management might perhaps suggest we have not understood the Church of England's unique role as the national Church in every community, and the opportunities that presents. Buildings are often painful precisely because they demand that we put down roots, that we commit, in this case to being God's people in this particular place.

Other voices

For better or worse, the clergy and congregation are not the only ones with an interest in 'their' church. If your building is listed, then it will be subject to another layer of legislation and interest from people outside the church community, such as Historic England (until 2015 part of English Heritage) and the national amenity societies – for more on external stakeholders, see Chapter D8. We ignore this fact at our peril – it is a criminal offence to make changes to a listed building without consent from the appropriate authorities. If you are considering external changes to your building (whether listed or not), you will also need to engage with your local authority planning department (and, if your building is listed, the conservation officer too). Church communities will save themselves a lot of bother if they recognize the importance of establishing and maintaining effective working relationships with the outside organizations and individuals who have a legitimate interest in their buildings. Given that planning (and conservation) functions are undertaken at the district level of local government, in all likelihood there will be a history to this relationship at diocesan level – it is worth discussing this with your archdeacon and DAC Secretary.

Look after the assets

The church building is usually the local church's biggest asset; it is the premises from which, and within which, the local church community conducts their core activity. It is essential that the church building serves the mission of the local church rather than inhibits it.

In part this is about stopping things from going wrong. The PCC has a duty in law to protect the assets from loss or damage. All buildings, but especially old buildings, need regular preventative maintenance. Perhaps the greatest hazard to a church building is from water getting in at the wrong place. Every church building needs a 'dry hat and boots', which requires a watertight roof, working rainwater goods and drains plus well-pointed external walls – see Chapter B3 for more on this.

To use another image, your church building is a bit like your partner in a dance – if either of you drags your feet you're both likely to fall over. Not only that, but it's important that one of you 'leads' and the other follows. The means by which a church community can 'lead' in this dance is to assert control of their property assets, other-wise they will find that events associated with the property assets will control them. Putting in place a forward-looking Asset Management Plan for the management of the church building will enable you to gain control of this relationship, so that you will know when the roof needs replacing and have the money in place when you need it. See Chapter B17 for an explanation of an Asset Management Plan.

Getting the building to earn its keep

Grants of public money for the repair or maintenance of a church will come with various requirements, including:

- Putting in place and carrying out a management plan of preventative maintenance for the church building into the future.
- Opening the building to the public on a regular basis.
- More specifically, a Heritage Lottery Fund grant will come with an expectation that you will improve public engagement with heritage.

All of these requirements are desirable in their own right. However, there are associ-ated implications, and the church community will need to be confident that there are sufficient resources (human and financial) to meet such requirements; for example, a maintenance agreement requires funds and opening the building may require people on site.

Insanity is doing the same thing over and over again, but expecting different results.
attributed to Albert Einstein

Healthy buildings are ones animated by human activity; wider community use of church buildings can therefore often help provide for their long-term sustainability. Busy churches are often able to earn an income and, because of the various activities going on inside, become self-policing so that security concerns are reduced rather than increased. Community use of church buildings requires the church community to 'give the building away and allow people in on their own terms'. Some church communities will need to work through the issues associated with letting go of what has come to be seen as 'their' territory. However, as we argue elsewhere, this giving of the building back to the community should also be seen as the righting of a historic wrong.

'No change' is *not* the solution

In our culture we are often anxious about change – indeed for some the point of Church is that it is a place to escape from the increasing pace of change in the wider world. It is tempting therefore to think that 'Going on as we are' is a viable option. Not only does this fail to recognize that church buildings and structures constantly changed throughout their history, it also ignores the longer-term trends that continue to see decline in church attendance.

'Going on as we are' and dribbling to decline results in closed church buildings that are lost to the community for ever. And of course the closing of a church building just shifts the problem from the PCC on to the diocese. The costs go to the Diocesan Board of Finance (ultimately adding to everyone else's Parish Share) and the question of finding a future for the empty building goes to the Diocesan Closed Churches Committee. Meanwhile the closed building loudly declares that 'God is Dead!'

Before giving up with the building, the church community therefore needs to make every effort to become sustainable, for example by exploring the possibilities to open up the building for community use. The key to this is to rediscover ways the building can be an asset rather than a liability. It is worth recognizing that a closed church in poor repair is far less likely to find an alternative user than one in reasonable condition.

Friends' Groups

One of the most significant causes of the emptiness of our church buildings is their detachment from their communities, and yet there often remains a marked affection within the broader community for what is still seen as 'their' church building. Friends' Groups are an excellent way to address this by generating interest, support and income for the church building from a much wider group than the regular congregation and fringe members. They are particularly useful and relevant in rural areas where church buildings still have significance to the majority of the local population. We deal with Friends' Groups in more detail in Chapter D10.

A7

Viable and Sustainable Churches

Part of the body – benefits and responsibilities

All parish churches in the Church of England benefit from the support of the wider Church. There is no truly independent and totally self-supporting parish church in the Church of England. Individual churches are part of a larger body.

Every Anglican congregation is part of a larger organization that brings the benefits of inherited assets, deployed clergy and the organizational structures of the diocese and province.

Each parish church is a separate charitable trust for which the PCC members act as the trustees. In the past the PCCs were 'excepted' from registration with the Charity Commissioners. PCCs of churches with large financial turnovers have been required to register with the Charity Commission in recent years. Nevertheless all PCCs are charities subject to the Charities Act and Charity Law.

It is the duty of charity trustees to ensure the proper financial management of the charity and to ensure the charity can always pay its bills (i.e. it is never insolvent). Trustees therefore need to know whether or not the charity is financially viable and has a sustainable future.

Money – the great unmentionable

All too often church communities do their best to avoid talking about money. It's an uncomfortable subject, the cause of disagreements and 'It's none of your business anyway.'

shhh.......!

The Greek word for fellowship is *koinonia*, and is often associated with the church (*ekklesia*). But *koinonia* can also be translated as enterprise or business. So we are, in running our local churches, not just a fellowship but also an enterprise and a business, which means we must get real about money. Just because we live in a society that sees wealth as little short of righteousness, this does not mean that in order to meet our calling to be countercultural we need to turn our back on money. Our calling is not to be otherworldly – that is the false dichotomy set up by a world that cannot imagine any other way of dealing with money. Indeed the gospel narratives show that Jesus spent a good deal of time talking about money or wealth and frequently challenging people about the way it was used.

Bluntly, without financial resources – and an appropriate 'theology of money' – the mission of the Church won't get very far. It is for this reason we have included this chapter.

An important distinction

The *Shorter Oxford English Dictionary* makes a distinction between viable and sustainable:

- **Viable**   Capable of living, able to maintain a separate existence.
- **Viability**   The quality or state of being viable.
- **Sustain**   To succour, support, back up.
- **Sustainable**   Supportable, maintainable.

Within the specific limits of a financial assessment, a *viable* church is one that can pay its own way and not rely on other churches to support it financially. By contrast, a *sustainable* church is one that can continue to operate and manage its own affairs, if necessary with some financial support from other church communities.

Because of the importance to the Anglican Church of retaining the mission and ministry across the country, and in response to the recommendations of their respective Pastoral Committees, the deanery and diocesan synods can choose to sustain those church communities that might not be viable as individual units on their own. This can be done by subsidizing ministry using national and diocesan funds, including the cross-subsidy between parishes by Parish Share. Such mutual support places a responsibility on individual churches to conduct themselves in a businesslike manner with openness and clarity of management.

Living churches

As well as making a judgement about a church's financial viability or sustainability, some sort of assessment will need to be made about the viability of that church as a community – the life and vibrancy of the people. It is best if this assessment is made within the local contexts of the deanery and the local ecumenical situation. *The Healthy Churches Handbook* (*HCH*) is a useful tool to help local churches in the assessment of their viability.[1]

Agreeing to engage in the process of the *HCH* is a sign of life in itself.

Each church community needs to be a 'going concern' in terms of both ministry and buildings. It is essential to be honest about the situation. It is all too easy to put in lots of time, energy and money to sustain something just because it is there rather than because it is really needed or is making a significant contribution to the mission of the Church as a whole.

Local church finances – we have to get real

It would be sensible to have an agreed way to identify those church communities that are not viable by themselves and require support (pastoral, ministerial and financial) in order to sustain them. Much of this may be difficult to nail with measurable data, but it shouldn't just be assessed by hunches and the sense of burden plus the ministry input required to 'push water up a hill'.

There are two main aspects to the financial outgoings for any local church: ministry costs and building costs.

- **Ministry costs** are the operational costs that include Parish Share, administration, heating, lighting, insurances and all the general costs of providing for services and the life of the church. The payment of Parish Share should be a high priority and essential commitment for every church community.
- **Buildings costs** can be split into three categories: Regular Maintenance to keep the building and its fittings in good working order; Capital Repairs to replace the items that wear out or fail; and Improvements and New Works which are the 'nice to haves' that make the building a better place. The Quinquennial Inspection Report and an Asset Management Plan will help identify the relative priorities of these three categories. Keeping the building dry will always be the most important – see Chapters B3 and B4.

A very rough and ready way of identifying whether a church has financial problems is to subtract the annual Parish Share assessment from the annual turnover. For a rural church, if the sum left is less than £10,000 it is likely the church will be in difficulties. Urban churches usually need to have about £20,000 in hand over their Parish Share assessment.

However useful this method is, it can quickly put any church with less than recommended sums available into a 'slough of despond' out of which it is difficult to climb. It may also give churches that exceed this figure a false sense of security – they may have bigger liabilities or indeed bigger opportunities. Perhaps therefore it is better to look for the potential to change and develop.

Viable and/or sustainable churches

There is a way of using available data from PCC accounts to measure the viability and sustainability of each church.

- **Viable churches** are those for which a church community can meet its ministry costs (Parish Share and operational costs) and keep the building(s) adequately maintained, with the Quinquennial Inspection items attended to.
- **Sustainable churches** are less clear-cut to identify. Because sustainability implies outside support, decisions will require discussion and negotiation across a group or deanery. In essence, if a church is able to meet its ministry costs and maintain its building (with agreed support from partner churches), then it could be considered sustainable. The complexity and condition of the building will be a significant deciding factor in considering the sustainability of a church, since this will determine the long-term liabilities.

This is not an exact science. The different types of community, the socio-economic factors, the condition of the building and the drive and passion of the people will all influence whether or not an individual church is viable or sustainable. A range of possibilities need to be considered but experience demonstrates that the finances of local churches usually fall into one of the following three categories, to which we've given traffic-light colour labels:

- **Green**   Parish Share paid on time and in full; sufficient funds available to meet operational costs; buildings well maintained, no outstanding Quinquennial Inspection (QI) items. Viable and sustainable.
- **Amber**   Parish Share paid in full but late; operational costs can be funded most of the time; basic preventative maintenance done; some QI repairs outstanding. Sustainable but not viable.
- **Red**   Parish Share and operational costs are a struggle; PCC is faced with the choice of either paying Parish Share in full or undertaking essential repairs; little or no preventative maintenance; QI repairs outstanding. Neither viable nor (possibly) sustainable.

These categories can be further examined by looking at the trends over three to five years using the parish accounts. This could prove especially useful to determine what the trends are and therefore in which direction a specific church is moving. For those amber and red churches (categories 2 and 3), this will give an indication of their potential for survival.

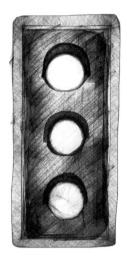

Moreover there is the potential to determine which of category 3 (red) could, with help, support and training, become sustainable; which of category 2 (amber) could become viable; which of category 1 (green) could support another church in another place to make it sustainable. This engages the Church in a tangible mission activity rather than being content with the status quo.

So before you go much further it may be useful to run the viability and sustainability exercise on your own church. Don't give up if the results aren't to your liking – there are a large number of possibilities to turn the situation round. This is what, in part, this book is all about.

Note

1 Robert Warren, *The Healthy Churches Handbook: A Process for Revitalizing Your Church*, London: Church House Publishing, 2004.

A8

The Church in Numbers

Lies, lies and statistics

As the established Church in England, the Anglican Church retains an important place and role in the life of the country. We are all familiar with news stories about the decline in church attendance, and in the popular imagination the Church is now nothing more than baptisms, weddings, funerals and an occasional 'Thought for the Day'. There is lots to support this view in the statistics that are collected, and you might think that all is lost and the organization is failing faster than it can cope with the changes. Certainly if you interpret the figures using a business model, it makes for uncomfortable reading.

Because of this uncomfortable reading it can sometimes be difficult to get hold of sufficient statistical information to make a sensible judgement. Depending on which agenda is being pursued, bad news may be buried while signs of life and hope are exaggerated in order to generate enthusiasm; conversely good news may be ignored in favour of another juicy scandal.

Choose 1:
☐ **lies**
☐ **d**n lies**
☑ **statistics**

The Church of England does publish some very useful statistics showing that across the dioceses cathedral congregations are growing while overall parish church congregations (with exceptions in some areas) are shrinking. Over the course of time this will impact on our ability to look after the parish church buildings. The inescapable fact is that the Church of England needs to change if it is to survive.

The other inescapable fact is that the Church of England, along with most other denominations, has continually developed and adapted to changes in society. Currently it is going through yet another phase of change, and we should not be surprised that this is accompanied by the usual difficulties and distress of the 'change cycle'. Just web search 'change cycle' and see what you find.

Current statistics

According to Peter Brierley in his *UK Church Statistics 2: 2010–2020*, across the UK as a whole there are over 50,000 church congregations; of course, not all of these have their own buildings.[1]

In England, as of 2015 there are 42 Anglican dioceses, each a geographical area that may or may not correlate to county boundaries. Across these dioceses there are over 16,000 church buildings currently in use as 'places of worship'. Of these, approximately three-quarters are listed because of their special architectural or historic interest, and the remaining quarter are unlisted. There are three grades of listed building:

- Grade 1 are buildings of exceptional interest.
- Grade 2* are particularly important buildings of more than special interest.
- Grade 2 are buildings of special interest, justifying every effort to preserve them.

Some 45 per cent of Grade 1 listed buildings are churches or cathedrals. Two cathedrals (Canterbury and Durham), Westminster Abbey and three parish churches are included in English World Heritage Sites.

According to research published by the Church of England,[2] 68 per cent consider their local church building an important part of their local community. Those who consider churches important include 45 per cent of people with no religion and 62 per cent of adherents of other faiths. Some 70 per cent believe the local church provides valuable social and community facilities and 57 per cent believe church buildings should be more actively used by the local community. Around 85 per cent of the population visit a church or place of worship each year.

The majority of the church buildings are looked after by volunteers who are members of individual church congregations.

In 2006 necessary repairs to all listed places of worship in England were valued at £925 million in the coming five years, equating to around £185 million per year. The current annual spend on repairs to Church of England churches is £112 million; since the great majority of listed places of worship are Anglican, there is a significant shortfall, which means that year on year there is a progressive deterioration in the condition of our church buildings.

Funding for church building repairs has to be raised by the individual churches – there is no central government or central Church of England funding for church buildings. Currently 70 per cent of this money is raised by the congregations and local community. Grants and Lottery funding forms the other 30 per cent.

Nearly half the population (46 per cent) think that central taxation, local taxation, the National Lottery or Historic England should be 'primarily' responsible for providing money to maintain churches and chapels.

A national review in 2011 of all 16,000 church building Quinquennial Inspection Reports identified that about 16 per cent of buildings are in poor or very bad condition with the majority in reasonable condition.

In the past 30 years stipendiary clergy numbers have halved to about 8,300 across England, and a similar pattern is repeated in other regions. In England, stipendiary clergy now represent 26 per cent of the total number of 29,000 licensed ministers.

Across the UK and other denominations

While there are considerable challenges facing the Church of England, the Church as a whole continues to grow. New churches, especially free non-aligned congregations, are starting up all the time.

According to Peter Brierley in his *UK Church Statistics 2005–2015*, the actual number of churches increased during 2005–10 and is expected to do so marginally during 2010–15.[3]

- 2005 total number of churches: 49,486.
- 2010 total number of churches: 50,709.
- 2015 estimated number of churches: 50,934.

Denomination	Opening	Closing	Net difference
Anglican	+34	−238	−204
Baptists	+84	−143	−63
Independent	+118	−154	−36
Methodist	+5	−337	−332
New churches	+267	−17	+250
Pentecostal	+668	−4	+664
Presbyterian	+5	−248	−243
Smaller denominations	+1460	−43	+1417

The new non-aligned churches are often looking for suitable buildings in which to meet for worship and from which they can operate. Town-centre sites are of interest to them but the traditional arrangement of Anglican buildings may (initially at least) be offputting; where there are ancillary buildings these may also be attractive.

Historic England

When it comes to the statistics for buildings, the following figures were published by English Heritage – as then was – as part of the Inspired! campaign.[4] This was to raise awareness of historic places for worship because, while they represent almost half of Grade 1 listed buildings, they actually only account for a small proportion (under 4 per cent) of the 375,000 listed sites and buildings in England.

- 16,151 parish churches in England, of which approximately 13,000 (80%) are listed.
- 2,765 Roman Catholic parish churches and 700 other RC chapels, oratories and churches open to the public, of which 625 (18%) are listed.
- 5,312 Methodist chapels and churches in England, of which 541 (10%) are listed.
- 1,115 United Reform chapels and churches in England, of which 290 (26%) are listed.
- 1,809 chapels and churches are members of the Baptist Union Corporation, of which 283 (16%) are listed.
- The Religious Society of Friends (Quakers) has 246 listed Friends Meeting Houses.
- There are 30 listed synagogues.
- There is 1 listed mosque.
- Of roughly 50,000 Christian places of worship in England, approximately 15,000 (30%) are listed.

These statistics demonstrate that the Christian faith is thriving in places and in forms that are less traditional and established. Traditional buildings and forms of worship are less attractive unless they are of the highest quality. More important in our more mobile society are churches that provide strong fellowship and the experience of belonging to a dynamic community.

Notes

1 Peter Brierley, *UK Church Statistics 2, 2010–2020*, Tonbridge: ADBC Publishers, 2014. For more on these official statistics, see www.churchofengland.org/about-us/facts-stats.aspx.

2 Church statistics 2009/10 published by the Archbishops' Council.

3 Peter Brierley, *UK Church Statistics 2005–2015*, Tonbridge: ADBC Publishers, 2011.

4 Archive material about the Inspired! Campaign can be found at https://historicengland. org.uk/images-books/publications/conservation-bulletin-61/.

A9

ABC of Church Structures

Legal status in the Anglican Church

It might seem a bit pedantic, but in the Church you need to know who or what has legal status as the holding authority and is therefore able to make decisions. Many people talk about 'the diocese' as though it was some kind of company or legally constituted body that managed and controlled a branch network. In fact the diocese is a geographical area and doesn't exist as much else!

So you need to know what the structures are, who has authority, who makes decisions and who might get into trouble if they are negligent or act improperly.

- The PCC of each parish is a trustee body, comprising the vicar, churchwardens and elected members.
- The Office of the Diocesan Bishop (i.e. not the individual person who inhabits the role) and the Diocesan Board of Finance are the legally constituted bodies.
- The diocesan synod has the task of governance but is not a trustee body.

The parish

The parish church is the base unit of the Church of England, with its parish priest, churchwardens and elected representatives, the PCC. The bulk of decision-making power in the Church of England resides at parish level.

Rather than the conventional corporate management structure that many outside the Church assume it to be, the parish structure is more like a network of independent outlets that cover every part of England but between which there is very little co-ordination. Unless there are significant rules that are being broken, little can be imposed on a PCC 'from above', whether by the bishop, the archdeacon or a Diocesan Board.

Parish independence is therefore a key characteristic of the Church of England, which means that consensus and agreement is essential to getting anything done. When it comes to running the diocese, the job of bishop can be a bit like herding cats.

The origins of the parish

Most simply, the parish is a geographical area or territory that originated in the Roman Empire, when it was used as a means of managing occupied territories. Each parish was administered by the emperor's representative supported by soldiers of the Roman army who ensured the civilians did as they were told and paid their taxes.

The Normans brought a substantial increase in the number of parishes by breaking up the old minster parishes of the Anglo-Saxon Church. The Norman parish formed the base of a taxation system that enabled the lord of the manor/rector to control the tithing with which to pay the taxes imposed on him by the king; this was the point of the Domesday Book, which was organized by parish.

The majority of parishes were designated when a lord of the manor (i.e. a baron loyal to the king) was appointed. The lord of the manor was responsible for keeping the peace, collecting the taxes and raising an army when required. In addition to the religious piety of the Norman invaders and in order to demonstrate his status and power, it was the lord who built (or rebuilt) the church and parsonage in the boundaries of his manor, and transferred property to create a glebe to maintain the church building and clergy – hence the term 'a living' for the position of being a priest in a parish. In addition the lord of the manor would have the parish advowsons – the right to appoint clergy to particular parishes. The bishop, without whose consecration the new church would have no religious and spiritual stature, had the right of confirmation of the appointment.

Over time, depending on the value of the glebe, endowments and property, many 'livings' became very valuable gifts and even commodities for the 'great and the good' to possess and of which to be the patron. This system of patronage continued through the Reformation when the rights of some manors were transferred to the friends of the king, to various winners of the political machinations of the age and to Oxford and Cambridge colleges. This is why in the twenty-first century the rights of appointment to some livings are still held by individuals, Oxbridge colleges and charitable trusts.

New parishes (initially funded by Queen Anne's bounty and later by the Ecclesiastical Commissioners) were created from the late 1700s onwards as the Enclosures and the early stages of the Industrial Revolution both forced and drew people from the countryside into new urban settlements. Many new church buildings were erected, often using government funds resulting from the Church Building Acts of 1818 and

1824 – these are known as Commissioners' churches or Waterloo churches. In addition to funding all or part of the cost of constructing church buildings, the Commissioners had powers to divide and subdivide existing parishes and to provide endowment funds for the payment of the clergy. The number of parishes increased but they were no longer linked to a manor and their geographical size was linked to the number of inhabitants, much as parliamentary constituencies are today.

However, from medieval times until the middle of the twentieth century individual parishes had individual funding – each parish church community was self-funding and independent from its neighbours. There was little or no central funding, nor was there much in the way of centrally agreed policies and procedures for financial administration.

Parish churches received (through endowments etc.) or raised (through tithes, church ales etc.) and spent the vast majority of their funding. Clergy were entitled to a proportion of the fees charged for 'occasional offices' (baptisms, weddings and funerals – although there was no charge for baptisms). Thus knowing the parish boundaries was important in order to ensure that the parishioners went to the 'right' church. Parish churches and their clergy could be very 'territorial', zealously guarding their fee income from neighbouring competitors. Hardly a recipe for the mutual support of each other as members of the body of Christ!

In addition to a proportion of the fee income, the clergyman's pay depended on the wealth of the parish. A good living was one with good income for the incumbent, but a poor living was quite the opposite. For example, in the late 1960s the living of Bishops Hatfield in Hertfordshire was worth about £35,000 p.a., whereas just down the road in the next-door parish of Hatfield Hyde the living was worth about £100 p.a. During the same period, in a Bedfordshire parish, the vicar's income was primarily derived from the glebe rents. He had to collect the rents from the farmers who were 'his' tenants. One particularly bad year he received less than 50 per cent of his due income so, for the first time in living memory in that parish, the vicar's wife had to go out to work.

Since the mid-nineteenth century the Church of England progressively made various moves to 'equalize' the situation and to make matters fairer for all concerned. When it came to matters financial it wasn't easy to get a fairer system in place. However, in the early 1970s, following much debate, the rules were changed. Clergy stipends were standardized and most of each individual parish's assets of money, land and property were transferred to diocesan boards and trusts with the income and capital receipts available for use across all the parishes of the diocese. The Church moved the majority of its income-generating assets (in the past land but today mostly financial stocks and bonds) out of the hands of individual clergy, parishes and bishops to the care of the Church Commissioners, which use these funds to pay a range of non-parish expenses, including clergy pensions and the expenses of cathedrals.

These radical changes weren't achieved without protest and dissent: some PCCs still talk about the terrible days when all 'their' glebe was taken by the diocese or 'their' rectory was sold off and the money kept by the church authorities. It can be difficult to convince some people that the money wasn't stolen and that it is still used to fund clergy, vicarages and the mission, but across the diocese, not just within the parish.

It is also difficult to get across the fact that these historic assets were intended to support the ministry and were not used to fund buildings. Even though the provision of the 'living' or the stipend is no longer a parish concern, each PCC is still responsible for insuring, maintaining and repairing the church buildings.

Parish and diocese – it's all about relationships

The historic and fiercely defended independence of parishes is (or at least should be) now a thing of the past. The mission of the Church is carried forward by each parish working in relationship with neighbouring parishes and the various committees and departments of its deanery and the diocese.

When it comes to parish church buildings there are a few key people with whom the vicar, churchwardens and PCC need to build and maintain relationships. The archdeacon(s) and the Diocesan Advisory Committee (DAC) are the starting point:

- Among his/her other responsibilities, the archdeacon as the bishop's representative has responsibility for the supervision of property matters.
- The DAC acts as the church 'planning committee' but do not themselves grant permission; their role, as their title suggests, is to *advise* the Chancellor,[1] who makes the decision to grant a faculty, giving permission for any changes to the church or its contents. Each DAC has a Secretary, who is the first point of contact.

Contrary to some popular opinion neither of these two parties is 'the enemy'. If they occupy that position in the minds of a parish church community then it is very difficult to get anything done. DAC Secretaries of course vary from diocese to diocese, but they are often both a great resource and a great ally. Much more will be achieved if you can learn to love your DAC!

If your church building is listed, it can be very helpful to build a relationship with non-church conservation stakeholders such as Historic England (the new name for the part of English Heritage that dealt with the statutory functions of listing, planning, grants and heritage research and advice) and the relevant amenity societies

who, by statute, have an interest in the church building. The people concerned may not always display much understanding or appreciation of the mission of the Church and, at times, you may feel that their heritage interests frustrate that mission, but they too are much better as your friends than considered to be your enemies. In Chapter D8 we talk more about who these stakeholders are and the limits of their authority.

Teams, multi-parish benefices and minster models

As well as the changes to the financial arrangements across the Church of England, there has been a continuing process of pastoral reorganization. The reduction in both numbers of stipendiary clergy and available funds has resulted in the amalgamation of individual parishes into teams or multi-parish benefices. Whatever the arrangements it is important to appreciate that the legal body responsible is still the PCC, even if some of these responsibilities are subsequently delegated to district church councils (DCCs), local church councils or PCC subcommittees.

In this ever-changing arrangement of parishes it is becoming evident that without the committed focus of the leadership body, the care and well-being of the church buildings can be overlooked. In teams or multi-parish benefices the PCC should ensure that sufficient resources are allocated to looking after the church buildings and that a properly delegated subcommittee is formed to ensure the assets for which the PCC as trustee body is responsible are protected from loss, degradation or depreciation; these basic responsibilities remain.

The PCC members can, in some situations, find themselves responsible for a small portfolio of historic buildings. Without sufficient expertise or finances to manage the portfolio this can be a fairly scary place to be. It would be sensible to seek help and advice if the PCC feels exposed or anxious about property matters.

Note

1 Terminology: each diocese has a Chancellor who presides over the Consistory Court of that diocese, dealing with disciplinary matters and issues relating to church buildings and their contents; Chancellors are generally judges or barristers. The Diocese of Canterbury uses the terms 'Commissary General' and 'Commissary Court'; all other dioceses use 'Chancellor' and 'Consistory Court' respectively.

A10

What Can We Do About It?

If a commercial organization treated its 'property portfolio' as the Church of England does, it could never survive. Which is not to say the Church should try to become a commercial organization but simply that if we ignore commercial logic, particularly with regards to cashflow, then we will succumb to that logic. It is, in that respect, no different from gravity – you ignore it at your peril.

We see three interlinked priorities for what our buildings should become.

1 Missional As the people of God we are, of course, called to be a missional people. If that is the case, then we need to consider every point at which we touch the community we are called to serve, whether in our regular worship, the way we deal with occasional offices (baptisms, weddings and funerals), our visiting and pastoral care, our communi-  cations (print, website, church notice board) and so on. Sitting squarely in the middle of this wide array of community contact are our buildings – they are our primary foot-print in our community and the means by which we are identified. Whether we like it or not, people view our building as an expression of what God is like. Our buildings are therefore not only the Church's face in the community but, in a sense, God's also.

We therefore need to think through how are buildings are 'read' by those outside the church community. Of particular concern will be the physical thresholds, which in many cases provide substantial psychological barriers to entry, as we examine in more detail in Chapter C7.

2 Used   We urgently need to rethink what we consider appropriate activities to take place within a church building; on the medieval model it is absurd to think of the use of the church being limited to Sunday worship. That sort of sensitivity is part of our Victorian inheritance, and therefore in relative terms very recent.

Much the best thing for the long-term health of an old building is for it to be used – it is better for the condition of its fabric, for its security, for the life within it and for its ownership by the wider community. For buildings to be more widely used they need a degree of flexibility – something the Victorians succeeded in frustrating by overfilling our churches with fixed pews. See Chapter B5 for more on the thorny issue of seating.

3 Strategic   As we discuss in Chapter A1, the Church of England is blessed with over 16,000 church buildings. This is like a retail network with a corner shop in every community. From outside the Church it seems bizarre that there is no co-ordination between the 'branches' in this 'network'. As we saw in Chapter A9, the much-cherished independence of the parish has deep historic roots, but this is increasingly a handicap in an ever more connected world.

And there are huge benefits to be gained from some co-ordination between 'branches'; how about, for example, a combined booking system for all the lettable spaces within a deanery? Such an arrangement has been shown both to increase bookings (and thus much-needed revenue) and also to begin to get individual clergy and congregations to think collaboratively and strategically.

And finally ...

The good news is that all that is needed is some imagination. Really? Is that all? Well, in a way, yes. For Walter Brueggemann modernity evokes in us:

- *amnesia* with no memory of our astonishing point of origin
- *greed, acquisitiveness, and idolatry* that assure a brutalizing present, and
- *despair* with no hope for our destiny or completion.[1]

Against this he calls the Church to subvert the increasingly dominant postmodern perspective:

Thus it is counter-imagination to:

- *remember* a rich past in the face of entrenched amnesia
- *entertain a covenantal present* in the face of a regnant commoditization, and
- *hope* a marvellous future in the face of an established, resigned despair.[2]

What is true of the Church is just as true of our relation to our buildings.

Notes

1 Walter Brueggemann, *Texts Under Negotiation: The Bible and Postmodern Imagination*, Minneapolis, MN: Augsburg Fortress, 1993, p. 55; emphasis in original.
2 Brueggemann, *Texts Under Negotiation*, p. 55; emphasis in original.

Section B   Practicalities

B1
What Sort of Old?

Know what you are dealing with

This Section B covers the theme 'Managing what you have'. In order to be able to care for a church building it is essential that you understand what you are dealing with.

Most churches and chapels in England are *old*, by which we generally mean they are older than our grandparents. But we need to be more specific – it isn't possible to lump all old buildings together with the assumption that they are all the same. Some 'old' buildings are relatively new and may be constructed differently from the 'medieval real McCoy'; they will therefore require quite a different approach to their management. So it is important to know what you are dealing with and how old is the old church building you have to manage.

How old is old?

If you ask a small child, the 'olden times' can be as recent as ten years ago, whereas most/many/at least some of those reading this will remember 'the olden days' before mobile phones. For others, 'old' means before the 1960s, when life in England was rather severe and formal, before we (they?) grew longer hair and turned on, tuned in and dropped out in those summers of love! But then, as they say, nostalgia ain't what it used to be ...

For buildings in general, and churches in particular, 'old' can usually include everything from before the 1920s because these are generally buildings of traditional construction built with solid walls held together with lime-based mortars. It is the solid walls and lime-based mortars that identify them as 'traditional buildings' and it is these two factors that make them behave very differently from 'modern buildings', which were and are constructed with cavity walls and Portland cement, or using other modern forms of construction. Chapter B2 looks in more detail at how these traditional buildings work.

The earliest church building in England is St Martin, Canterbury, which dates from AD 597. However, like most old buildings, because it has been around for so long, St Martin's has had any amount of changes and alterations, so some of it isn't nearly so old – only about 100 years old!

Knowing what you have and how old is your old

There are a number of ways to learn about a church building. The relevant volume of the 'Pevsner' guides (properly The Buildings of England series, extended to Wales, Scotland and Ireland, structured county by county) should have specific information on your particular building, and then more general books such as Richard Taylor's *How to Read a Church* will give you more general background.[1] If the church is listed then you will be able to find the listing description via your local authority planning department or the online database run by Historic England – see www.historicengland.org.uk/listing/the-list. There may also be information in local guide books or even a specific guide for the church.

Even though such an approach is a bit academic and book based, local guide books can be full of incorrect information based on speculation, assumption and hearsay! Far better is to use the written information to accompany you or refer to while you take the time to look at the building inside and out, together with its setting and how it relates to the nearby buildings and/or landscape. This can be very enjoyable detective work and will give you a much greater understanding of the church than the written words alone.

Early churches in England (i.e. around AD 500) were probably built of timber and only later rebuilt using stone. The Celtic and Anglo-Saxon churches were often associated with pre-Christian sacred sites but were modest single-cell structures that existed alongside what was already there. The Norman Conquest brought with it an extensive church-building programme, which in part at least was about the assertion of power, status and control. As England prospered, many buildings were enlarged, embellished or rebuilt. During the Reformation, Commonwealth and Restoration, church buildings were subject to significant change and re-ordering dictated by wider political and liturgical change. Victorian wealth, new ideas of the sacred, reforming social action, population growth and so on brought about another wave of new building, rebuilding and re-ordering. Aside from learning about the archaeology of the building, careful inspection of a parish church and an understanding of how it has developed through the ages can provide a remarkable commentary on the social history of the parish.

But this exercise is of more than academic interest – it is useful to do this research because it will help you to look after the building and be able to spot problems before they become a crisis. And since an old building without crises is one that can be enjoyed, everyone is a winner. All this is simply explained in the diagram of the Heritage Cycle in Chapter C8.

When it comes to looking after the buildings, knowing 'what sort of old' you are dealing with helps in that you will come to know a bit more about the building's quirks and shortcomings. Early buildings were seriously 'over-engineered' (look at the thickness of those medieval walls) but this has enabled them to last so long. Embodied in the way the materials are used is a great deal of practical knowledge and craft experience of how buildings work and decay. That said, don't forget that in many cases some of the 'old' has been significantly changed by subsequent alterations, adaptations and improvements. This means the 'old' isn't necessarily all the same age; usually there are different eras of old in an old church, even within a single element of a unified appearance. The implication of this is that we should expect the building fabric to wear out at different rates, so like the Forth Bridge, there will always be something that needs maintenance, repair or replacement!

Sometimes the messing about that has happened to the building through the ages really is a mess, sometimes it is a delightful embellishment that adds a great deal. Pre-Norman old is very special because it is so rare. It may be very simple but its massive construction and rather dark and gloomy interiors can make it difficult to use in the twenty-first century.

The Normans, and church builders after them in the later medieval period up to the early sixteenth century, were always keen to use the latest building technologies available to them. Some of these buildings are feats of engineering and innovation that pushed the limits of what was possible, and remain hugely impressive accomplishments even by today's standards.

Of course, not all 'old' was well built. The worst, of course, never survived, but even what remains can be very variable in quality. For all of the delights of classical design, the Georgians could at times be the very worst 'jerry-builders' deploying the deceits of 'facadism' (ashlar stone exterior layer with lath and plaster interiors) hiding the most terrible bodgery of poor brickwork, hidden timber and skimpy construction.

The Victorian delight for 'scraping' to reveal the bare stonework inside and out not only created vertical walls of 'crazy paving' and consequently gloomy interiors, but has also removed the protective exterior renders essential for some types of stone that are soft and prone to decay. A similarly bad idea was the fashion for removing the drip moulds from around the windows of churches with the consequence that the rainwater is positively encouraged to find its way into the building.

The materials used for the new churches built during the reign of Queen Victoria (i.e. built between 1837 and 1901) have either reached, or will soon reach, the end of their first phase of life. About 150 years is the very maximum for the materials to last before the processes of decay (which started as soon as they were used in the building) begin to demand their repair or replacement. So if your old building is Victorian and you haven't had it re-roofed or the walls repointed, you should expect to have to do so soon.

Paradoxically, very old buildings can often be easier to maintain. It is often possible to access all parts of a medieval building using a 12-foot ladder along with the stairs, high-level walkways and hatches provided in the construction. Georgian and Victorian buildings rarely include sensible routes to enable access for regular maintenance and can nowadays require expensive access equipment. Some buildings that previously had good access have this compromised by later changes (e.g. new bell-frames often prevent safe roof access, sometimes simply for lack of a little joined-up thinking).

Finally, some repair methods have caused damage in their own right and positively serve to *increase* decay to church buildings; this can be very expensive to put right. The legacy of Portland cement repointing is currently a significant problem to thousands of churches. It is only in the last 20 years or so that we have regained a proper understanding of how traditional construction needs to be allowed to breathe. Understanding a breathable building is the most important principle for you to appreciate in managing what you have, and we deal with this in more detail in the chapters that follow.

Note

1 Richard Taylor, *How to Read a Church: Pocket Guide*, London: Rider, 2007.

B2
Rubble Sandwiches – Traditional Wall Construction

The first thing you should understand about your church is that it is most unlikely to be built in the same way as the house in which you live. Traditional buildings (as a rule of thumb those built before 1920) built from masonry have solid walls made of porous materials that both absorb moisture and allow it to evaporate; by contrast, modern buildings (post-1920) are constructed with physical barriers and impervious materials that exclude moisture. This chapter is about traditional stone-wall construction, which is generally the same whether it is medieval or the Victorian equivalent, and its peculiarities. If your building is built of Victorian brickwork then you can skip the first half of this chapter and rejoin at the 'Keep breathing' heading below.

Sandwiches anyone?

Stone walls generally look solid, don't they? In practice that appearance of solidity is somewhat deceptive: the nice presentable inner and outer skins of stone are facings that hide a mish-mash of rubble fill in between. This fill will include whatever was readily available at the time the wall was built – often irregular stones gathered from the nearby fields, perhaps with some broken brick or tile depending on the age, all held together with mortar of sand and lime. Effectively you have a vertical sandwich – two visible faces of attractive 'bread', with a motley filling of tuna, mayo, sweetcorn (and whatever else was in the fridge at the time), which remains hidden.

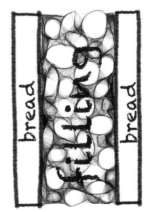

rubble sandwich

So why were these walls not built more solidly, using just the decent quality stone all nicely bonded together? Basically because stone was expensive, both in its quarrying and cutting, but particularly in its transport. Traditional building (i.e. before the Industrial Revolution transformed the transport infrastructure of the UK) always used the materials that could easily be brought to the construction site; which, incidentally, accounts for the great variety of regional vernacular building styles in pre-industrial societies. Leaving aside a very few buildings of the highest status, traditional construction is an expression of the geography and geology of each particular locality.

Given the quality of material in the filling of the 'sandwich' you could be justified in calling this 'rubbish construction'. Yet it is a form of construction that has stood the test of time. By its nature it results in the much thicker walls we are familiar with in medieval churches and castles, and their width gives these walls an inherent stability. Provided the building is adequately maintained, there is very little that goes wrong with this form of construction, as there are no cavity ties to rust or plastics to perish. As a result, there are many medieval buildings constructed in this way that have stood for up to 1,000 years, and which, if properly maintained, should be there in another 1,000 years.

So what's not to like?

This 'sandwich' construction relies on the lime mortar in the rubble 'filling' to keep the whole 'sandwich' acting as a single structural element. If water gets into the sandwich then the lime and sand mortar can be washed away. Without this void-filling 'glue' between the rubble the construction as a whole loses its integrity and instead of a single solid element you have something more like a bag of marbles – the construction will no longer be able to support as much load and the whole lot will begin to slump. Where you see stonework walls bulging, whether on the inside or the outside, this is what is most likely happening.

'BLT' stands for:

☐ belief, lime & tradition

☐ bacon, lettuce & tomato

☐ ...

The risk of delamination (i.e. separation of the layers) of the sandwich that occurs when water gets into the construction underlines the crucial importance of the regular clearing of gutters and basic maintenance to ensure that the building retains a 'dry hat and boots', which we discuss further in the next chapter, B3. This delamination can be very serious, potentially resulting in the sudden collapse of the wall, and therefore of the roof and so on above. Your inspecting architect should be on the lookout for signs of this, and if necessary a structural engineer should be consulted. The good news is that walls showing signs of delamination can often be made sound again by injecting a grouting mix to fill all the voids and re-establish the integrity of the sandwich.

Keep breathing

Another key difference between traditional and modern construction is the way each deals with moisture. Modern construction generally relies on impermeable barriers to control moisture, such as a damp-proof course in a wall or a damp-proof membrane in a floor. By contrast, traditional construction controls moisture through evaporation. Both are perfectly respectable approaches, and it can be argued that the more natural breathable approach is better for human health. Where trouble arises is in the mixing of the two approaches, by adding an impermeable material to construction that is trying to breathe. For example, replacing lime plaster with modern gypsum plaster greatly reduces the ability of that section of wall to breathe; rather than stopping the damp as may be imagined, the new impermeable plaster draws the moisture further up the wall as it outflanks the new barrier, often resulting in a more pronounced 'high water mark' where the new plaster stops, and also an increased risk of frost damage externally.

A word on foundations

Traditional walls often have very shallow foundations; where current Building Regulations would expect a new wall to have a foundation at least one metre in depth (and often more depending on soil type and ground conditions), traditional walls may be founded on nothing more than bare earth just a foot below the surface. This is not of itself a problem – many buildings have stood happily on such foundations for many hundreds of years – but it does make them vulnerable to a lack of maintenance.

Once again this is a question of dealing appropriately with your rainwater. If a gulley at the foot of a downpipe becomes blocked then with every downpour the rainwater will be soaking the ground around that downpipe. The danger is that this concentration of water will begin washing away the soil on which the wall rests, thus undermining it, as well as making the wall itself damper than it should be. If this is left unchecked, the wall may well need underpinning, which will be hugely more expensive than the much simpler task of maintaining the rainwater system in good order – a clear case of a stitch in time saves nine, or in this case more like 99.

Lime mortars and plasters

The use of lime in building fell out of fashion in the first half of the twentieth century and was replaced with the near-universal use of the bagged 'cement' (Ordinary Portland cement) that any general builder will be familiar with. Lime is now enjoying something of a comeback, and there are many more builders who are now familiar with it and can use it responsibly. It is worth understanding the pros and cons of each material:

- **Cement** is a much **stronger** material than lime, and sets more quickly. For this reason it is almost invariably used for general masonry construction (e.g. of a new house) because a builder can build a wall more rapidly using cement than they can using lime mortar, and crucially can build more each day, making the process considerably more cost-effective *for the builder*, and in the short term.
- **Lime**, however, is much more **flexible** than cement. Lime gives a mortar a 'springiness' that allows a wall to accommodate movement, whether that movement comes from heavy traffic, seasonal ground movements or from daily and seasonal changes in temperature. All of this means that a lime-based construction is much less likely to crack than a cement-based equivalent. Remember that the mortar joints in a wall are there to keep the individual stones or bricks apart, not to glue them together, and in most circumstances lime does a much better job of that.
- In terms of **environmental** considerations, lime is the much better option. The production of cement consumes great quantities of energy and therefore has a large carbon footprint, whereas the use of lime in construction is actually carbon negative – the process of creating lime for use in building from the basic limestone, and its curing when used in mortar, actually consumes more carbon dioxide than is produced in its manufacture.
- Lime is also **breathable**, where cement is not. You should expect a traditional wall to have some moisture in it; as we discuss further in Chapter B4, some moisture, provided it is controlled, is no problem at all. To retain their integrity, the individual stones (or indeed bricks) in a traditional wall need the surrounding mortar to be breathable to allow the moisture in and out. Repointing a traditional wall with cement mortar, as has so often been done out of well-meaning ignorance, can quite literally destroy that wall. Without breathable mortar, more of the moisture is in the individual stones or bricks, which leads to frost damage. Each time there is a frost the water in the stone or brick freezes and then of course thaws again; in time this freeze–thaw cycle will blow off the face of the individual stones or bricks, and the face becomes progressively eroded. As a consequence, many a church architect spends time arranging for the removal of cement pointing and its replacement with lime.

Brickwork

Brickwork construction may or may not follow the same principles outlined above for traditional stone walls. The rule of thumb is that the thicker the wall, the more likely it is to be a sandwich construction. The basic (imperial) brick module (i.e. the brick itself plus the width of a mortar joint) is 9 x 4.5 x 3 inches; in new money that translates into roughly 230 x 115 x 76 mm, though this often varies. You would expect a wall up to 455 mm (18 inches) thick to either be solid or well bonded together, but beyond that it is anybody's guess, and you will only know for sure with some structural investigation.

Just like stone, brick (at least of the sort generally used for the walls of churches) is not 'waterproof'. Both the brick and the mortar used in the joints are water permeable. The same principles as for traditional stone construction, particularly the need to keep a dry hat and boots on the building, therefore apply.

B3

Dry Hat and Boots

The importance of keeping dry

dry hat and boots

The greatest danger to a church building is not fire but water. It is perhaps helpful to think of a traditionally built church as *soluble* – expose it for long enough to water in the right way and your building will 'dissolve'. For that reason, allowing water to get into the structure or the interior in the wrong place, often termed 'water ingress', is the greatest threat to the long-term life and survival of a church building.

Conversely, if you can keep a 'dry hat and boots' on the church building, this will keep it weather-tight, and as a result the building will last for centuries. By a dry hat and boots we mean a sound roof, effective rainwater goods (gutters, downpipes and gulleys) and the external surfaces (pointing, brick and stonework) in reasonable condition.

It really is as simple as that: pay attention to these essentials and you will ensure a long-lived future for the building.

Water ingress

Aside from the roof covering itself, the rainwater goods are the most important items to maintain to ensure the building is dry. Blocked gutters overflow into the interior space and blocked downpipes cause damp walls and 'blown' plaster. Worse, as described in Chapter B2, blocked gutters or leaking roofs can direct water into the rubble core of a traditional masonry wall and wash away the mortar that binds the wall together. Blocked gulleys at the base of the walls can result in your church building sitting in a pond; water is fed into the walls, a bit like a flower arranger's oasis, and the soil beneath your minimal footings will be washed away.

The individual stones or bricks in a traditional wall are held together (or more accurately apart) by mortar, which is a mix of sand and a bonding agent which, in old buildings, is lime. The pointing is the final application of mortar at the face of the wall that forms the visible join between the individual stones or bricks. For any masonry construction, the mortar should always be weaker than the stone or brick, because in this way any movement in the building (which is inevitable) is distributed between all of the joints, leaving the stones themselves intact. Where mortar is stronger than the stones, movement is concentrated into one or more much larger cracks, with the crack passing uninterrupted through any of the stones unlucky enough to get in its way – this would be a serious concern.

Part of the wisdom inherent in traditional construction is that the mortar is softer than the stone or brick. This allows the structure both to move, and also since the mortar is lime-based, to breathe. However, the implication of this is that the external faces of the exposed mortar (the pointing) weathers away and every so often it has to be replaced, an activity known as repointing. This is not a bad thing, but rather the way it is meant to be; the mortar acts sacrificially, as it were 'laying down its life' for its friends, the stones.

Sadly, since the 1920s a wonderful, super-strong, progressive and thoroughly modern material called Portland cement became widely available. Subsequently much repointing was done using hard cement mortars, which exacerbates a number of problems:

- The stone or brick decays faster.
- Cracks form between the cement pointing and the stone/brick, which allows water into the structure.
- Moisture that does get in is then trapped in the building fabric because the mortar is impervious.

A cementitious interlude

We are of course simplifying. The Romans first developed cement, using it, for example, in the dome of the Pantheon in Rome and – because it could set underwater – to construct the harbour at Caesarea Maritima in the Holy Land. 'Roman cement' was patented by James Parker in 1796, and was used in the nineteenth century because it could cover poor quality construction and be made to look like ashlar stonework by introducing joint lines. However, its waterproof qualities are a liability when inflicted on traditional masonry construction, for the reasons stated above. Roman cement was largely replaced by 'Portland cement' in the 1850s, but it was not until the early twentieth century that it became widely adopted in the forms of construction you are likely to meet in a church building.

Rainwater goods

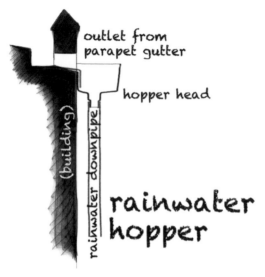

outlet from parapet gutter

hopper head

(building)

rainwater downpipe

rainwater hopper

Gutters are up high, often out of sight and beyond easy reach. Leaves, silt, sticks, bird droppings, dead pigeons and plastic bags block them really well. Subsequently the combination of silt and fertilizer makes them the ideal location for vegetation to grow – grass, flowers, trees even. Blocked gutters can cause water to pour down the inside or the outside of the walls, particularly where the gutter is hidden behind a wall (known as a 'parapet gutter', the parapet being the part of the wall rising above the level of the roof). Parapet gutters direct the collected rainwater through occasional openings in the wall, each with a 'hopper' that collects the water or a pipe to throw the water clear of the building; if these openings or hoppers are allowed to block, the water will be directed into the building. The downpipes that take water from the hoppers, or direct from an overhanging gutter, can block easily, resulting in water washing down the exterior face of the wall and soaking through to the inside.

Downpipes take the water from the gutters down to ground level. Whether they are cast iron or plastic, neither type is maintenance-free. They can become blocked or split. Cast iron will need painting every five years and the plastic versions (aside from being inappropriate for a historic building) tend to fail completely after about 25 years. If you're considering new rainwater goods, think about cast aluminium, which has a similar appearance to cast iron but (obviously) doesn't rust. When looking for potential problems, pay attention to damp walls or green algae on the pipes, joints and around the hopper heads, which may indicate blockages.

Gulleys are located at and/or below ground level. They receive water from the downpipes. Gulleys can have u-bends, which means you should be able to see water in the gulley just below the grating – you need to know what kind of gulley it is. Some have silt traps, which need emptying regularly – especially if the building is sandstone. It is good practice to empty a whole bucket (approx 10 litres) of water down each gulley every month. This will both keep the gulley clean and provide visual confirmation that the drains are running freely. Because the gulleys are adjacent to the walls of the church, it is essential to get the water away from the building as efficiently as possible.

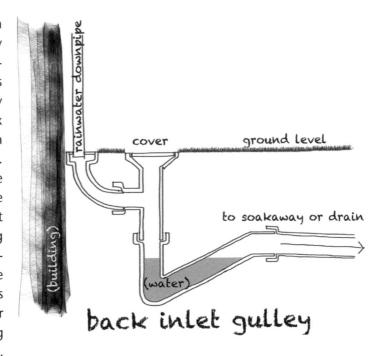

back inlet gulley

You need to know where the water goes to from the gulleys. Does the water go into a drainage system? If so what kind of drainage system – soakaway or into the sewerage? Does the soakaway work or is it blocked? Most soakaways need digging up and cleaning out every 10–15 years. Take precautions before you go poking around in the gulleys: they can be traps for sharp and dangerous objects – syringes and broken glass. Wear gloves and use a ladle to remove the sludge.

Pointing

This takes a bit more experience and expertise to identify what is going on. You will need a bit of training and advice from the church architect. However, look out for areas of the wall material that are eroding around the lines of pointing, or areas where the pointing has fallen out leaving gaps between the individual stones or bricks. There may also be dark stained patches or areas of algae on the walls, which indicate areas of damp caused by trapped moisture.

Finding sources of water ingress

Finding the leaks and places where the water is getting in requires some diligent observation. It isn't just what you can see; what you can't see is just as significant. So you have to be a bit of a detective when it comes to keeping a dry hat and boots on the church.

   The best way to check is to make the inspection of the roofs and rainwater goods at least every six months, when it is raining or immediately after heavy rain. There can be a surprising number of fountains on a church in the rain. If your church has fountains it means blockages. Many Quinquennial Inspection Reports number the downpipes and gulleys, which is very useful when describing which one has the problem.

Externally

In addition to any fountains spouting from the joints of blocked downpipes and over the top of blocked gutters, look for how the water runs off the coping stones of parapets and gables (the coping is that last course of stone that provides the capping to a wall). If it isn't running off it might be running in via the gaps between the stone where the pointing has failed.

   When it is dry, damp patches or dark stains on the sections of wall behind the downpipes or around the hopper heads indicate that there might be a problem. Also signs of soil being washed away near the walls or being spattered up from the ground at the base of the walls suggest the gutter above isn't catching the water.

Internally

Look for damp patches high up on walls, ceilings and the junctions where the roof meets the walls. You may well need some binoculars and a torch to see sufficiently.

   If the church has a combination of damp floors, lifting parquet or rising damp climbing the walls blowing the plaster or turning surfaces green, this is caused by water ingress. Water is getting into the building down from above or up from below, and sometimes even horizontally in from the side.

   If you are confident that the roof is sound and the gutters and downpipes are all working well but the interior is still damp, then it could well be that the below-ground drainage isn't working. Blocked gulleys and silted-up soakaways result in rainwater, once down off the roof with nowhere to go, sitting in an ever-growing puddle and seeping into the church through the walls. Another possible cause of damp is condensation – we'll have more to say about this in Chapter B4.

All of this is hardly exciting, and can seem a million miles away from the core activity of the Church. However, keeping a dry hat and boots on your building is essential if the building is still to be there in 50 or a 100 years' time, and therefore to the long-term well-being of the Church's ministry. And it also makes a substantial difference in the short term – it is difficult to care for people if you are trying to do so in a building that speaks of lack of care.

Have a plan of action

So what should you do? It is never too late to start thinking about the appropriate strategy to keep your church's rainwater goods, gulleys and ground drains flowing freely to protect the building from the damaging effects of water ingress. As should be clear, the objective is to get the rainwater off the roof and away from the building as swiftly and efficiently as possible; key to this is achieving and maintaining the dry hat and boots every church needs for its long-term survival.

The best strategy for keeping the rainwater goods working is to have a contract with a local builder or specialist who will visit the church at least twice a year to clean gutters, hoppers, downpipes, gulleys and drains.

Each building will have its own particular access challenges. Ladders might be quite sufficient for some while others will require specialist access platforms to reach high-level or inaccessible areas. Doing nothing because the gutters are too difficult to reach is neither good for the building nor any good as an excuse! So if you cannot reach those parts of your building that need to be reached, find a specialist who, with the right kind of equipment, can.

Interestingly most areas of a medieval church building were reachable relatively easily with little more than a ladder, but the Georgians and Victorians created many high and lofty buildings where access to the gutters is both difficult and potentially dangerous.

There may be a cost, but simple preventative maintenance pays thousands in dividends. Recently, in 2008, a Lancashire congregation had 'saved' £200 per year for ten years by not cleaning out the parapet gutters of their church building. They then had to raise and spend just under £250,000 to put right the extensive dry rot and blown plaster caused by the resulting water ingress. The Society for the Protection of Ancient Buildings (SPAB) has calculated that every £1 'saved' by not doing preventative maintenance costs £20 in repairs within five years. Think of it as the most fantastic financial investment!

When it comes to church buildings, 'a stitch in time saves nine thousand times nine'. Chapter B17 has more information about regular preventative maintenance, which is the essential requirement to keep your church dry.

B4
Damp and Moisture Control

Most of us live in houses built using relatively modern construction methods, typically with a cavity construction (two separate skins of masonry, with or without insulation between) or perhaps timber frame (with insulation between the studs and brickwork or whatever other external facing). What all modern construction has in common is that water is kept out by means of an impermeable waterproof skin. And just like a plastic raincoat, you then need to deal with any moisture generated internally – hence the Building Regulations now demand that all bathrooms, kitchens, utility rooms and so on have mechanical extract fans.

Modern construction achieves its waterproofness with lots of plastic and cement. A concrete floor will have a damp-proof membrane ('dpm') – basically a thick plastic sheet – which in turn is lapped with a damp-proof course ('dpc') in the walls. Breathable membranes are now used in pitched roofs and timber-framed walls, but these are solutions to the problem of condensation trapped in what is otherwise an impermeable construction.

If modern construction is like a plastic mac, then traditional construction is more like a woollen great coat or a breathable fabric such as Gore-tex. A medieval church will have no waterproof layers anywhere – not in the floor, the walls or the roof (see Chapter B2 for a discussion of traditional masonry-wall construction). The result is that moisture is an ever-present reality in a traditional building, and so too is the movement of that moisture from one part of the structure to another. This may sound alarming to modern ears, but is nothing to worry about provided we understand that a traditional building needs a different form of care.

We talked in Chapter B3 about the importance of your church building having a 'dry hat and boots' – this is about controlling the amount of moisture getting into the structure. This current chapter is about some of the principles involved in dealing with the moisture that you will inevitably find in old structures.

A tale of two sponges

Aside from the moisture in the floor and walls, the other major factor to consider is the moisture in the air that the building contains, because the two work together. Now for a bite-sized morsel of physics in the shape of the idea of **relative humidity**. Warm air is able to carry a lot more moisture than cold air – this is the basis of cloud formation and rain, and it is why condensation forms on your bathroom mirror when you take a shower: moisture condenses where warm air meets something cold because as the air cools it can no longer carry as much moisture and has to 'put it down'.

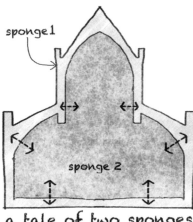

a tale of two sponges

A historic building is like two sponges: the first 'sponge' is the fabric of the building itself – particularly the walls and floor – and the second is the air contained within it. If the air of 'sponge 2' is warmed up, then it will be able to absorb more moisture – it becomes 'thirsty' – and it sucks this moisture out of 'sponge 1' (the walls and floor). As the air cools down, the process is reversed.

Implications

There are a number of implications of this:

- Sporadic heating of historic buildings (e.g. only on Sunday mornings) is bad for the building. Heating a building in this way causes the moisture to shuttle back and forth between our two sponges, which over time may cause the masonry to deteriorate. It is much better, if possible, to keep the building at a steady-state temperature, either by heating the people instead of the air space, or if you have more continuity of use of the building through the week, by keeping it heated all the time, at least to a background level – see Chapter B10 for a discussion of the different options for heating churches.
- Impermeable surfaces should not be added to an old structure – see below for some ways we have dreamt up to destroy our buildings.
- Given that the building is 'breathing' all the time, ventilation will be important. You do not want too much because then it will be impossible to heat the building; but nor do you want too little because the internal 'sponge' will become too wet and then encourage mould to grow.

How to destroy your church building

The best way of damaging a historic structure, short of resorting to arson, is to add impermeable materials to construction that is trying to breathe. These are some of the main culprits:

Carpets and floor coverings   Many modern carpets have a rubber or foam backing, which prevents a traditional solid floor from breathing. The effect is to force the moisture sideways into the adjacent floor and walls. So if you are putting down carpet, make sure it has an appropriate breathable backing.

Gypsum plaster and cement render   These are great materials, but not in a historic building. If you use a modern plaster at low level on an old wall because it is damp, you will make the problem worse by forcing the moisture further up the wall. The correct material to use is a lime-based plaster, which does allow the wall to breathe.

Paint   Modern emulsion paints work by forming an impervious film over the surface that has been painted. As with gypsum plaster, this traps the moisture in the wall, which will in time cause the paint to bubble and flake. The correct material for decorating an old wall is limewash which, because it breathes, is much less likely to fail as described.

Cement mortar   As already discussed in Chapter B3, cement makes a much stronger but less flexible mortar than lime, which was traditionally used. The weakness of lime mortar is its strength, so to speak. By contrast, harder cement mortar puts more stress on the face of the stone, often causing it to crack, and by being much less breathable it makes the stone wetter and thus more susceptible to frost damage. The combined effect can be to cause the rapid erosion of the wall, as though the cement mortar were 'eating away' the stone.

B5

The Wonderful World of Seating

Are you sitting comfortably? Then we'll begin

Most churches have seating from one or more of five basic periods. What follows is of course an oversimplification, but since it accounts for a good 90 per cent of examples, we suggest it is a useful generalization. Many churches, if they are old enough, will have gone through all of these stages, though some stages may have been missed out.

Victorian Poppy Head

Empty When a medieval church was first built it would have had no fixed seating. Many churches of course grew from something very small by multiple stages into the sort of medieval buildings we are now familiar with. At most there would have been some seating around the perimeter, which is where our saying about 'the weak going to the wall' comes from – you went 'to the wall' because that was where you might find a seat if you were unable to stand. The beauty of 'pewlessness', of course, is that the space is able to be used flexibly for all sorts of communal activity. And it should be remembered that in many settlements, the medieval church was the only community building.

Early pews From the late twelfth century until the Reformation, medieval churches became subdivided into a series of sacred spaces run by guilds, parishes and individual families, and naves began filling with 'worship stations' in the form of altars, statues, paintings and so on. Fixed rows of pews began to be introduced, some of which survive, while the Reformation swept away the rest. It is clear that medieval churches, on account of their 'mixed economy' of uses, were not fully pewed in the way we are now accustomed to in a 'traditional' church.

Box pews Gradually this became formalized and further elaborated, and by the Georgian period it was normal for churches to be full of box pews; one example of this is Holy Trinity Church at Goodramgate in York (now in the care of the Churches Conservation Trust). Georgian pewing effectively divided the church into a layout of open-topped rooms, individual families having their own pews for which they would pay rent. Sometimes these 'rooms' were elaborated to include fireplaces and other creature comforts. Filling a church in this way meant that communal activities would take place in vestries, bricked-off aisles or chapels, or in attached buildings like the National Schools or churchyard buildings. In practical terms, box pews do reduce draughts and are great for keeping toddlers in one place.

Benches What we are so familiar with in a 'traditional' church are Victorian 'benches'. In sweeping away the system of pew rents, the new benches were much more demo-cratic – previously if you could not afford to rent a pew, you would be relegated to a few benches set aside for the poor, or you had to stand. Instead of a series of inward-facing family clusters everyone could now see and be seen, the congregation would display an appropriate attitude of devotion and (in principle at least) anyone could sit anywhere.

Chairs Chairs are not a new idea, as witnessed by the two-year correspondence in *The Ecclesiologist* in the 1950s mirroring contemporary discussions of over-pewing, flexibility of space, quality of welcome, stackability and so on.[1] In most cases benches won the day, but they began to be replaced by chairs as early as the Edwardian period, when side chapels, baptistries and children's corners began to appear. Churches are increasingly removing their Victorian pews and replacing them with chairs. At its best this transforms the building's flexibility and returns it to its community roots; at its worst it replicates one static arrangement with another, and in the process reduces the numbers accommodated. More on this to follow.

Over-pewing

The Victorians were keen to increase the number of places in our churches, in response to the nineteenth-century growth in population and the rise of Nonconformism. This variously involved the building of new churches in new urban areas, the demolition and rebuilding of some existing churches and the extension and re-ordering of others. The main central conduit for funding was the Incorporated Church Building Society, which provided substantial grants for all these classes of work. In seeking to create more 'sittings' in churches, the ICBS unwittingly encouraged the cramming in of as many pews as possible, since the more sittings you could accommodate the greater the possible grant.

It is this more than anything that seems to account for the 'over-pewing' of our churches, imposing a single rigid format on the building and removing the flexibility it had traditionally had for use in a variety of formats. To a modern eye there also seems to have been an element of social control, of church being about sitting up straight and doing what you're told; like a tightly bound corset, pews often restrict movement and enforce a pattern of behaviour. Whatever the case, our churches were made much poorer with the eviction of much community activity, and with it the loss of ownership of the building by the wider community.

We think of this as a 'process of sclerosis'.[2]

Construction

Usually pews are set on wooden platforms, raised perhaps 100 mm (4 inches) from the general floor level; these raised platforms are usually in timber, with aisles often tiled or flagged. Wooden pew platforms are a great deal warmer than stone flags or tiles, making for warmer congregations. This difference in level means that removal of the pews also entails removal of the pew platforms. So what does this mean in practice?

The typical construction of the pew platforms is floorboards on timber joists with a clear air void underneath. At the bottom of this void is usually bare earth. This construction is no different from the ground floor construction in a typical Victorian house, and suffers the same typical problem of a potential lack of ventilation. Where these floor voids are vented, this is usually by means of holes in the sides of the pew platforms, which may or may not be adequate. But if, as is often the case, they are unvented, and if the soil is damp because your water table is high, you may have some rot in the joists and other timber members. If the floor feels springy in places, then this is the most likely reason. And even if you are free of rot, you will be creating favourable conditions for woodworm and other forms of beetle attack.

In physical terms, the pews themselves are usually very straightforward to remove and put back in place. This makes it possible to take away a bank of pews temporarily (leaving the platform) to demonstrate what the openness might feel like (ensure you mark the new trip hazard adequately with warning tape to all edges). This can be done with an archdeacon's licence rather than needing to go through the process of a faculty application to the Chancellor, and is a temporary arrangement that can last approximately a year (but talk to your archdeacon). Once you come to remove the pews properly, the floor needs to be remade to suit the main level of the church. Care is needed here to make sure that by filling in the pew platforms (and therefore preventing those areas of soil from breathing) you do not create a problem by driving the ground moisture into the walls and columns. As always, seek professional advice.

The other practical implication to the removal of pews is that it may also affect your heating installation, since they do offer a discreet means of introducing radiators into the middle of what is often quite a wide space, at the front and/or back of a bank of pews. Individual pews can also be fitted with electric heaters underneath or with heat-pad pew cushions. With removal of pews of course goes removal of these heating facilities, so the pews may well demand an adjustment to, or even a complete rethink of, your heating.

Chairs – what to look for

In specifying church chairs there are several things to look for:

Stackability   If you are serious about using your church building flexibly, then it is very important to be able to move your chairs around, and preferably to stack them to enable the space to be cleared altogether. If you are going to clear the space, then you need to think through where the chairs would stand when stacked – at the edge of a space or in a separate store? Some designs will safely stack 40 chairs in less than a square metre; others won't stack at all, or only three- or four-high safely.

Linking   Make sure you have a design that easily links and comes apart and that you understand how to do this. In particular, if you want the flexibility to arrange seating in arcs (which makes for a much more inclusive feel as the gathered people of God), then you will need a chair design that links together at the front leg only.

Upholstery (or not)   Many will assume that to be comfortable, a chair must be upholstered. In reality, whether a chair is comfortable to sit on or not is much more to do with the ergonomic design of the seat and back than with the padding. We of course bring a degree of padding with us (some more than others …), so we would urge you to go into the chair-choice conversation with an open mind on this. The downside of upholstery is that it has a much shorter life than a non-upholstered finish, so even if the initial costs are lower they may be greater in the long run.

Back design   Look at the design of the back of the chair. If the back is bent in one direction only, it will be comfortable to sit in when sitting up straight, but if you attempt to move your bottom forward and lean back you may find that the back of the chair cuts into you. By contrast a back that curves in two directions – concave horizontally and convex vertically – will be more comfortable to sit on for an extended period because it allows a greater variety of sitting positions.

Legs   If the chair has a crosspiece linking the two front legs below the seat, as many do to give it lateral stability, the height of this bar affects how readily you can tuck your feet under the chair when sitting more upright.

Arms   A design with an option for arms is helpful for older people. These may need to be stacked separately, but can tie in well visually.

Width   Most contemporary chairs are much wider than the earlier models of rush- or wooden-seated chairs, so you will need to think about how many chairs will fit. The usual width required for a single chair is 510–540 mm (20–21 inches); allow a 'pitch' of about 900 mm (36 inches) (i.e. from the back of one row to the back of the one in front).

Books and kneelers   The more of this stuff your church uses, the more you will struggle with chairs. Some designs allow for a bookrest to the side between you and your neighbour. Some churches with chairs hand out kneelers to those who want them as part of the welcome process.

Storage   If you are serious about clearing away the chairs, how they stack is important. The most practical designs include trolleys made to take the design of chair and allowing them to be wheeled away to a storage area.

Testing, testing, testing ...

Different people sit in the same chair in quite different ways, so it is important to get a good number of people to sit in examples you are considering, and to listen to their comments. Chair manufacturers are generally very happy to loan a sample or two of their chairs, but may not have one in the exact colour or finish you are considering, so it is important to separate issues of finish out from more basic aspects of the design. Comfort when sitting is a very personal thing, so do not expect to find an option that pleases everyone!

One very popular stacking chair used in many churches was designed by David Rowland in 1964, and is known as the Howe 40/4. This is both elegant in design terms and easy to stack – up to 40-high on trolleys, enabling a space to be cleared completely. It has been widely used in historic churches, including a number of English cathedrals. Depending on finish, this costs around £150. In recent years various manufacturers have been trying to develop similar stackable designs at a cheaper price, and the Church Buildings Council ran a 'Design a Church Chair' competition in 2012 to help stimulate the market.[3]

Happily there is now a broader range of choices, including some designs around £100 and even down to £40 or so, which challenges the (appallingly awful) banqueting chair. Be clear, however, that each design is different, and while £150 may sound like a lot for a chair, compared with the cost of buying the wrong chair, or building storage to accommodate chairs that are less stackable, even at that cost the right chair is a bargain.

Your flexible friend

The great benefit of removing pews and installing chairs is the ability to reconfigure the internal space of your church for different uses. Rather than imposing a single rigid format (the great crime of over-pewing), a variety of formats enriches the building hugely. How about being able to accommodate funerals and weddings (formal inherited format), café church (multiple small tables), harvest supper (larger tables), a ceilidh (cleared to the sides) or a meditative service for 20 (intimate seating in the round)? Whether your particular church is called to any or all of these activities, the typical parish church should both be capable of (and expect to be) hosting a wide variety of activity – because fundamentally your church is a building for the whole of the community.

Of course all this flexibility comes at the cost of an additional 'caretaking load' – the time and physical effort required to shift between formats. It is really important that you are realistic about this, and know how you are going to manage the moving of furniture. It is also really important, if you intend to clear the space at times, that you think through where the stored chairs are going to be placed. A few stacks of 40 chairs on a trolley in a side aisle may be fine, or you may design in specific storage cupboards (in which case this needs to be co-ordinated with the choice of chair). What is not acceptable is to have chairs that stack only six or seven high littering the edges of a space and that can be pulled over by a small child, or indeed twice as many safer stacks of three chairs that take up much of the potentially available space!

As always there are other options, including short pews that are movable. While many Victorian pews were cheap 'flat pack', ordered from a catalogue and assembled on site, others were beautifully made from quality materials with a great deal of love and care. Where they were made specifically for the building it is often the pew ends that have the fine carving, and it sometimes works to make shorter pews out of the long ones, thus retaining and reusing the carved ends. These can in principle be made movable, and in this way a church can gain much of the flexibility it is hoping for while preserving the best of the workmanship.

Sometimes pews may be made up of medieval carved ends, joined by much later ends and backs. Again the strategy of reducing the length may be appropriate, as at St Mary, Wortham in Suffolk, an example featured in *Pews, Benches and Chairs* by Trevor Cooper and Sarah Brown.[4]

Emotion

Seating can be a surprisingly emotive issue. Rightly or wrongly people can get very attached to 'the pew my mother sat in all her life, and her mother before her', and the question of whether they attend church themselves is neither here nor there. If you are seeking to make the argument for change, you ignore these sentiments at your peril since, whatever else they may be, these views will be sincerely held. It is perhaps no accident that it is precisely the thing that you touch and that supports you that people become most attached to. The implication of this is that any discussion of pews, however mundane they may be, will likely bring with it more profound pastoral issues of security, anxiety around change and of course mortality.

Notes

1 See ch. 15, 'Movable benches or chairs?', in Trevor Cooper and Sarah Brown (eds), *Pews, Benches and Chairs: Church Seating in English Parish Churches from the Fourteenth Century to the Present*, London: Ecclesiological Society, 2011, pp. 237–56.

2 'Sclerosis': coined in the fourteenth century and roughly translating as a 'morbid hardening of the tissue'.

3 See   www.churchcare.co.uk/about-us/campaigns/news/604-church-chair-competition-update.

4 See Cooper and Brown, *Pews, Benches and Chairs*, ch. 29.

B6
Fonts and Baptistries

BAPTISM
Danger of Death
(and New Life)

Baptism, of course, is the rite of initiation into the Church and is recognized across the Church as an introduction into and affirmation of membership in the Christian community. The argument over infant baptism is an old one, going back at least to Origen and Augustine (both in favour) and Tertullian (against). While this is the subject of a range of sincerely held opinions, this is not the place to rehearse the arguments for and against. Instead this chapter will look at the practical implications of how we carry out baptisms, of whatever form, in our buildings.

How much?

Almost any traditional church will have a font, usually of stone, and often medieval in origin, in which infants will have been baptized over many centuries. If our Church is in the business of bringing non-churched adults to faith, then we must also cater for adult baptisms, which of course can also be done in a traditional font. Many churches prefer the option of full-immersion baptism for non-infants, which more directly and dramatically spells out the symbolism of the rite. Naturally a full-immersion baptistry requires a good deal more water than a 'sprinkling' in a traditional font; given that water and building fabric do not always mix happily, this needs some careful thought.

The first observation is that a pool for full-immersion baptism need not necessarily be permanent; some churches bring in a small demountable swimming pool for the task, which requires a supply of warm water and a pump to empty the pool afterwards. When such a church undergoes a re-ordering there is often the request for this arrangement to be formalized and made permanent, since baptism is seen to be central to the life of the church. A permanent baptistry is usually in the form of a pool that is often covered over with removable flooring when not in use; the basic structure is either preformed in plastic or cast in concrete. Clearly in the case of historic churches this may have implications for below-ground archaeology; you might discover earlier buildings on the site (very interesting to uncover but may delay your programme) or burial vaults for the great and the good. The presence of burials under the floor is sometimes indicated by ledgerstones, which are inscribed memorial stones set into the floor and covering the entire grave (though they may well have been moved as part of an earlier restoration or re-ordering).

Thought needs to be given to how any pool, temporary or permanent, is to be filled and emptied, and how the water is to be heated. While it is possible to do all of this with permanent services, given the relatively infrequent use the baptistry will be put to these are often best done with temporary services. The pool can be filled from a cold feed or a hose, heated with a submersible electrical element and then emptied by means of a submersible pump.

In terms of size, you want a pool that is large enough for three people – the baptismal candidate plus two doing the baptizing. However you heat the water, having some insulation to the walls, floor and steps is sensible – otherwise the heat you put into the water will be absorbed quickly by the structure of the pool. You also need to think about where the candidate for baptism will come out of the water and then stand, as water will be streaming off them on to the floor. Clearly a tiled or stone finish here will deal with the water better than carpet or wood, though some churches simply use plastic sheeting and lots of towels.

Location

Since baptisms usually take place in a service in the midst of the church community, the location of the font or pool needs to allow people to gather round – a font surrounded by pews or a baptismal pool stuck in a corner is unhelpful. Baptismal pools are often incorporated in staging, which has the combined advantages of raising the focus of the sacrament while also reducing the amount of digging required, which is particularly relevant if the pool is naturally drained. Alternatively a location somewhere between the middle and the front of the nave can provide more opportunity for the community to gather round – provided of course the seating can be moved.

There is also a sound tradition of placing the font on view close to the entry into the church, emphasizing that baptism signifies initiation into the new life of the Christian community. Hence the font is often located near the main door or centrally at the back of the nave. While this works well symbolically it should not be at the cost of creating a visual barrier on entry (which makes the building feel defensive), nor in a position where it is possible for only a handful of people to gather round.

Canon F1 of the Canons of the Church of England allows the flexibility for the font to be placed in other locations, but is clear about its respectful setting:

1 In every church and chapel where baptism is to be administered, there shall be provided a decent font with a cover for the keeping clean thereof.
2 The font shall stand as near to the principal entrance as conveniently may be, except there be a custom to the contrary or the Ordinary otherwise direct; and shall be set in as spacious and well-ordered surroundings as possible.
3 The font bowl shall only be used for the water at the administration of Holy Baptism and for no other purpose whatsoever.[1]

New life

Christianity of course does not have a monopoly on the symbolic use of water. Indeed many churches in Britain are built where they are to allow the appropriation of pre-Christian holy sites, which were often associated with springs. In medieval times baptisms often took place out of doors at these springs or holy wells, or indeed in rivers. We see nothing wrong in continuing these traditions, particularly in communities where that older understanding lives on.

The theology of drainage

There is an understanding still common within the Church that the font should drain away to consecrated ground. Clearly this makes the prospect of moving a font more disruptive as it requires remaking a drainage connection, which means digging up a part of the floor. While this understanding presumably had some older precedents, this is a relatively modern concern and was principally promoted by the Oxford Movement. Furthermore emptying a full-immersion baptismal pool straight into the consecrated ground underneath a church will not do the foundations any good nor help keep the building's boots dry.

Other uses for a font

Any pre-Reformation church had a stone font since infant baptism would then have been standard practice. Many of these medieval stone fonts remain and are in themselves often artefacts of considerable interest. Perhaps because they are relatively easy to move within a building (later concerns around drainage aside) it is not uncommon for a fully rebuilt Victorian church to retain a medieval font from an earlier building on the site; your font may therefore be the oldest part of your building.

Churches that have a tradition of full-immersion baptism will often not know what to do with their old stone font, particularly if they do not wish to offer infant baptism. Again this theological 'hot potato' is not a subject for this book, but that doesn't mean your church shouldn't think about it and come to a sensible, agreed and coherent decision that works for the community in which you're located.

Aside from the issue of having more than one place of baptism, the old font can in its way remain useful. In particular it remains a visible expression of death and rebirth that is at the heart of Christian community. It is therefore an object that can prompt useful questions in the casual visitor, whether the individual tourist or the child on a school trip. And in more settled communities the idea of several previous generations of a family having been baptized in that particular font remains a powerful draw, particularly in an age in which so many people feel rootless. Why would we not want to use something of such symbolic power if it would help draw people into the community of the Church?

Note

1 Canons of the Church of England, Section F, 'Things appertaining to churches', 'F1: Of the font' – see www.churchofengland.org/about-us/structure/churchlawlegis/canons/section-f.aspx. Note the 'Ordinary' is the bishop, or the archdeacon acting on his/her behalf.

B7
Multimedia

Scope and ambition

This chapter looks at some of the issues involved in installing audiovisual (AV) equipment into churches. Any consideration of this needs to start from a decision about what you want this equipment for. For example, the optimal means of amplification for the spoken voice will be different from music and different again for a band compared with a choir. It is also important to understand how the acoustics of your building work at present – before designing in a new system as part of a wider programme of re-ordering it is important to consider the reverberation time of the space (how much it echoes) and whether the overall acoustic of the space can be improved by changing the acoustic absorption of the surfaces.

The rest of this article assumes you have decided you need at least some form of amplification or other technology. The needs of people with disabilities should always be part of your considerations when thinking how to introduce or improve the technology in your church building. This is a legal requirement since the introduction of the Disabled Discrimination Act 1995 and its successor, the Equality Act 2010.

Mission control

As soon as you consider amplification you need to think about where the sound is to be controlled from. In planning your space you will therefore need to decide early on about the location of any sound desk or control point because this will be the hub for a whole network of cables. Recently this question has become more flexible as it has become possible to control a system from an iPad or other mobile device. This allows the person doing the controlling to move around in the building, but you still need a central point to which all the cables come; and of course the iPad option requires some form of (reliable) WiFi network in the building. Whether you are twiddling physical knobs or controlling it from a tablet, in terms of location, the person operating the system will find it much easier to operate if they are able to hear the sound in the space in the same way as the rest of the congregation. In practical terms it is

also helpful if you have easy access to the front of the space, in case you need to go forward to adjust a microphone or whatever.

Generally the sound desk is best located towards the rear of the space and slightly raised to allow the operator a line of sight to the front over people's heads when the congregation is standing. It can therefore become a substantial element within the space. If possible it is best to avoid areas with a substantially lowered ceiling, as this area will have a different acoustic. If the system is reasonably complex you will have various pieces of rack-mounted equipment, some of which may be very expensive. This raises the issue of how much of the equipment is locked away, which in turn depends on the pattern of use of the building and how well supervised it is during the week.

Lights, camera, action!

Many churches make good use of projection equipment. The beauty of it is that it enables you to dispense with a lot of the hand-held clutter that can be so unfamiliar and offputting to first-time visitors, and free worship up for everyone. It also allows for a much wider variety of forms of presentation.

For some churches, particularly those built on the Hillsong model, the use of multimedia is so central that the architecture of the building is designed around it – the church is essentially a theatrical black box without any windows to let in natural light. Undoubtedly this is preferable if video projection is your top priority and you have the luxury of designing a church from scratch. The trickier issues arise when trying to implement this model within an existing (and particularly a historic) building. In this case you will need to plan your projection with sunlight in mind, and consider how much you will try to black out the windows, particular those at high level. You will need to think about how people who are visually impaired will manage to see or read off a screen. While projection is a huge improvement for some people, it can actually make matters worse for others.

Another obvious issue when dealing with an old building is that sight lines will not be as favourable as in an open-span modern space, and the location of screens will need a good deal of thought. A traditional church with side aisles was never designed as a space where everyone would have an uninterrupted view but instead as a family of interconnected rooms with complementary functions. If you are introducing projection into such a church it is very likely you will need repeater screens to deal with blind spots, for example in the aisles. How all of this is attached to the existing fabric, and how cables are run, needs careful thought beforehand. If you are planning a new installation as part of a re-ordering, then it is advisable, if possible, to use the building in something like its new format(s) before finalizing the projection and AV.

Finally, think about the feel of the building when it is in other patterns of use. In an old building it is important to be able to hide projection screens away – when not in use a large blank screen has a significant (and generally unhelpful) impact on the feel of the space. Some churches are experimenting with live streaming of the words of the prayers, songs and responses and so on to the congregation, who follow on hand-held tablet devices or mobile phones.

Flexibility

Designing a multimedia system for a space with a single pattern of use is one thing, but many churches want to have some flexibility for how the space is arranged, and crucially where the focus of attention is. If that is the case for you then you will either need a location for your control desk that works for each of the main layout options or some mobility, which will come at the cost of a more complex system and most likely a higher price tag.

At the same time think through which other spaces you may want to have video and audio relayed to. It is often a good idea to do this for a foyer/narthex space, particularly if parents might use this to take restless children out of the main space but still want to be part of what is going on.

Induction loop

Don't forget to make allowance for an induction loop to cover the whole space; this is a simple ring of copper wire or tape hidden around the perimeter and linked to a small transmitter, which enables those with hearing aids to hear much better. A loop is not difficult or expensive to install, but like all these things is much better planned in than fitted as an afterthought. As well as the loop, you will need to have some visual signage informing people that you have this bit of technology because those with hearing aids will need to turn a switch on their earpiece.

General principles

- **Technology is wonderful**, but it is a moving feast that is developing all the time. It is now possible to control a complex installation from a tablet or smartphone. This introduces greater flexibility but usually at the cost of additional complexity.
- **Pay for some good advice** from an AV consultant, who should be able to help you with developments in what is available and, if they're doing their job, help you cut down your wish list to what you really need. It is very important to be clear about what you're hoping to achieve and not simply to be wowed by all the sweets in what can be a very exciting sweet shop.
- **The best advice is KISS** – 'Keep It Simple, Stupid!' Any system, particularly for a community building, either needs to be durable enough to last several decades or important enough that you are happy to replace the key bits every few years. Much modern technology is, sadly, surprisingly fragile, particularly in environments with higher levels  of humidity; no matter how clever it is, if it breaks easily it will be no use at all.
- **Aim to be moderately future-proof** by trying to anticipate which sort of future changes would be disruptive of the space as a whole, while not trying to cater for every conceivable future need. In practice this may be as simple as laying spare ducts to enable cables to be run across the space without being festooned around the walls. Many cables come with the connectors already in place – in practice this means wider ducts are very helpful to allow space to thread through not only the cable but the connector on the end as well. Any floor boxes should be strategically located and big enough to accommodate additional outlets if needed.

How much is enough?

Multimedia is one area where needs and wants can easily become confused. Bad audiovisual installations are an embarrassment, will make you look incompetent and may therefore impact negatively on your ministry. Equally there are churches where the installation is clearly out of proportion to the real needs of the worshipping community. So while multimedia is important, and offers some exciting possibilities, it should never become an end in itself. Take a sanity check at each stage of developing a multimedia design, and always be clear about who wears the 'ministerial trousers'.

B8
Heating Basics

It's a 'modern' phenomenon

Heating churches is in a sense a modern phenomenon – it seems that before the nineteenth century few church buildings were heated. Nevertheless people went to church even in the coldest months, though there is evidence they weren't always happy about it. Modern expectations are quite different; most of us live in centrally heated houses, and this cultural shift has unsurprisingly had an impact on our expectations of comfort levels within church buildings, no matter how old.

> The frost … froze last night the Chamber Pots above stairs … No Service again at Church this day (and which should have been in the Afternoon) owing to the cold.
>
> *Parson Woodforde, 25 January 1795*

However, it is worth remembering that even though it was never heated, a medieval church building in its original form might have felt a good deal warmer than it does now. When first built, many of these buildings had plastered ceilings below the roof which, in the rural areas, would have been thatched and thus well insulated. This, along with the insulation provided by earth floors strewn with rushes and lime-rendered walls, would have made a significant difference to the ability of the building to retain such heat as was generated by activities within the church, or the residual heat 'stored' by the building from spells of warmer weather. High box pews, once introduced, would also have provided welcome protection against the draughts.

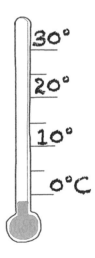

Great expectations

Nowadays there are any number of issues and problems associated with heating church buildings, many of which are connected with changing expectations and life-styles. In the twenty-first century we expect the environment around us to keep us warm whereas our forebears found ways of keeping warm in what they expected to be a cold environment.

Many of the church buildings in central Europe, and especially the former communist-bloc countries, still lack heating even today. The temperature in churches during the winter months might be below minus 20°C but the buildings will be packed for services. Human bodies are of course excellent heat emitters, so a full church will be a lot warmer than an empty one. Apparently some Russian congregations have summer and winter churches, the winter one sometimes being above the cattle shed in rural areas for warmth to rise to the people above.

In essence, therefore, to put heating into a medieval church building is to implement a significant physical change in response to a cultural change. There is nothing wrong with this – indeed 'twas ever thus – but it is important that this change is made in a sensible and thoughtful manner that respects the grain and nature of the original building. Badly installed services are one of the principal means by which the integrity of historic buildings are compromised. It is quite possible to destroy the appearance, and even the structural stability, of a historic building through the insensitive installation of a heating system. Temporary tents have been erected in some churches to provide a smaller enclosed and separately heated space during the coldest months.

Many historic Anglican churches are in need of heating installations that are both efficient and sustainable, and of finding ways to improve the insulation of the building that doesn't cause damage to the fabric. Rarely is this straightforward to achieve, and some areas of improvement in historic buildings may not be possible at all. There are a number of factors to consider, so it is important that time is taken to arrive at a good solution that contributes to the long-term health of the building.

It's the clothes we (don't) wear

One factor we all forget is that our forebears wore multiple layers of clothes, many of which were made from wool (the very rich might have silk undergarments – mmm very nice!). Clergy cassocks and cloaks are a remnant of historic clothes and, as any vicar will tell you, they are excellent for keeping the warmth in and the cold out! (At one point in our country's history, in order to protect the wool revenues, clergy were ordered by Canon Law to wear woollen undergarments!) The word 'surplice' (the white cotton cape-like thing that is worn over the cassock) comes from Latin meaning 'over the fur' – clearly previous generations were well prepared for the cold!

There is evidence that sometimes the people took matters in hand in their efforts to keep themselves warm in church. In the late 1700s the new vicar of Spalding in Lincolnshire complained that many of the gentry had set up braziers in their box pews, which spewed smoke and fumes into the open space of the church. (Even more remarkable is that, in addition to their personal heating arrangements, sideboards and cupboards were installed in their box pews for food and drink, which they consumed somewhat riotously and sometimes during divine service! The new vicar was not amused and cleared the whole lot out.)

Of course, it is never difficult to wear a vest but it is difficult to have your cake and eat it. Recently Hexham Abbey PCC had a choice whether to go one step further. Faced with bills of over £20,000 a year to heat the building to the constant 17 °C required for the well-being of the pipe organ and the comfort of the people who worked in the church, the PCC sought expert advice to find a cheaper and greener solution. But there was no cost-free solution, and the cheaper greener solution would be to put the organ in its own temperature-moderated box, encourage the congregation to dress appropriately and also provide 50 woollen 'Hexham Habits' for visitors to put on over the clothes they came in. Unfortunately this sustainable solution, which would have been much cheaper than heating the whole of the building, was considered unacceptable. The PCC decided to continue to fund burning fuel in order to provide a minimal level of comfort throughout the church.

Being cold was (once) a fact of life

If you look for the evidence there are very few church buildings that bear the traces of any form or method of heating earlier than the Victorian period. St Thomas' in Dudley (the town at the centre of the Industrial Revolution) was completely rebuilt in 1818. The architect's plans for the new building had no provision for any kind of heating, even though it is located in a coal-mining area. It was the railways, the new technologies of the later industrial period and the cheap coal that saw the introduction of heating systems into public buildings, churches included. Heating was installed in St Thomas' in about 1878.

It was thus the mid- to late-Victorian period that saw the introduction of heating installations, hot-air vents, cast-iron 'tortoise' stoves, boiler rooms, large-bore cast-iron heating pipes and fireplaces in the vestries, all with their attendant chimneys and flues. This was partly a response to changing tastes but also to an increased need, since our churches were actively becoming *colder*. One by-product of the growing influence of

A. W. N. Pugin and the Ecclesiologists was the removal of the plaster ceilings that were a common of feature of medieval churches in order to raise the interior height of the nave and chancel. This had the advantage of creating the 'ecclesiological wow-factor' of a more dramatic interior but the attendant downside of providing an uninsulated 'cold roof'. As a result the church buildings lost heat more quickly, while the 'scraping' (removing the lime render to stone walls inside and out) of churches in response to the new 'gothic' fashion for the 'honest' expression of bare stone exacerbated the problem by removing what little insulation the walls possessed.

Heating – what do you want and why do you want it?

Before looking for specific solutions it is worth stopping to think about the motivation behind your considering a new heating system or change to your existing one. What is it you are really hoping to achieve from any proposed changes? It could be because you want to:

- make the interior warmer
- make people happier
- save money
- replace an existing installation that is on its last legs.

As well as wanting to be warm and to provide a warm welcome, many church communities are keen to reduce their fuel bills. As a result, congregations often consider using modern technologies familiar from other settings, such as double glazing, applied insulation materials and commercial-style hot-air blowers over entrance doors. However, in many cases these measures will be inappropriate in a historic setting. The guiding conservation principle for a historic building is that the heating should be quiet, visually unobtrusive and have minimum impact on the fabric of the building. One example of the intelligent incorporation of modern technology in a historic building is St Michael and All Angels Church, Withington, which is claimed to be the UK's first zero-carbon church. This was achieved through reduction in energy consumption, renewable energy generation from a biomass boiler, and photovoltaic panels – all in a Grade 1 medieval Cotswold church.[1]

Perception is reality to those doing the perceiving

Creating an acceptably warm environment is not just about temperatures; people's perceptions are also crucial.

One truism of construction science is that damp buildings always feel colder than dry ones, even when the temperature is the same. This is because a dry wall reflects back to you more of the radiant heat that strikes its surface than does a damp one. So before you embark on improving the heating installation, make sure the building is (reasonably) dry. Then see what can be done to control the air exchange, which will reduce the draughts (while still allowing the building to 'breathe'), and don't use materials that trap and hold moisture, such as carpet on a damp floor.

Another factor that affects peoples' perception is the *thermal coefficient* of different materials used in the church. This influences how they feel to the touch and how they feel affects how cold we perceive them to be. For example, limewash really does feel warmer to the touch than emulsion paint; lime plaster feels warmer than gypsum plaster; wood feels warmer than stone, ceramic or metal materials.

Which system?

When choosing a heating system there are a number of conflicting issues to juggle with, such as:

- installation and running costs
- frequency and the number of people using the building
- the cubic capacity of the space to be warmed
- different temperature requirements for different activities (congregational worship where people move around more can be at a lower temperature than a concert or lecture where they remain seated)
- the availability of services to the site.

There is simply no one-size-fits-all solution, so the needs, possibilities and restrictions of each building and site must be assessed individually.

Churches are community buildings that are run by a changing band of volunteers and clergy and that may well, during the course of a week, be used by a wide variety of people. A good rule of thumb when it comes to installing technology is, as we said in the previous chapter, **KISS** – 'Keep It Simple, Stupid'. Which is to say that there is no point installing a system that, on a day-to-day basis, needs an engineering graduate to operate it. The multiplicity of users is more of an issue in community buildings than in buildings of any other type; this is something many of those who design services installations fail adequately to account for, so you will need to understand what is being proposed and you may well need to push back against an initial set of proposals.

The good news is that there are an increasing number of examples of good practice from which lessons can be learnt. Furthermore as a result of changes to the Building Regulations, these are now backed up with data and evidence.

Do the research and consult first

Research

As a starting point it is essential to understand your current installation – what you have and how it should be used to obtain the best performance. Just because the system is old doesn't mean it is no good. Indeed when it comes to older boilers, these sometimes are better than current models since the basic technology is more robust than the cleverer but relatively fragile modern equivalent.

Take time to think about how you use the building. If you can, monitor what happens to the temperatures inside and outside the building, both when the heating system is in use and when it is not, and through the seasons of the year. Use smoking joss sticks to identify where the draughts are coming from. See what happens across a variety of different circumstances, for example when:

- the main door opens and closes
- the wind is from the east, west, north and south
- the building is heated from cold
- the background temperature is kept steady and then raised from this when needed.

Try to monitor how much fuel is consumed an hour when the system is running at flat out compared to when it is providing background warmth. The basic message is to do the research *specific to your particular building* before making any decisions.

Consult

Armed with this information it is then advisable to consult the Diocesan Advisory Committee (DAC) heating advisor and your church architect. Do this before you embark on any conversation with a manufacturer or contractor; however well meaning they may be, these people will be in a specific line of business, which translates into an interest in selling you their specific wares. It is important, therefore, to be clear in your own mind as to what question you are seeking an answer.

And as always, don't forget that any changes to the fabric and fittings will require a faculty from the Chancellor. The ChurchCare website (www.churchcare.co.uk) has some very useful guidance notes about heating for churches.

Archaeological advice

Installation of a heating system, and in some cases even the simple replacement of a boiler, may well have archaeological implications to the fabric above and below ground level. A PCC undertaking work in a church or churchyard is legally a 'developer' and is required by law to be responsible for the costs of any archaeological work that may need to be done or observations that must be made before, during or after the works. This is not an option for PCCs but an obligation in the same way that it would be for a commercial company developing a historic building or a piece of land. Similarly laying services (roads, drainage, water, gas, electricity or telephone) to a historic property or across a historic site will have archaeological implications. Once again your first port of call should be the DAC.

Note

1 See www.inspiredefficiency.co.uk/case-study-st-michael-and-all-angels-church.

B9

Energy Efficiency

Not just for anoraks

The current need to improve the energy efficiency of the nation's building stock is a necessary modern response to the urgent modern problem of our profligate and unsustainable use of energy. This chapter is concerned with how historic buildings should best address this modern problem.

Historic church buildings were not explicitly built with energy efficiency in mind – indeed as we have seen they were not built to be heated at all. Vast expanses of single-glazed leaded light windows, cold roofs and solid masonry walls leak heat fast. So now that we expect our buildings to be heated we have created a problem to be solved, and of course the higher the expectation of heating the greater that problem is.

To keep such buildings warm requires either substantial amounts of energy input to overcome the energy losses, or significant interventions to reduce the energy losses and reduce the energy input. In principle, better insulation rather than more heat is the sustainable route to keeping warm.

But – and it is a big 'but' – traditional buildings need ventilation and the movement of air to keep them healthy. Sealing them up as we do our houses and workplaces with non-breathable insulation, double glazing, plastic materials and expanding foam gunk is not good for the fabric. There are few modern products that will work well in traditional church buildings.

So what possibilities are there for improving the thermal performance of historic building fabric? Draught-lock porches or thick curtains across the doors are an excellent place to start. Replacing ceilings that the Victorians removed can help. There may also be potential to insulate the roof construction, but you need to be extremely careful not to cause problems by introducing condensation where warm air meets cold materials, which will lead to the rotting of roof timbers. On the other hand, in the context of replacing the roof covering there may well be opportunities to incorporate an uninterrupted layer of insulation that will present fewer condensation risks, and any such opportunities should be taken. Underfloor insulation is also well worth exploring, again particularly in the context of more significant work.

A storage refrigerator

Many traditional church buildings feel like refrigerators. More accurately, solid masonry construction works like a cold-storage radiator (i.e. it doesn't refrigerate all the time and will actually radiate some warmth if the weather gets cold enough). The structure requires such a huge amount of heat to warm it up that it constantly feels cold except perhaps in the early autumn when the warmth held in the walls, which have been heated by the sun during the summer, is at a higher temperature than the ambient air and so for a brief period the walls act as radiators. Church buildings are usually cool in the summer and cold in the winter. Some churches can be such powerful cold-storage radiators that they suck the heat out of you faster than your body can replace it.

Heating traditional buildings (with solid walls and uninsulated roofs) to the expectation levels of the twenty-first century can be difficult and very costly.

Energy efficiency in historic buildings

Retro-fitting energy-efficient materials and systems to historic buildings is both difficult and expensive. There are a number of drivers pushing the energy-efficiency agenda in England. However, without becoming too political about the subject, it is important to acknowledge that surrounding the energy-efficiency agenda there are a variety of conflicts of interests and different desires of outcomes.

The Building Regulations are one of the principal means the UK government uses to improve energy efficiency and so meet its ambitious carbon-reduction targets. Up until now the protected status of listed buildings has trumped the competing claims of the Building Regulations where these have been in conflict, but it is likely that this may change with future revisions. If that 'heritage veto' is removed or qualified, then the demands of energy efficiency will result in significant change to historic buildings, which will need to be carefully managed. Effective conservation is the 'management of change' which, in the case of energy efficiency in historic buildings, needs thought and reliable data.

It should come as no surprise that there is no quick fix nor any fully tried-and-tested solutions for historic buildings. The Society for the Protection of Ancient Buildings (SPAB) and Historic England are producing good guidance information. The Church of England is committed to the 'Shrinking the Footprint' initiative and is able to give advice and guidance to PCCs.

Given that the available technologies are changing quite fast it is therefore essential to get well-researched, objective and up-to-date advice. Successful outcomes will most probably be reached by compromise and 'best fit' solutions, agreed decisions being made on a case-by-case basis. Just because the church down the road has a biomass boiler feeding an underfloor wet system doesn't mean it is automatically the right thing for your church.

Heat loss – knowing your VHL from your FHL

When dealing with a traditional church building you need to distinguish between the heat lost through draughts and leakage (Ventilation Heat Loss or VHL) and the heat lost through the structure and into the ground (Fabric Heat Loss or FHL).

The place to begin is to reduce the VHL. This the most cost-effective option, whereas reducing the FHL can involve some very expensive or visually unacceptable alterations. Begin by making every effort to understand what is happening and identifying the areas of the VHL in your building. Use smoking joss sticks to track where the draughts are, both when the heating is on and when it is off. Track the temperature changes when doors are opened and closed as people come and go.

The remedies for VHL are all about draught prevention. These may include the provision of a draught-lock porch with a door at each end so one is closed before the other is opened. To have any chance of achieving only one door open at a time means a generous distance between the doors – a minimum of say 2.5 metres (8 feet). Another relatively easy improvement is loft insulation above ceilings – though be careful to keep the roof space ventilated. Underfloor insulation can make a huge difference to a suspended timber floor that is well ventilated below, so could be considered with pew bases. Heavy curtains are one of the simplest solutions – putting them across doorways and arches is more visually acceptable than in window openings but you may have to be radical. Failing lead cames in leaded and stained-glass windows cause lots of draughts: it isn't just that the windows are single glazed – there can be gaps between the lead and the glass.

Reducing the VHL may bring some challenges to the current conservation status quo. Secondary glazing is currently unacceptable to historic church windows but maybe one day we will change our minds. Another route with a significant potential impact is that we should begin to consider is putting back the plaster ceilings that the Victorians took out of nearly every medieval church.

In all the efforts you make to reduce the VHL, beware of oversealing the church building. It is essential for a medieval building to breathe and it must be possible for it to be ventilated. Just as weeds can be defined as plants in the wrong place, so draughts are areas of uncontrolled ventilation.

Reducing the FHL can be more of a challenge as solid walls leak heat. However, consideration should be given to replacing the interior lime plaster (with its reasonable insulating properties) that the Victorians, in their enthusiasm for scraping, removed from so many churches. Heat will leak through solid floors. Many earth floors (through which heat will leak quite slowly) were replaced by uninsulated concrete, which leaks heat at a faster rate. It may be possible to retro-fit an insulating material over the concrete but the change of level may be problematic, or then again it may resolve other issues you may have with disabled access. It will also, of course, change the appearance of the floor, which needs careful thought. Before taking that step it is essential to do the research and see how fast the heat is actually being lost.

Dedicated followers of environmental fashion?

When it comes to traditional buildings, compromise is the only option. To make the right choice of which compromise, it is essential to understand what is happening and how the building functions both when it is heated and when it is not.

In all the effort we are making to both reduce the carbon footprint and improve the energy efficiency of buildings, we should beware the 'hype cycle' and ensure that we're not being motivated by guilt. Many of the emerging 'sustainable technologies' are hyped up long before they have completed full trials and can be considered tried and tested with adequate data that demonstrates they really will make a difference. Do not rush out and get the latest gizmo for your church building – wait until there is good, considered and objective advice. In this case it is a good thing that conservation processes put a brake on fixing innovations to historic buildings – otherwise by now we may have had lots of church towers sporting wind turbines!

The application of a sustainability agenda to historic buildings is not a settled science; as with any emerging discipline, the supposed experts sometimes get it wrong. For example, the data used to calculate the Energy Performance Certificate (EPC) for a domestic house has been found to have loads of discrepancies; the software many inspectors use is inadequate and makes far too many assumptions. The U-values given for houses with solid floors and solid walls suggest that similar buildings (e.g. churches) deliver a woefully bad thermal performance, which then sets up a guilt cycle among the congregations. SPAB is leading research that is already suggesting the assumed U-values for solid walls are incorrect and that in reality they perform very much better than the assumptions behind the computer modelling allow.

With rising energy prices and an increasing demand for a warm community space, the need for effective, low-cost, environmental and conservation-friendly heating systems has never been so important. But so too is the need for accurate, well-researched and relevant advice, data and information, and at the moment this is largely lacking.

B10
New Heating Systems

An A to Z of things to think about or be aware of ...

If you are thinking about installing a new heating system or significantly upgrading the present installation, it is likely that you will need to instruct a heating consultant to advise you on what is most appropriate for your building.

Beware that some heating consultants and M&E (mechanical and electrical) engineers love the latest technology with lots of complex computer-controlled systems. The damp environment and pattern of use of a church building can play havoc with highly strung delicate electronics! Remember the importance of 'KISS' – 'Keep It Simple, Stupid'.

There will be a number of conflicting issues that PCCs will have to juggle:

- funding
- frequency of use of the building
- size of the space to be warmed and the numbers in the congregation
- availability of services to the site.

You need to ensure your advisors are thinking about all of these issues, not just some of them.

The consequence of this is that finding the right heating solution for your church building will take time. The ideal outcome will be a heating installation that is quiet, visually unobtrusive, affordable to run and that will cause

minimum impact to the fabric of the building. Ultimately the system you choose will be a compromise between a wide range of factors.

In addition to this introductory list, don't forget to look at the guidance notes on the ChurchCare website.

Access – for fuel delivery, installation, maintenance. It seems obvious but all too often the benefits of straightforward easy access can be forgotten in the design process or badly compromised by the constraints of the building, site or heritage interests. Pumping fuel oil or blowing wood pellets over long distances is full of hazards. The churchyard gates and paths will need to be wide and strong enough for the delivery lorries. Oil, bottled gas and biomass require the right structures and sufficient space, some aspects of which are governed by the Building Regulations. Any M&E items (boilers, pumps and controls) will at some point fail and need an engineer to visit; so make sure the installation is easy to access and the place in which it is located is not liable to become a junk store. Take care not to create an access problem for the future.

Aesthetics – external and internal. How things look is a hugely important factor in the architectural harmony (or more often lack of it) of any building. Church buildings can be ruined by intrusive amounts of heating equipment located in the wrong place. Items such as air-source heat exchangers can be visually unacceptable, and siting needs to be carefully considered.

Availability of equipment and spares, fuel supply, space. Tried-and-tested technology is best in a church building. You need to be confident that the hardware and the fuel have a proven track record and will still be available in years to come.

Background heating at a constant low level (9–11 °C) has been found in some church buildings to make the church feel warmer, and is cheaper to run when boosting up to 17–19 °C for services and so on. Providing a solid stone or brick building with constant background heating of about 10 °C does work and is much better for the long-term health of the building. Each church will respond differently, so a variety of temperatures and times will need to be tested to find the best long-term option. Controls (that you can fully understand and operate) are crucial to this strategy working cost effectively. See also 'Temperature' below.

Controls have enormous possibilities. Depending on the use of your building, the controls may require flexibility to cover a variety of activities on a variety of days at a variety of times at a variety of temperatures in different parts of the building. Zoning may be necessary, with control settings relevant to the context and activities. Simple programmers may be difficult to find but whatever you do fit, make sure the controls are tamper-proof. A dummy thermostat on the wall of each room is a surprisingly effective way to satisfy the fiddlers without them actually interfering or being able to change the settings!

Cost of installation, maintenance, utilities/fuel. Establish the future running costs as well as the installation costs before deciding which systems to fit. The 24/7 costs of running a gas-fired underfloor system has taken some PCCs by surprise; modern condensing boilers do not necessarily burn less fuel. Some makes of modern boilers have been a job-creation scheme for service engineers; most condensing boilers have a much shorter lifespan (circa 10–15 years) than old-fashioned types (circa 25–40 years). You may need to start saving for the replacement when its predecessor is fitted. Fossil fuels may continue to be expensive and will continue to be subject to price rises. Controversial fracking may reduce gas costs, but then again may not …

Effectiveness, efficiency, heat output, heat quality. This includes the percentage of fuel you put into the system that is converted into heat you get out. Electricity is very efficient on site but its generation in a power station is relatively inefficient. The location of heat emitters is significant to people's comfort. Costs may determine whether you have the slow and steady heat of a radiator system or the intense blasts and swift cooling of blown hot air or the boiling head and freezing feet of overhead radiant heaters.

Environmental impact includes a huge number of issues about which there may be a similar number of opinions. For example, issues include flue emissions, fuel generation, whole life of the installation. What pollutants are being put into the environment? How sustainable is the fuel, where has it come from and what is the environmental impact of its extraction and transportation? Will the equipment last and can it be recycled when it is disposed of?

Flues/chimneys will be found in many churches that have redundant Victorian fireplaces. If possible, use the flues associated with such fireplaces rather than adding new steel pipes externally. The flues/chimneys should be checked for structural integrity and have the correct liner fitted, as modern fuels and modern boilers burn very differently from the older ones for which they were designed. For example, a modern condensing boiler produces a great deal of water vapour. That water will condense out in a pre-existing flue/chimney if it is vented out that way, which will make the building damp unless an appropriate liner is fitted. Oil-condensing boilers have much easier flue options than conventional ones, especially if you use '28 second' kerosene rather than diesel.

SECTION B PRACTICALITIES

Fuels used in virtually all installations will be electricity with some other fuel or heat source. Less common is electricity on its own, but see 'Renewables' below. Some all-electric systems require a three-phase supply, perhaps 450 volt, in order to be able to run the lights and so on when the heating is switched on. Biomass (wood chip, wood pellet, acanthus grass or straw) is currently a financially attractive option attracting a government subsidy, based on consumption – 'The more fuel you burn the more money you get.' However, biomass requires a great deal of space for the fuel store and boiler. Fossil fuels have well-publicized environmental impacts – but so too does electricity in its generation. Of the fossil fuels, mains gas is currently a better option than oil.

Ground- and air-source heat pumps need careful consideration. Subsidies may still be available but these change frequently, so do your research. Talk to other churches who have installed them; early installations have had mixed outcomes. The optimum efficiency is 400 per cent (i.e. 4 kilowatts of heat out for 1 kilowatt of electricity in). The heat produced works well with underfloor heating, which operates at much lower temperature than radiators. However, the rate of heat loss from a traditional building can be greater than the rate at which heat pumps can provide the heat. Air-source exchangers (which look like air conditioning units) can be unacceptable in some historic settings, and some heat emitters can be equally unattractive.

Heat curtains are very popular in shops and foyers of public buildings. They are cheap to install, expensive to run and they don't really work in churches. Better if you can to use a heavy fabric curtain instead.

Heat emitters (radiators, fans, lamps etc.) need to be well researched before being chosen. All heat emitters need to be kept clean; paint finishes on radiators can make a surprising difference to the heat they emit so take care and get advice about what type of paint to use when redecorating. A high-temperature radiator system (82 °C flow with 71 °C return) can present a scalding hazard for children. Underfloor heating (see below) is wonderful for buildings where people sit or play on the floor – great for Youth Church and Under 5s.

Installation costs are affected by practicalities, but sometimes the very practical may be unacceptable in terms of aesthetics. Many contemporary adaptations in historic churches are required to be reversible. Few heating systems are easily reversible but some can be more so than others. Digging up floors to install underfloor heating has a massive impact on the fabric, the outcome is not reversible but it is virtually invisible.

Legislation requires that new heating or changes to existing installations have permission, so along with obtaining a faculty from the Chancellor, you may have to conform to Building Regulations, depending on what you are proposing. If the proposals involve changes to the outside of the building, then Conservation Area and/or listed building consents and planning permission will also be needed.

Maintenance is a regular essential for any mechanical or electrical installation. A straightforward practical system can save your PCC lots of money. Follow the manufacturer's recommendations – make sure the system is properly maintained on a regular basis by a competent engineer. Don't wait for a crisis before finding the right person.

Noise levels from loud fan-assisted radiators or hot-air-blowing systems are no good in a church. They need to be rated at 25–30 decibels maximum. Industrial and barn-space heaters using gas or oil burners or electric elements with blower fans are totally unsuitable, especially during the sermon and the prayers.

Operation should be practical and straightforward, without the need for a rocket scientist or brain surgeon volunteer member of the congregation to run it. Remember to 'KISS'!

Quality of equipment must be right for the job. Domestic fittings are not robust enough for a church, which is a public building and as a consequence will be subject to rough or ill-informed treatment. Domestic radiators and standard copper piping are damaged too easily, so for all their attractive cheapness they will rarely save you money.

Renewables that generate electricity (aside from ground- and air-source heat pumps mentioned above) include photovoltaic (PV) panels. These require planning permission, and can be a great idea when they work effectively. They can be used to feed your heat pumps, though of course you generate less of your electricity at the times of year you run your heating. For PVs you need to do the cost-benefit analysis – they can be a very expensive way to generate electricity. Wind turbines rarely work on buildings of any kind, and on historic churches they are a non-starter.

Temperature can have a significant impact on a church building. Damage can be caused by rapid changes of temperature and moisture levels (see Chapter B4). Constant stable heat is far better. The people using the building very often want effective sudden warmth for the time they are in it but don't want to 'waste' money on keeping a moderate level of heat running when nobody is inside. There has to be a reasonable balance between these needs and expectations. Rapid changes of temperature cause changes in humidity and condensation, which will damage plaster and wall paintings, encourage rot and pest activity in timber, corrode lead roofing from the underside and so on.

Underfloor heating systems use hot water in pipes set into a solid floor or just under a timber floor, and deliver heat to where people are; most other systems (including conventional radiators) rely on heating the air, which is particularly inefficient because in tall leaky buildings the heat rises and is quickly lost. Underfloor heating is much better for the building (see 'Temperature' above), and there are no hot pipes for children to burn themselves on. It can be used with almost any heat input, including heat pumps, because the system runs at much lower temperature. However, installation can be disruptive because you usually need to remake your floor, so in practice underfloor heating usually accompanies a more extensive re-ordering. If you want your church building to be a community hub that is working during the week it can be ideal; but if your building is only used on a Sunday morning, underfloor heating is not for you as it will prove very expensive.

Wear and tear will cause some parts of a heating system, such as fan-assisted radiators, to wear out sooner than others, so factor in their earlier replacement in your forward-looking Asset Management Plan programme and budget (see Chapter B17).

B11
Lighting – Strategies and Issues

A modern phenomenon

It is only very recently (in the last 50 years or so) that we have come to expect high levels of illumination in our churches. However, with some congregations now using projected images and words for worship, lower light levels are now required in order to read the words on the screen.

Early churches were dark and mysterious. Where there was lighting it would have been oil lamps or candles. By the fifth century church leaders saw the potential of candles to emphasize the Light of Christ and so they came into regular use for church worship. However, candles were relatively expensive until the late 1800s.

Lighten our darkness...

In early church buildings openings in walls were used to let light in, but they were not windows as we understand them. These openings usually had wooden shutters which had to be opened to let the light in – along with the weather and the biting insects! In the smarter buildings oiled vellum, alabaster, linen sheeting and other translucent materials were used to keep the worst of the weather and bugs out.

Glass windows began to appear in what we now call Romanesque buildings and so natural light become possible during the day. However, glass was expensive, so glazed window openings were small. The later medieval period saw increasing use of glass but it was still hugely expensive. During the Commonwealth (with the Protestant focus on the Word) and Georgian periods, clear glass was used extensively in the church buildings, admitting more light than painted or stained glass.

In terms of artificial light, oil lamps and candles were in widespread use until the mid-1800s. Gas lighting first became available from the 1820s; it was quickly adopted by churches but there was some resistance to its use because the light it produced was considered dull and flat. The gas mantle, which produced a much brighter and whiter light, only came into use after 1890. The introduction of large amounts of Victorian stained glass was only possible because of the artificial light provided by oil and gas lamps.

The National Grid (1920s) enabled a huge increase in the use of electricity for lighting across the UK. Most church lighting schemes date from after the 1920s and in many rural areas electric lighting was only installed in the 1950s.

Think first, act second

If you are thinking of making changes to the lighting in your church, look at the building and its uses before instructing or even consulting anyone. Do not leap to get a contractor round to look at your building before you and the PCC members have thought through some basic issues. It's 'your' church, not the consultant's or contractor's, so you need to take responsibility for it.

Be clear about what you do now and what you want to do in the future. Understand what you have and how it works, such as where the dark areas are and where good lighting is essential. Look at the building with and without current lighting, in a full range of conditions – when overcast and sunny, in the morning, afternoon and night, and at different times of year. Poor or inadequate lighting is rarely noticed by the church community, so the PCC needs to consider why it is being proposed to improve or change the current lighting. Who is making the suggestion and why? Is it a question of fashion or because you have spare funds that are looking for a project, or because there is a real need? Think hard about what it is that you are trying to achieve.

Begin with the broad-brush issues:

- How is the space to be used? List all the different activities that currently go on or you intend will go on in the building in its various spaces. Identify the ages and sight requirements of the users. Do people need to read words off a page or simply to see what is going on?
- What is the liturgical plan? List the various forms, styles and patterns of worship. How could lighting enhance (or inhibit) what you want to do?
- What resources are available (i.e. how much money are you prepared to spend on capital equipment, energy and spares and consumables)?

Help me, please …

Once you are clear about why you are changing your lighting, most PCCs will need help to source the equipment that will provide the optimum solution; the local DIY store is not the place to start. It is likely that the PCC will need to engage a consultant to help. It is essential to go and look at lighting schemes the consultant has provided in other churches and talk to the people who are using them. The Diocesan Advisory Committee can provide names of people to talk to and names of churches to visit.[1]

Beware the free lunch! If any contractors or designers offer you free advice, you need to be aware that it may come with the hidden agenda of selling you the kit they want you to buy. Lighting is another area (like audiovisual installation) where it is easy to get carried away by the technology and end up with a system that costs a small fortune, all to service a building that may only be in use for just a few hours a week. It is important, therefore, to consider the costs involved against the benefit provided, and to do so in the context of the overall needs of the church community. Note also that contractors are not designers and that they may therefore not be very competent to manage the aesthetics of lighting.

Mind your language

There can be some confusion about the language used in the rarefied world of lighting, so here are some words of clarification. A particular term may well mean something slightly different in the mouth of a specialist as opposed to in general usage.

The **lamp** is the bit you replace (often thought of as the 'bulb'). Some lamps are bulb-shaped, some are tube-shaped and some are thin and flat. You cannot always tell what type of lamp it is from the shape.

The **luminaire**, or light fitting: the whole thing, includes not only the bit you might need to replace, but also the body – the hardware that holds the lamp.

The **luminary** is best used to describe a prominent person (e.g. the bishop).

A **bulb** is an incandescent lamp (i.e. it emits light as a result of heating a thin strip of metal). Think of Thomas Edison. This form of lamp is hugely inefficient, converting only 5 per cent of the energy to light – the rest goes to heat. Typical life: 1,000 hours. Gradually becoming museum pieces.

A **fluorescent** lamp produces light by fluorescence – the 'neon light'. Much more energy efficient, but the light is often a bit dreary; no good for spotlights. Typical life: 10,000 hours.

An **LED** lamp produces light by electroluminescence. Much more flexible because LEDs can be used for general lighting or for spot lighting. Costs are rapidly reducing. Typical life: up to 100,000 hours, which makes these the only sensible choice for light fittings that are inaccessible (e.g. high up in churches).

Colour temperature describes the colour tint of the white light and is measured in kelvins. 'Cool' white has a higher 'temperature' (e.g. 4,000–5,000 K) whereas 'warm' white is lower at 2,700–3,000 K. This can have a big impact on the mood that is created in the space; it also depends on the colour of the surfaces being illuminated. Higher-temperature light can feel cold and clinical, so if in doubt, go warm. Decide which to go for and then stick to that – mixing them can look awful.

The remainder of this chapter covers the issues to think through.

Aesthetics

Think about what the installation hardware (i.e. lamps, luminaires, brackets, candelabra etc.) will look like. How will the building look when the all the lights are on? How will it look if certain lamps are on or only some parts of the building are lit? If at all possible, and especially if the proposals are for radical change, get the consultants to conduct trials and, if necessary, set up 3D models – computer or even physical scale models.

Above all, what are you trying to achieve? Recognize the potential for lighting to influence how people feel in the building. A zoned installation can provide a combination of settings to achieve different moods. High levels of illumination are not always necessary and can in fact make the interior of a church feel more like a factory or a supermarket than a place of worship. Contrast is more important than lots of light or flooding the space with excessive amounts of artificial light.

Mood can be significantly influenced by the type of light the lamps produce – see the comments about colour temperature above. At the two extremes of white light, some lamps produce very hard bright light, others can produce warm soft fuzzy-edged light. You need to know what you want and what you will get.

Arrival, approach and entry to the interior of a church (and the reverse on leaving) are often overlooked. Any lighting scheme needs to consider how the external experience complements the internal experience. Think about the experience of the first person to arrive (perhaps to unlock) and the last person to leave (perhaps having locked up) on a dark and stormy night or in an inner-city setting. The adequacy of lighting and the position of the switches as one approaches or leaves the church can be significant.

Preservation of the historic fabric and artefacts

The routing of cables and service ducts, and health and safety requirements, can all have an impact on the historic fabric and also have considerable logistical implications. Electricians are notoriously insensitive to historic fabric and unless they are properly instructed and carefully controlled they will make holes for cables and trunking through historic fabric without much thought. This is one of the most common ways the fabric of historic buildings gets damaged. For more on routing of services, see Chapter B12.

Internal lighting in churches will date from about the 1920s; it is worth looking for the scars from the earlier system(s), which could be used for cable runs and so on. Also note that some lamp types can cause harm to historic materials – check that you are not putting fabric and artefacts at risk.

Technical

Lighting can very easily become a 'KISS'-free zone. At the risk of scaring you off from taking an active interest in the proposals to change the lighting in your church, here is a summary of technical issues, including the hardware of lamps, luminaires and control systems. Once again this is intended to make you familiar enough with the area to enable you to work with a specialist.

Lighting products change very fast; the technology is always developing. Lighting designers and consultants acknowledge that the equipment they specify can be out of date very soon after it has been installed, sometimes as soon as it has been chosen.

Low-energy fluorescent and LED are developing very fast. LED illumination is remarkable and can be used in a huge variety of ways but it cannot do everything. As a consequence of the continual improvement of lamps, especially LEDs, it is likely that in the future there will be fewer lamp changes but more equipment changes.

Dimming of most lamp types is now possible but it needs careful research, thought and understanding of how the various technologies interact. Many LED lamps come in dimmable and non-dimmable forms – beware! Some dimming systems with certain types of incandescent lamps can cause a range of audible noises, including high-pitched whining, groaning and even singing-type sounds! And cheap ones are more likely to fail in buildings with higher humidity, like historic churches.

Control systems are becoming more and more complex. It is essential to check their compatibility with the various lamp types and dimming systems. Wireless control systems offer huge potential with high-level and inaccessible lamps. Some remote WiFi control systems have had clarity issues and have even unwittingly received instructions from mobile phones. More complex installations have more complex control systems, which go way beyond simple switches and have become termed sophisticated 'user interfaces'. Frankly these high-tech gizmos are no good if the people using them are technophobic or just want to turn the lights on or off. Make sure you get a system fitted to both the people and the building, not just the imagination of the lighting designer.

Compatibility can be a complex problem where different bulb types, manufacturers and fittings are used. Concerns about compatibility creates pressure to stay with one manufacturer for all the various bits of kit in order to be confident the control system will be able to make it all work. However, a single-source supplier might not deliver the best price or the best lighting solution for your building. As with computer systems, it is best to avoid 'closed-source' systems that lock you into a particular manufacturer. The better option is to try and get 'open-source' products that are supplied by a variety of manufacturers.

Spares, and their availability on the open market, should be established before committing to using a particular fitting.

Maintenance

It might be assumed that a new lighting installation should not require lots of maintenance. Unfortunately, even with new systems this is not always the case.

Make sure your lighting installation comes with a handbook that includes the technical data and specification of all its various bits of equipment. It needs to link the various lamp types with the various light fittings with the manufacturer's part numbers of all the items listed. This will both avoid confusion and make the job easier when someone new takes over, but may need asking for at the time the scheme is priced.

You can expect to have a new system demonstrated to you at handover, but there will be a lot to take on board and you will most likely forget. It is essential that this training is done with more than one person, and it can be really helpful if you video it – because you will always forget what was said. Ideally then produce your own idiot's guide.

Some dimming-systems hardware has proved to be remarkably fickle, requiring a clean, dry and dust-free environment in order to function properly – something of a challenge in many church environments. Some luminaires have proved to be excellent dust traps or the most perfect accommodation for insects, whether dead or alive.

Depending on height and ease of access, some installations are best re-lamped all at the same time, while with others you can replace lamps as and when they fail. You need to be confident that the various lamp types necessary for your installation are readily available. Some lamp types may have to be ordered from specialist suppliers. For the lamps that are replaced on an as-and-when basis, keep one or two lamps of each type in stock.

Running costs

Along with the energy costs you need to identify the other running costs. Clarify the costs of replacing the lamps (ideally do your research before you agree to the system that is specified). Some lamps can be over £50 each which, if a number are replaced all at the same time, can make a significant dent in the budget. Hire costs for a special motorized high-level access platform can be in the region of £500 per day, which needs to be included in the running costs. Many PCCs have been very taken aback by the annual maintenance cost for the new 'high-tech' dimming and scene-control systems – these can be in the region of £1,500 to £2,500 per year, with extra charges if one of the sophisticated individual circuit-control units needs replacing. It is essential to get this information from the manufacturers and/or the servicing agents before agreeing to have the system installed.

Energy use and environmental considerations

The aim of 'Shrinking the Footprint'[2] and the desire of many PCCs to reduce costs mean that all churches are concerned to keep their energy use to a minimum. This can be achieved in a variety of ways. It isn't just about the lamp types – there are some cost-benefit calculations to be done and design/specification choices to be considered.

If a particular lighting circuit is rarely used, the capital cost to install LEDs may be far greater than the occasional use of incandescent bulbs. Then again the calculation will be different if the change only involves changing the lamp itself.

Be aware that not all dimming systems reduce the amount of energy used – some just reduce the amount of energy flowing through the lamps.

Note too that the design and location of switch panels can encourage or discourage all the lights being turned on.

External lighting

There is a growing body of opinion that the external lighting of buildings not in use at night should be prohibited altogether, or at the very least turned off by 11.00 p.m. External lighting can contribute to 'light pollution' and the loss of dark skies. Bats and other animals can be disrupted by high light levels at night.

Floodlighting of a church requires both a faculty from the Chancellor and planning consent. It would be sensible to consult with the local residents and be sensitive to their views. On the other hand, floodlighting for specific events, festivals or celebrations can be a way of bringing attention to the building, setting it at the heart of the community – but again you need to consult and to be considerate.

Notes

1 The Society of Light and Lighting has produced a new guide for lighting churches – see D. Holmes, *Lighting for Places of Worship* (LG 13), London: CIBSE, 2014; www.cibse.org. Historic England has some very useful guidance – see http://historicengland.org.uk/images-books/publications/external-lighting-for-historic-buildings/;   http://historicengland.org.uk/images-books/publications/bsest5-principles-of-conservation-practice/; http://historicengland.org.uk/images-books/publications/new-work-in-historic-places-of-worship/.

2 See www.churchcare.co.uk/shrinking-the-footprint.

B12
Routes for Services

When we say routes for services, we're not talking about processing with the choir … This chapter is about the damage that cables and pipes can do to a building, and how to avoid it.

The requirements of modern technology, or even the installation of a modest kitchen or WC, mean bringing services in and out of the church building. How those services are run has a significant impact on the fabric of any building, particularly historic ones, so these issues need thinking through. Even if your church is not historic, incorporating services gracefully makes a huge difference to the feel of the space. If done badly the church will feel cluttered, smaller, *diminished*; if done well the routes for services will be 'invisible', allowing the building to speak for itself.

It is a bit like someone standing in church to read while wearing a false nose and moustache; if your eye is drawn to the peculiarity of what they are wearing then attention is directed to the person rather than the reading. The job of reading well in public is for the reader to 'get out of the way' and enable the audience (in this case the Church) to encounter the reading (in this case the Word); anything else is role playing or 'mere performance'. So too the job of the mechanical and electrical services is to facilitate the seamless working of the building while remaining as discreet as possible.

New stuff needs other stuff to make it work

Some services come into the building, such as water, gas, electricity and telephone, while others go out, such as sewerage connections and ventilation. Most of these connections will require making holes in historic fabric that may well be listed, and it is well known

beware making holes…

within the conservation sector that this is often the greatest cause of damage to historic buildings.

The good news is that with a little forethought, most of that damage can be avoided. The key thing is to think carefully *before* you start knocking holes in walls, floors, windows or roofs, to consider what routes are available, and to identify which are the best options in terms of balancing protection of the building with the efficiency of the services. It is essential that you consult with the Diocesan Advisory Committee (DAC) as soon as you identify the need to make holes in the historic fabric.

The same concerns apply to areas outside the church building. Churchyards are usually sites of sensitivity as well as considerable antiquity, so digging trenches across them to bring the services in and out requires similar thought and care. Whether it is Mrs Bloggs, a medieval knight or a serf who gets dug up, you need to be careful of what you are doing and have the right permission and safeguards in place.

You will probably need an archaeologist

Most of the holes to be made in a listed building or trenches dug through the churchyard will require the PCC to take archaeological advice beforehand and possibly engage an archaeologist to have a 'watching brief' during the work.

This requirement for archaeological input, as we have said before, is not an option for the PCC; it is a legal obligation. In making changes or improvements to a church or churchyard, the PCC is acting as a 'developer' and is required *by law* to be responsible for the costs of any archaeological input that may be needed before, during or after the works. This is exactly the same legal requirement that applies to a commercial developer or a private property owner who is developing land or laying services across a historic site or into a historic property.

Minimize the impact

This requirement for archaeological input means that the cheaper routes for pipes and cables are often those that require less intervention into the historic fabric because they require less archaeological input. The key principle is to minimize the impact on the historic fabric, which will help to minimize the price. For example, knocking a new hole through the base of the tower will be much more expensive than a longer pipe-run within the building that exits via an existing Victorian ventilation hole under a suspended floor.

Sometimes finding the best route will be a matter of compromise, but wherever possible it should be the change or the improvement that should be compromised, not the historic fabric.

Take advice from the DAC and your professional advisors, who will have experience of similar problems elsewhere. You will need to ask them about ways to minimize the archaeological impact of the PCC's proposals and the appropriate level of archaeological work required. They will be able to offer the PCC clear advice, an explanation of the situation and guidance on any given proposals. Where necessary the DAC will usually provide, at no charge to the PCC, a brief summarizing the extent of the archaeological work needed, so that the PCC can get comparable competitive quotes and be confident both that only the required work will be done and that the price for the job is reasonable.

Trenches in churchyards

The impact of any proposed work will depend on the depth, length and width of the required trenching and whether the services can be routed using directional drilling, impact moling or some other form of trenchless digging.

Normally pipe/cable runs can be installed with minimal archaeological impact by routing the run to use existing trenches or laying it along an existing pathway. As a rule of thumb, disturbances of less than 30 cm (12 inches) in depth are not considered to be archaeologically sensitive, but note that there will always be exceptions.

Where assessment indicates the likelihood of archaeological deposits other than unspecific human remains, it is usually only necessary to employ an archaeologist to monitor the digging of trenches. On rare occasions the trenches will need to be dug by an archaeologist.

Making holes in the historic fabric

Do not do this without taking advice and asking permission. There is nothing more to be said on this – no ifs and buts, no exceptions to the rule: **Do not make holes in historic fabric without taking advice and asking permission.** There are too many wonderful church buildings that have been damaged by insensitive (and sometimes totally stupid) routes chosen for service pipes and cables.

In the past the utility providers usually chose the shortest, cheapest and most direct route to bring their services into the building. Until the 1980s, utility providers were usually government or local-government agencies and the recipients had to take what they were given, with little consideration about the impact on the building. Nowadays the PCC is the 'valued customer' and the significance of historic fabric is much more important. While we may not be able to undo all the mistakes of the past, we can make sure we don't make them again.

It isn't just bringing services that requires making holes in the fabric of the building. Some holes are bigger than others, but the impact of that hole isn't always to do with its size. Fixing a microphone on a pulpit is at one end of the scale, and knocking through a wall to make a doorway at the other; however, if the pulpit is Jacobean and the wall contemporary, the significance of the impact is the other way round.

It is not usually necessary to undertake archaeological monitoring of every hole made, unless the work is large scale or in a highly sensitive location. But before you make the hole you need to have a good understanding of the likely impact. This is why you need to take advice and ask permission. The DAC's evaluation of the project will include an assessment of how great the intrusion is, what fabric it affects, the historic significance of that area of the building and whether the damage is reversible.

Cables and pipes within the church building

This is not just about aesthetics, but all about a proper understanding of conservation as 'the management of change'. The difficulty often comes down to the (lack of) experience of the electrician or plumber doing the work – the 'rules of engagement' for a historic building are quite different from those for a modern house. So all routes for services need thinking through and agreeing beforehand. Otherwise it can be like tacking your cables across the *Mona Lisa*. (Yes, really.)

Following the general principle of 'minimum intervention into the historic fabric', chasing the cables and pipes into the walls and floors is not usually an option. Instead the cables and pipes will need to be surface mounted. This means they are on show and can therefore have a significant impact on the appearance. While this might not be so serious a problem, a whole load of spaghetti drooping round the walls or running across stone pillars, arcades and arches will look dreadful. You will also need to investigate the surface on which cables or pipes are to be mounted. For example, if it is lime plaster you need to know it is strong enough to carry the load and be confident there are no wall paintings beneath.

The PCC needs to think very carefully what the finished effect will look like, take advice from people who understand these things and specify clearly where the cables and pipes are to be located and how they are to be fixed in position. It is essential not to let the contractors or the tradespersons (on site on the day) make the decisions as to where the pipes and cables will run. They will usually choose the shortest and easiest route between A and B. They will not be thinking of the aesthetics or the conservation principles.

Some buildings are so special and their aesthetic of clean lines and uncluttered surfaces so significant that surface-mounting pipes and cables is unacceptable. In such cases some intervention into the historic fabric is necessary but again it has to be done with considerable thought and care. There is an established practice of chasing cables into the joints of the stonework and then repointing over the top.

(Re)gaining your faculties

This is a list of the kind of information that will be needed for a faculty application to bring services into the church building:

- A Statement of Significance for the church and churchyard.
- Information about known burials or vaults in the areas affected by any pipe/cable runs and when the last interments took place along this route.
- Photographs illustrating the situation (snapshots are enormously helpful).
- A plan of the church and churchyard, preferably to scale, showing the source of supply and the position of pipes, taps, trenches, entry point into the building and so on. This should also show options open to the PCC if more than one route is a possibility.
- Details of the trenches: depth, width, route, proximity to paths, graves, trees or other features, how they will be dug (e.g. impact-mole, hand, mini-digger).
- Details of waste disposal/water supply/electrical supply (e.g. distance to mains, natural fall away from church).
- Information on how the service(s) will be introduced into the church building and the internal routes of pipes or cables.
- Information about the end point of the water supply, whether an outdoor tap or sink inside the church. If the PCC intends to use the water supply for a kitchen facility or in a WC it would be sensible to provide the DAC with as much information about this at the outset, although the PCC may wish to do the work in phases and apply to the Chancellor for two separate faculties (phase I, provision of services and phase 2, the installation of the WC/utility area).
- Information about the distribution board and electrical arrangements inside the building.
- Details of whether the church architect/surveyor has been involved in the project.

Wider consultation

For drainage works the local authority Building Control department should always be consulted at the outset to see what scheme would, in principle, be acceptable. If you are intending anything different from a connection to the mains sewer you may need to consult with the Environment Agency.

It is usual that Historic England (or Cadw, Historic Scotland as appropriate) will need to be consulted about proposals. The church insurers should be informed of the proposed works and approval obtained.

If the specification has not been drawn up by the church architect or surveyor, it is very likely that the DAC and all the other interested parties will recommend that she or he should be consulted about fixing and location of equipment, pipe/cable routes and design of fittings that might have a visual impact on the church. The PCC should do this at the outset rather than after the other parties and consultees have discussed the proposals.

B13
Kitchens and WCs – the Essentials

Kitchens and WCs are surprisingly powerful things! Many types of social encounter are eased with food and drink, and church-based activities are no exception. WC facilities are now seen as a basic requirement for any public venue. These changes in expectation and social practice mean that buildings that lack them become increasingly difficult to use. Adding such facilities might, for example, enable you to host concerts and other community events. These facilities can be missional game-changers because they bring with them all sorts of life and activity, which is what many of our churches are so lacking. Don't underestimate the transformative power of the humble WC and kitchen! See also Chapter E5 for some examples of the various solutions discussed.

What you need and where to put it

Generally speaking it is more sensible, practical and cheaper for essential facilities to be provided within the existing structure of the building rather than in an extension.

Before you contemplate putting the facilities outside, make the effort to explore each of the internal possibilities, listing all the various pros and cons. Then do the same for an external building to house the necessary facilities. An extension option will almost always be more expensive than an internal solution (think double the cost); it also has the disadvantage of handing a veto over the scheme to the local authority planning department, who cannot be expected to understand your mission as a church.

WC decorum

If you can justify the need for a WC, then next you should think hard about where to put it. In someone's home you would be very surprised to find a WC opening directly off, say, a dining room – it would feel odd, since we normally expect a greater degree of separation between the noise and potential smell of a WC and the heart of a house. So too in churches – if possible it is much less obtrusive to go out of the main worship space to find the WC. A WC put in the wrong place will not be used, and this is particularly true for older generations, who will need to use the facilities more frequently. Remember this important rule of thumb: the further liturgically east a WC is located in the building, the less use it will see.

If you have one, the base of a west tower can work very well, as this is easy to divide from the main space. An extension may work, but this, as already noted, will be more expensive. If it is not possible to locate your WC outside of the main space then a 'pod' solution – a free-standing structure that requires minimal alteration to historic fabric – located discreetly towards the west end of the church can work well. Once again think hard about where you place the door – preferably not in full view.

If you are going to go to the expense of putting in a WC within the building then it should be to current disability standards – generally 1,500 x 2,200 mm (5 foot x 7 foot 3 inches) internal dimensions. Note, however, that where this WC is the only one in the building, Building Control will require a second basin (at normal height for ambulant disabled use), which will further increase the space required. And if it is to be a wheelchair-accessible WC then you will of course need to think about level access – see also Chapter B19 on accessibility.

When is a kitchen not a kitchen?

Kitchens come in many guises; indeed 'kitchen' may not be a helpful word. For many churches the need is for a simple refreshment facility that can be used to provide drinks – a tea station – or perhaps to serve pre-prepared foods – a kitchenette. There is therefore a spectrum from a kettle and sink at one end to a full-on commercial catering kitchen at the other.

Whatever name is used, be clear about what it is you want the facility to do – literally, what you're catering for – because that will determine not only the space the

kitchen will take up and the equipment to be accommodated but also the size of holes that will need to be made
in walls and/or roofs for water, waste and ventilation pipes
and electric cables, and therefore the types of permissions
required. A kitchen that has to produce 100 three-course
dinners for a lunch club or wedding reception is very
different from one required only to produce tea, coffee
and light refreshments.

Note also that the full-on catering options will bring you
into contact with the local authority Environmental Health
department, which may have a significant impact on what
you are and are not able to achieve.

Consultation and discussion

As with much else about church buildings, the best solutions usually come from early
consultation and discussion. Sometimes such consultation results in the rejection of
the originally proposed scheme but usually this is followed by a creative dialogue that
produces a good (better?) practical solution. A good scheme will meet the following
objectives:

- Facilities that serve the changing needs of the church and the wider community,
  preferably allowing flexibility for them to grow.
- A positive contribution to the character of the building.
- High-quality workmanship and attention to detail.
- The provision of mains water, foul drainage (see below) and ventilation with mini-
  mal archaeological impact above and below ground.
- A scheme that is within the PCC's budget, phased to accommodate fundraising if
  necessary/possible.

What comes in must go out – sewerage

Both kitchens and WCs produce 'foul water', which must be disposed of properly; foul
water cannot be allowed to enter the rainwater disposal system or simply be chan-
nelled into a soakaway. Health and safety legislation and environmental protection
legislation require proper disposal to the public sewer wherever this option is open to
the PCC. It is possible to pump sewage quite a long way and it would be sensible to

take advice before you rule out connecting to the mains sewer; both your local authority and the Environment Agency should be consulted at an early stage.

Where there is no accessible public sewer, the alternatives are:

- Cess pit (holding tank that has to be emptied).
- Septic tank (containing a mini sewerage works – some require pumps).
- Trench arch drain (a clever long-run earth closet).

These alternatives should only be considered for exceptional cases where there is no reasonable access to mains drainage, for instance a church building in an isolated field. The latter two systems produce a certain amount of liquid outfall, which will have to be discharged within the churchyard (i.e. not on a neighbour's property unless you have all the necessary permissions). Note that there are some areas of the country where trench arch drains are not permitted and others where the septic tank must be of a particular specification.[1]

Note also that cess pits and septic tanks require deep and wide holes in the churchyard. The holes are often dug by machine and the location of such tanks and the route of the associated pipes should take into account the possibility of disturbing archaeological deposits. To assist in the decision about where the tanks should go, the DAC and archaeologist may ask for test pits to be dug in various locations to assess the depth and nature of any below-ground archaeology (usually just burials, but you never know what may be found).

It's nice to smell nice; it's nice not to smell

Aside from drainage, ventilation is the other essential factor to consider when locating, designing, specifying and managing the kitchen and WC.

A simple 'tea station' should not be too much of a problem. However, don't leave a water boiler simmering away – this can release several litres of water vapour per hour, which will have to condense somewhere and will increase the problems of damp within the church.

WCs located inside the church will usually have to be mechanically ventilated. There are ways to create a 'stack ventilation system' but both the diameter and height of the chimney may be unacceptable. Given the tendency for damp and only occasional use, it is very easy for an enclosed WC to suffer from the unpleasant combination of 'dead air' and damp. Both the design and specification must therefore address the need to ventilate the WCs effectively and efficiently when in use and when not. The small fans we are used to at home are virtually useless in churches.

How the waste air is taken out of the building can be another challenge but before you decide the only solution is to knock a hole in the wall, have a look at the possibility of taking the vent up the wall, over the wall plate (a timber member fixed to the top of a wall, to which the roof is then fixed) and under the rafters to the outside.

Beware of domesticating the sacred space

Statutory bodies such as Historic England, together with many DACs and Chancellors, have objected to proposed schemes for cupboards and sinks because they are considered 'too domestic'. Where kitchen schemes have initially been refused for churches it has often been because the design, materials or finishes were inappropriate for a church building. Experience through the dioceses over the years has distilled out some fundamental principles of good practice:

- **Walls** should be more reversible and not require foundations excavated into the church floor. Timber framework is much better than blockwork.
- **WC partitions** should be a sound-insulated framework. 'Noises off' from within the WC can be very distracting within the church.
- **Wall and ceiling finishes** should be suitable for what may be a damp building – timber panelling may be a better choice than plaster.
- **Locating the WC** further liturgically east means it will be used less. This is a cultural thing – when you need the WC you don't want to advertise the fact. Experience demonstrates that for the most-used loos – 'go west'.
- **Screens, cupboards and finishes** should complement the existing fabric of the building and be of a comparable quality.
- **The standard of materials and quality of workmanship** should equal or surpass what is already in the building.
- **WC doors** should be designed in such a way that they do not open directly into the nave. A lobby providing a buffer between the WC and the main space is not a requirement of the Building Regulations but is still a very good idea. Where this is not possible, ensure you can open the door without anyone in the nave being able to see into the cubicle.
- **Kitchen sinks** should not be visible except when in use, even when, for example, they are concealed in a side aisle.
- **A tea station** in a side aisle can be built into well-made woodwork, with a lid over the taps and draining board so that when not actually in use the installation appears as a handsome vestment chest or cupboard.

- **Cupboards against external walls** can be problematic because they trap the damp and/or provide homes for vermin. The solution to this is to space the cupboard off the wall, and ensure the gap is well ventilated.
- **Kitchen cupboards** should be of cabinetmaker quality, design and construction (i.e. not standard kitchen units from high-street outlets). A good joiner will be able to make the cupboards from the salvaged timber from old pews.

Compost!

A cheaper option for WC provision in remote locations (and fast being considered the sounder environmentally appropriate option) is to fit a composting WC outside of the church building. It is early days for modern composting WCs in the UK and therefore it is advisable to research the latest developments when you need the information necessary to make decisions.[2] It is important to ensure the composting WC is suitable for the English climate; it seems the types developed in Australia, South Africa and the Mediterranean do not work well in the colder climate of the UK.

The caravanning and boating fraternity have developed the technology of sewerage-free loos which, coupled with the legislation requiring WCs on building sites, has led to the ubiquitous site 'portaloo'. This solves the problem in a cheap, straightforward, practical manner, even if its plastic construction and high-visibility colour score low for aesthetic sensitivity …

While you are testing the possibility of wider community use of the building and determining the potential level of usage, you could install a temporary 'portaloo', which could then be upgraded to a composting or fully flushed WC at a later date. Don't forget that consents are required, even for temporary facilities. So don't do anything without consultation.

Notes

1 For trench arch drains, see: http://ew.ecocongregation.org/downloads/TrenchArch.pdf.

2 For more on composting WCs, see Darby, 2012, *Compost Toilets: A Practical Guide*, and http://toilet-composting.com/. Specifically for churches, see www.natsol.co.uk/category/site/church/.

B14

Bats

There are two issues to concern us when we are dealing with bats and church buildings. The first is the impact that the presence of a colony of bats has on the day-to-day life of a church community; this is the issue of 'cohabitation', and is chiefly a question of policy. The second, for those churches that have bats, is how one deals with carrying out building work around them without harming them. Of relevance to both these questions

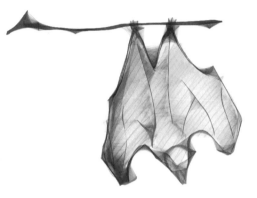

is the fact that bats enjoy a significant level of protection under the law; causing harm to a colony of bats can lead to a fine of up to £5,000 and a prison term of up to six months.

The natural place for bats to roost is of course in the wild, in trees, caves and so on. Increasingly, whether through loss of natural habitat or increased activity in the countryside, bats in Britain are making greater use of buildings, and some species are now 'buildings-dependent'. This of course affects rural churches more than urban ones. Given the legal sanctions this is not an issue one can ignore; rather the question is how to resolve what are competing claims over the building. We need, of course, to abide by the law; the excellent ChurchCare guidance note sets out a responsible but proportionate response.[1]

The trouble with cohabitation

Bats can destroy church communities. Perhaps that sounds overstated but ultimately it's what is at stake. A significant bat colony makes it much harder for a church to function; it hugely increases the cleaning load, damages potentially sensitive building fabric and furnishings and, perhaps most critically, reduces the range of functions to which a building can be put. There are, to say the least, substantial issues with mixing small children with animal faeces, however discreet the pellets might be. Few of us tolerate animals defecating in our homes (and any who do are likely to attract the attention of social services …); yet for some reason churches are expected to do so.

At the same time it is of course right that endangered species should be protected. The issue is how best to reconcile the two 'communities' – the *noctilionine* (yes, that

seems to be the adjective for bats) and the *ecclesiastical*. The demand that church communities put up with a bat population, seemingly at whatever cost to the life of those communities, either fails to recognize the fragility of many of these church communities or perhaps is blind to the church representing anything of any value at all. Whatever the understanding, an approach such as this reduces parish churches to a network of 'bat hotels' and makes for a troubled relationship.

The Church Buildings Council (CBC) has of late put a great deal of effort into lobbying central government to achieve a better balance between the needs of these two 'communities'. As well as producing an excellent guidance document,[2] the CBC also draws attention to some DEFRA-funded research by Bristol University that looked at improving the success of mitigation measures where bats occupy churches and other historic buildings (you can find the report by doing an online search for 'WM0322 bats'). This particular piece of research looked at the mobility of colonies of soprano pipistrelle bats and found that 'The availability of suitable alternative roosts is an important factor in determining the impact of future exclusions on these bats and [they] are able to make use of a wide variety of both natural and man-made structures for roosting.' This offers some hope that in future it will be more possible to find ways of encouraging a colony to emigrate from the church building elsewhere, perhaps to roosts created for that purpose in the churchyard.

Building work

When a person reasonably believes that their action would not result in disturbance to bats, but in the process of undertaking works accidentally causes disturbance it is unlikely to be an offence. However, if bats are disturbed during works, continuing with the works would be likely to constitute a breach of the law.[3]

The time when bats are most likely to be disturbed is when a church carries out building work, whether that be maintenance or a larger project. If your church is embarking on building work you are strongly advised to find out whether you have bats present well in advance; if you do have a colony present it is essential to plan the work to minimize disruption. If you have a significant population of bats then one or more surveys will be required before a licence will be granted by Natural England (or regional equivalents[4]); however, surveys are generally undertaken during the summer months when bats are most active. If you start and subsequently find you have disturbed a colony of bats then you will have to stop work while you obtain a licence to continue, involving an inevitable delay to the construction contract; you might find yourself paying for a contractor to stand around doing nothing for a number of weeks, which could prove extremely expensive.

Note, however, that bats are less susceptible to disturbance at some times of year than others. Times of particular concern are the summer maternity period and the winter hibernation, but the exact time of year these fall will depend on the species of bat with which you share your building. Disturbing a colony during these sensitive times can have a significant impact, including the death of adult bats, the abandonment of young or even, in extreme cases, the collapse of the colony; from a bat's point of view the stakes are high. However, it should also be noted that there is often flexibility depending on how bats are using the building – they will often be restricted to particular areas, which may have little impact on the works to be carried out.

Licences

The Church Buildings Council has published guidelines that have been drawn up in consultation with DEFRA and Natural England and should be followed when undertaking all works to a church building. Not only is this the most authoritative source of guidance, but given the CBC's mission to change policy, this is an area where we can hope to see some change, so look out for updated guidance published on the ChurchCare website.

CBC's guidance helpfully classifies building work into three categories – minor, routine and more extensive – and sets out the appropriate response in each case:

NOCTILIONINE EVENING NEWS

Churchgoer Colonies Invade Medieval Roosts!

an upside-down world...

Minor works such as routine maintenance, repairs, redecorating and so on can usually be undertaken without bat surveys.

Routine works, including works to mechanical and electrical services, replastering, timber treatment and so on; the recommendation here is to arrange a visit by an ecologist or a Volunteer Bat Roost Visitor. This is a service co-ordinated by the Bat Conservation Trust; given that it relies on volunteers it can take a while for a visit to be arranged. The visit should result in written confirmation of the advice given.

More extensive works are likely to require a licence, issued by Natural England. This should be issued within 30 days of the application, but before applying it will usually be necessary to commission a survey from an ecologist, which can represent a signifi-cant cost and will take some time. Natural England provides detailed advice on how to obtain a licence – see www.naturalengland.org.uk.

One frustration with the way the legislation has previously been applied is that it is a one-size-fits-all system – the same process had to be followed regardless of the conservation status (i.e. sensitivity) of the roost. Recently Natural England has trialled a new type of 'low impact bat class licence', which would allow for works that affect less sensitive roosts to be licensed on the basis of briefer survey information, which is where much of the cost and delay is encountered. For more information refer to CBC and Natural England.[5]

A radical option

A medieval church is in essence a very simple building but, as we discuss elsewhere, will usually have gone through many episodes of change in its life. In most 'traditional' church buildings you will see the timber trusses, rafters and boarding of the roof struc-ture, and this, of course, is one area where bats are more likely to roost. Many medieval churches would originally have had horizontal or vaulted ceilings of lime plaster; in some cases, particularly where the roof has not been elaborated with rich carving, it may therefore be worth considering reintroducing a flat ceiling in traditional materials. This is not a cheap option, and is thus not a measure for the faint-hearted, but may be worth considering if it is the best way of sustaining the church community while enabling the bat community to remain (and hopefully to prosper). And as discussed earlier in this book, the insertion of a ceiling also presents significant opportunities to improve the thermal performance of an old church by introducing insulation where there is none, and removing significant draughts, thereby making the building both more sustainable and more comfortable. (See also Chapter B4 on moisture in historic buildings.)

Notes

1 See http://churchcare.co.uk/about-us/campaigns/our-campaigns/bats; alternatively, just web search 'churchcare bats'.

2 See www.churchcare.co.uk/churches/guidance-advice/looking-after-your-church/bats.

3 From ChurchCare, Guidance notes, 'Bats in churches – undertaking works' – http://churchcare.co.uk/images/BATS_APRIL_2014.pdf.

4 The regional equivalents of Natural England are Scottish Natural Heritage, Natural Resources Wales and Department of Environment Northern Ireland.

5 See also 'Roost', 'a resource developed by the Bat Conservation Trust (BCT) to aid in the gathering of information on bat roost mitigation, compensation and enhancement techniques' – http://roost.bats.org.uk.

B15
Timber Decay

There are various possible causes of rot or beetle attack on your church building; this chapter deals with a few of the most common ones, and gives you some initial suggestions as to where to start in addressing them. If you suspect you have an infestation of some kind then it is important to take it seriously and get it investigated. It is equally important to follow Corporal Jones' immortal advice in *Dad's Army*: **'Don't Panic!'** Remember also that almost all examples of timber decay in old buildings are caused by bad design and/or maintenance elsewhere in the building; in addressing any form of decay it is essential, therefore, to ask how it got there in the first place.

Creepy crawlies

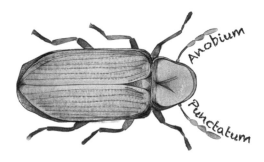

The two main pests for churches to worry about are **Woodworm** (*Anobium punctatum*), generally known as the common furniture beetle, and **Deathwatch Beetle** (*Xestobium rufovillosum*). The two are related – cousins, if you like – and have much in common, though there are a few important differences, which we will get on to.

Starting with the similarities, both are woodboring insects native to Britain; adult woodworm are 3–6 mm (1/8–1/4 inch) long, deathwatch 6–9 mm (1/4–3/8 inch) long. Both leave holes in wood – these are the flight holes for the adults – and yes, both have wings and can fly. With both species, the bulk of the damage is done by the larvae, who like to feast on the cellulose of the timber; woodworm leave tunnels up to 1–2 mm (1/16 inch) in diameter while deathwatch make tunnels 3 mm (1/8 inch) in diameter. Both produce dust, known as 'frass', as they munch their way along (generally following the grain of the timber), and this is often the first sign of a colony. A bit like digging the Channel Tunnel the beetles chew through the material in front of them and push the waste out into the tunnel behind them. Note that the emergence of dust is not necessarily a sign of current activity – it is possible for old dust to emerge due to vibration in the building many years after it was produced.

So what about differences? This is mostly a question of taste. Woodworm prefers sapwood (the wood nearest to the bark of the tree from which the timber was cut) whereas 'Cousin Deathwatch' prefers heartwood (wood from the centre of the tree), and particularly oak. This makes deathwatch both less accessible to treat and more serious in terms of its ability to compromise the integrity of structural timbers. Heartwood is, however, pretty tough stuff, and these beetles only usually find it palatable when the timber has already suffered from fungal decay – feeding on material that might euphemistically be described as 'previously enjoyed'. Big timbers, if used unseasoned as they often would have been, take many years to dry out, allowing suitable conditions first for the initial fungal decay and then a nice environment for the larvae to thrive.

The good news is that these beetles are actually quite picky about the conditions they need in order to thrive, particularly the level of moisture in the building. It is reckoned that the beetles like timber with a moisture content over 15 per cent, whereas below 12 per cent the larvae die; so if you can get the moisture level of your timber down to that level, problem solved! There are therefore two obvious things we can do to guard against beetle infestations. The first is to maintain the building properly, clearing gutters regularly and so on; this is another area that underlines the importance of maintaining a 'dry hat and boots' (see Chapter B3). The second is to use the building more; this is an example of the maxim 'Use it or lose it'. Buildings in frequent use are warmer, and the timber drier; buildings infrequently used are likely to have a higher moisture content generally, and specifically in the timber.

How to treat it

Chemical treatments may not be as effective as they at first appear, particularly for the more reclusive deathwatch. These treatments are unlikely to reach much beyond the surface of the timber, leaving the central parts of the timber, where the colony is most likely to be, unaffected. It is also a very blunt instrument, and has the huge disadvantage of killing the spiders that are the natural predator of the beetles. Yes, whether you like them or not, in this context spiders are our friends …

If possible, the best thing is to start with an accurate diagnosis of where live infestations are. There are two minimally invasive processes that are becoming available and that if used should enable any intervention to be targeted to the source of the problem. Some have used ultrasound to determine what is going on inside the timber and therefore where any damage is located, without cutting into the timber at all. A second means of surveying is via microdrilling, which produces holes of just 1 mm in diameter. These holes both determine where any infection is located and will then allow treatment to be syringed into the affected areas, offering a much more 'surgical' approach.

Stopping the rot

'Wet rot' and 'dry rot' are confusing terms, which together have probably led to more unnecessary destruction than any other misunderstanding in conservation.
Iain McCaig and Brian Ridout, Practical Building Conservation: Timber[1]

As with beetles, there are a variety of types of fungi that might rot your building, but of the possible culprits the usual suspects are wet rot and dry rot. The names are misleading – both sorts of rot are caused by fungi and neither will grow without high levels of moisture.

Dry rot is one type of the larger class of brown rots; it leaves a powdery residue and was named 'dry' rot from erroneous eighteenth-century explanations of its cause. We now know that it is caused by the fungus *Serpula lacrymans*, which principally attacks softwood and can produce extensive surface growth, with long 'threads' that can find their way through brickwork. This of course makes it the stuff of nightmares, evoking the fear that dry rot is a cancerous growth that is unstoppable and that, to use another *Dad's Army* quote (again), 'We're all doomed, doomed.' A great deal of myth has consequently arisen around these fears.

In fact like other forms of rot, dry rot will only spread to areas with sufficient moisture; it cannot grow at all where moisture content of timber is below 20 per cent, and will not thrive unless the moisture content is a good deal higher than that. Typical timber moisture content in an unheated building is 16 per cent or less, so dry rot can only develop where there is an additional problem with moisture entering the building. There is also a mistaken belief that dry-rot threads conduct water to new areas to moisturize the timber, and so it spreads without limit; while it is true that the threads may conduct some moisture, this is not in sufficient quantity to support further growth. Remember: **dry rot is not 'timber cancer'**.

Ironically, so-called wet rots such as cellar rot (*Coniophora puteana*) require lower levels of moisture to thrive, though still well above the 16 per cent mentioned above.

Integrated pest management

Integrated pest management (IPM) is the name given to a graduated and measured approach to pest control within buildings that focuses attention on identifying and locating the specific pest, considering how it comes to be there and how the condition of the building can be altered to discourage or eliminate it, and then to use chemicals only if the issue cannot be addressed in other ways and in a localized and targeted manner. Not only is a less invasive approach a better means of building conservation, it is equally preferable in terms of sustainability and nature conservation.

It should also be remembered that you may have protected species, particularly bats, within your building, and that any treatment process should not jeopardize these; Natural England maintain a list of pesticide treatments that are compatible with bat colonies.

The end of the matter

The moral of this story is to return to where we started: the key to dealing with all these forms of decay in buildings, including so-called dry rot, is to address the levels (and therefore the sources) of moisture in the building, not to wreck the building or its ecosystem by pulling it apart or resorting to 'chemical warfare'.

Note

1 Iain McCaig and Brian Ridout (eds), *Practical Building Conservation: Timber*, Farnham: Ashgate, 2012, p. 197.

B16
Maintenance

'Stave off decay by daily care.'

This phrase is often used by the Society for the Protection of Ancient Buildings (SPAB); the words are the advice of William Morris, who founded SPAB in 1877 (the same William Morris of Arts and Crafts fame).

Decay is a fact of life; every building starts decaying as soon as it is built. Sadly some people seem to believe that the need for maintenance is an admission of defeat and that the building must somehow be defective. These are true disciples of modernity, and their reluctance presumably relates to an unwillingness to acknowledge our own inevitable mortality. They are also men and women of true faith, in this case faith in the myth of the maintenance-free building. Whatever the causes, in no previous era was anyone so foolish and credulous.

The speed at which the decay happens is affected by a number of factors but the main cause of early, premature or rapid building decay is simple neglect. While not expecting anyone literally to undertake *daily care*, Morris' short sentence sums up the best way to approach maintenance and how such an approach will save your church thousands of pounds in more expensive repairs. So effective is the prevention of repairs by daily care that such maintenance is often called *preventative* maintenance. Preventative maintenance is the key factor when it comes to the all-important task of keeping a 'dry hat and boots' on your church, as discussed in Chapter B3.

SPAB runs a brilliant scheme called Faith in Maintenance to help people care for and conserve historic places of worship (mostly churches but also including historic chapels, synagogues, mosques, temples and gurdwaras). As well as practical training sessions there is a huge amount of really useful information on the SPAB website.

Recently SPAB has launched a new programme of relevance to church communities called the Maintenance Co-operatives Project to train and support groups of volunteers in a local area to work together to care for a number of places of worship and to pass on the knowledge, information and skills to other people.[1]

Maintenance is looking then doing

At its simplest, maintenance involves two activities: looking and then doing. Neglect, by contrast, involves closing your eyes and sitting on your hands. The difference is primarily one of attitude – of whether or not anyone really cares.

It is also important to appreciate that maintenance is different from repair. Where maintenance is actively preventing things from going wrong, repair is replacing bits that have gone wrong. More specifically, repair could be either:

- the work to put right defects in design, specification or construction, or
- the work to replace materials that have been the victims of significant decay or elements damaged by other factors and forces.

Any building, historic or otherwise, will need both maintenance and repair; the second costs much more than the first but the more you do of the first, the less you need to do of the second. Or put another way, you can either 'spend' care now or money later; it's your choice.

There is also an important question of who does what. Those legally responsible for the church building (vicar, churchwardens, PCC members) need to know that the people who are undertaking maintenance, repairs and improvements are competent and able to do the work without putting the fabric or its fixtures and fittings at risk – or, of course, the people who use the building. However, this doesn't mean you have to employ a professional or tradesperson to do everything. There is a great deal of DIY maintenance work that can be undertaken provided certain principles are followed. One of the great strengths of old buildings is that they are relatively simple in the way they are put together; hence, for example, the same basic principles of maintaining a dry hat and boots and ensuring that the building can breathe apply to every old church. Our buildings might in the first place have been built by master masons (the 'professionals') but thereafter were generally speaking looked after by the local community (the 'amateurs').[2]

Care in the community

The great advantage of the amateur 'care in the community' approach is the sense of ownership that accompanies the community taking responsibility for daily care, and which is the single biggest factor in ensuring the survival of a historic building. Historically, however, this often didn't happen; by the end of the eighteenth century many of our historic churches were in a terrible state after generations of neglect, and it was the Victorians who saved them. It was also in the first half of the nineteenth century that the idea of the professions developed; the Royal Institute of British Architects, for example, was founded in 1834. The upside of this change was that things were done more 'properly'; the downside was the disempowerment of local communities, who became more detached from their buildings, leaving their care to the 'experts'. We are still both enjoying the benefits and suffering the drawbacks of this cultural change.

So what exactly is the problem? It is a combination of:

- a lack of knowledge and understanding about traditional buildings
- a lack of experience with traditional building materials
- modern building materials that promise instant solutions.

These three issues are fixable by means of training and support of the volunteers who do the DIY maintenance.

Do it yourself – carefully and intelligently

The most effective way to harness the enthusiasm and interest of people who volunteer to help look after your church building is for the PCC to appoint a clerk of works and subcommittee to provide the forum for training, support and supervision. In this way you can do it yourself carefully and intelligently.

DIY stands for:

☐ Do It Yourself
☐ Destroy It Yourself

Choose one answer

Your PCC needs to be prepared to fund or even organize some practical training for the volunteers who are looking after the church on behalf of the PCC. SPAB can provide support and advice on how to do this. Or even better, try to organize this at deanery level; it will be much easier to get a critical mass of people together, and you can begin to share local expertise and experience.

Wherever it is organized, the members of such a 'fabric team' need to be familiar with the information provided by the SPAB Faith in Maintenance (FiM) programme in *The Good Maintenance Guide*, available via the SPAB FiM website.[3] As well as getting the subcommittee to be familiar with this information, check whether there is a new SPAB Maintenance Co-Operatives Project operating in your part of the country.

Your church fabric team needs to be able to carry out a 'baseline survey' of the church building in order to be able to spot possible problems and identify the building's particular 'pinch points'. In addition, a one- to three-day practical lime course can save your church a lot of money because it will enable it to have a number of volunteers properly trained and able to carry out repointing of the stone or brickwork; for the importance of getting this right, see Chapters B3 and B4. Although this kind of work will need the supervision of the church architect and (depending on the extent of the work) a faculty from the Chancellor, it can give the church a considerable sense of achievement to undertake such a practical and beneficial exercise.

The maintenance work may be simple (e.g. keeping the gutters, downpipes and gulleys in good working order) but don't forget that if the team is to be able to do the job asked of it by the PCC it is essential to provide them with the right tools for the job, plus adequate protective clothing and a safe access system.

Use your professional advisor

Simple principles about materials and how they are used seem obvious but can all too easily be ignored. Historic interiors need a bit of care and attention to detail and this is in part why we have the faculty permission process (for more on this see Chapter D8) and why PCCs are encouraged to consult with their church architect.

In addition to finding information and advice from books and from both the Church-Care and SPAB Faith in Maintenance (FiM) websites, don't forget to ask for advice from the inspecting church architect/surveyor. This is your dedicated professional advisor who knows the building and is competent to advise you about its maintenance and repair. You need to be clear at what point the advisor will start charging you – he or she may be happy to take telephone queries without charge. Some PCC members are scared that asking for advice will cost them money, or perhaps they think it's all right to pay a lawyer for legal advice but not a qualified professional for advice about the building – a bit mad, particularly since such 'savings' may result in significantly greater and wholly unnecessary expense.

Regular checks prevent sudden cheques

Pea-sized problems can be managed, so it is important not to let a problem become a boulder or it will crush you. We usually treat our church buildings in much the same way we treat our homes (i.e. by ignoring the building maintenance until there's a problem). The trouble is that when it comes to old buildings we usually don't wake up to the problems until there's a crisis, by which time putting right what has gone wrong can be time-consuming and very expensive. This is of course compounded by the usual church approach to problems – 'If I ignore it for long enough maybe it or I will go away.' Well the building won't, and neither will the problem, so unless you're prepared to move house it would be best to face up to reality and do something about it! Little and often is much better than neglect and crisis.

There are significant financial benefits to the church community from undertaking regular preventative maintenance for the church building. A checklist of things to look for and any subsequent action points will provide a methodical approach to the maintenance of the building(s). You will probably need to prepare a checklist specific for your building because each church building is unique and individual. The size and complexity of the structure will influence both the extent and content of the checklist.

It would be sensible to look back through the Log Book (see Chapter A4) and previous Quinquennial Inspection Reports and consult with the church architect to identify any particular repeating problems or specific pinch points where trouble occurs due to the building's design, construction or materials. These items should be incorporated into the checklist, which will ensure all the important elements are included and can be properly inspected and assessed.

SPAB have the knowledge – it's yours for the reading

We end where we began, with SPAB, whose advice on maintenance is excellent.[4] There seems little point in trying to replicate this; instead we're signposting you to it, so please follow it up.

Notes

1 For the Maintenance Co-operatives Project, see www.spabmcp.org.uk.

2 For more on the historical state of church buildings, see 'A Restoration Tragedy: Cathedrals in the Eighteenth and Nineteenth Centuries', in Jane Fawcett (ed.), *The Future of the Past: Attitudes to Conservation 1174–1974*, London: Thames & Hudson, 1976.

3 Sara Crofts, *The Good Maintenance Guide: A Practical Handbook to Help Volunteers Care For and Preserve Our Historic Places of Worship*, London: SPAB, 2008. This may be ordered from the SPAB office, a local SPAB group or via the Faith in Maintenance website – see www.spabfim.org.uk/pages/resources_home.html.

4 Crofts, *Good Maintenance Guide*.

B17
Asset Management Plans

If it's bad news I don't want to know

Church buildings need to be looked after and properly maintained if they are to do their job well. Church of England legislation therefore requires all church buildings to be inspected every five years by a qualified architect or surveyor. This Quinquennial Inspection (QI) identifies in a report (QIR) issued to the PCC the repairs and maintenance works required to ensure church buildings are kept in good condition. While only church buildings are covered by the QI procedure, the recommendations made in this chapter can be applied to any church property.

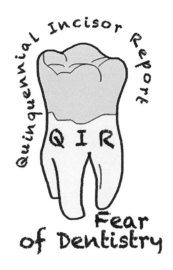

For all the benefits of the QI procedure, church communities often dread receiving the QIR, fearful it will highlight a long list of urgent works. It's a bit like combining the widespread fear of the dentist with the discomfort of spending large amounts of money on something we don't understand; we can all too easily adopt the ostrich approach in an attempt to ignore the issues. This merely compounds the feeling that the building is a monster that cripples the life of the church by diverting attention from mission and ministry.

Slaying that monster involves taking back control. One drawback of both the QI procedure and the local church's response is that they are reactive: the QIR is the reaction to the problems the inspection identifies; the church community then reacts to the recommendations of the report. All of this perpetuates the process of reactive management of our church buildings (i.e. after the event rather than at or before the time).

Any organization responsible for large amounts of property knows that reactive management is not a good way of caring for any building. Responding to the latest crisis results in a loss of direction and focus because the priorities for action are set by the problems rather than by an intentional policy. The key to taking back control is to be proactive rather than reactive.

Maintenance plans

In recent years grants from English Heritage – and now the Heritage Lottery Fund (HLF) – have come with a requirement for the recipient church to prepare a maintenance plan listing all the tasks that need to be done to keep the building in reasonable condition. The maintenance plan, which is usually written by the church architect in preparation for the main repair works, has the benefit of helping church communities address the need for regular maintenance of the building (sadly many such plans remain unactioned, but that is another story).

While the requirement to prepare maintenance plans is limited to church buildings receiving grants, there is potential to develop their benefits into a proactive tool for church communities to use for the maintenance, repair and improvement of the church (and any other buildings for which they are responsible).

Asset Management Plans

Building on this, we would therefore like to promote the concept of the Asset Management Plan (AMP) as a proactive management tool that allows for the care of the building(s) in the context of the broader priorities of the church.

A key aspect of the AMP is the development of a process to ensure that the management of the building is planned, budgeted and actioned. The AMP enables the church community to:

- evaluate the sustainability of their church building(s)
- make financial plans and budget for work to the fabric
- have buildings that serve the church's vision for mission and ministry.

The AMP therefore helps the local church community to ensure that the existing built assets and any capital funding is used as effectively and efficiently as possible in promoting the church's mission and ministry.

REGULAR MAINTENANCE

Item	KNOWN CYCLE	COST per CYCLE	ANNUAL COST	2	5	10	15	20	25	30	other	COST over 30 YEARS
Clean Gutters and Downpies	3 months	200	800									24,000
Clean Gulleys and drains	3 months	50	200									6,000
Boiler Service	annual	200	200									6,000
Ventilation Service	annual	200	200									6,000
Portable Electric Appliances Test	annual	125	125									3,750
Vermin and Rodent Control	3 months	70	280									8,400
Cleaning window glass	2 yr	500	250	*								7,500
Lightning Conductor Test	2 yr	100	50	*								1,500
Fire Extinguisher Test/replacement	annual	150	150									4,500
Electrical Installation Test	5 yr	3,000	600		*	*	*	*	*	*		18,000
Painting Exterior metal/wood	5 yr	5,000	1,000		*	*	*	*	*	*		30,000
Churchyard Grass-mower service, fuel	annual	300	300									9,000
Churchyard Landscape/Trees	annual	500	500									15,000
Churchyard walls pointing & clear ivy	5 yr	1,000	200		*	*	*	*	*	*		6,000
Repointing Various Areas	2 yr	3,000	1,500	*								45,000
Total			**6,355**									**190,650**

CAPITAL REPAIRS — When work will be required

Item	KNOWN CYCLE	COST per CYCLE	ANNUAL COST	2	5	10	15	20	25	30	other	COST over 30 YEARS
Churchyard Paths	10 yr	5,000	500		*		*		*			15,000
Felt roofs to boiler roof and organ loft	20 yr	10,000	666		*	*		*		*		20,000
Repair/replace window feramenta	as & when	3,000	300			*		*		*		9,000
North Aisle Mullions	100+ yr	25,000	834				*					25,000
Pinnacles to tower	100+ yr	60,000	2,000					*				60,000
High Level Internal Cleaning	10 yr	3,000	300		*		*		*			9,000
Lead Roofs patch repair	10 yr	3,000	300					*				9,000
Lead roof replace (100 years old)	150 yr	150,000	3,000								50	90,000
Electric Lighting upgrade	25 yr	25,000	833						*			25,000
Electric Power upgrade	25 yr	15,000	500						*			15,000
Heating & Boiler upgrade	25 yr	35,000	1,166						*			35,000
Kitchen & Toilets upgrade	15 yr	12,000	800				*			*		24,000
Ventilation System Replace	20 yr	18,000	600				*					18,000
Total			**11,799**									**354,000**

IMPROVEMENTS & NEW WORKS — Project Target Completion

Item	KNOWN CYCLE	COST per CYCLE	ANNUAL COST	2	5	10	15	20	25	30	other	COST over 30 YEARS
Fire Alarm & Emergency lights install	one off	18,000	3,600		*							
Re-ordering, new rooms & office	one off	130,000	13,000			*						
New Mower	one off	500	100	*								
Total			**16,700**									

AMP annual total (£) to be raised: 34,854

Example Asset Management Plan: By combining real tasks and costs of Regular Maintenance with projected tasks and costs of Capital Repairs, Improvements and New Works, the AMP produces annual and long-term budgets for the building, enabling both preventative maintenance and saving for large capital items.

SECTION B   PRACTICALITIES

The AMP separates building-related work into three categories:

Regular cyclical maintenance refers to items that need to be done on a short cycle from every three months to five years (e.g. cleaning rainwater goods, lightning conductor test, gas installation servicing and test, electrical test, paths maintenance) together with 'little but often' work and minor repairs to things that break or wear out (e.g. pointing, painting metal work etc.).

Capital repairs refer to items that run on a longer cycle from five years upwards, covering the repair and or replacement of major elements of the building and site (e.g. roof coverings, stonework, electrical installation, central heating installation and WC and kitchen fittings, boundary walls, gates and railings etc.).

Improvements and new work consist of alterations to the existing building to meet legislation (e.g. Equality Act requirements) or liturgical needs (e.g. nave altars, space for musicians) together with the changing expectations and desires of contemporary church life and society in general (e.g. WCs, kitchens, and audiovisual and multimedia facilities).

To write to your AMP you will need to gather information from the following sources:

- Log Book.
- Current Quinquennial Inspection Report.
- Accounts (last three years) to look at spending patterns on the building.
- Annual Reports (last three years) to APCM about the building.
- Other records about maintenance, repairs and improvements.

Using the historical information as the basis and working in conjunction with the architect and possibly a Quantity Surveyor, the PCC can put together a forward-looking programme (20–30 years) of works together with realistic cost estimates. With the costs broken down into the annual sums, the AMP will enable the PCC members to assess their ability to sustain the buildings and to address their responsibility for the church building in a more manageable way. The proactive process of the AMP will provide the church community with sufficient information to stop living in fear of the Quinquennial Inspection, and with its 30-year time frame, it enables a church to do the right thing by the next generation.

An example is shown on the accompanying spreadsheet. All church buildings are different and will have differing needs and priorities, but the items shown are common to many. The totals may look scary but the PCC members need to know accurately the scale of the task before them. If the local church is not making sufficient investment as identified by an AMP, then the capital required when a building element fails will be even more difficult to find.

Delegate and resource the task properly

Ideally every church community needs from among its members a 'clerk of works' for its building(s). The clerk of works should be someone who is physically fit, preferably with a head for heights, a practical bent and the understanding and willingness to get to grips with the maintenance requirements.

The PCC could authorize this person, together with a small subcommittee of volunteers equipped with a budget, to take responsibility and ensure the essential maintenance items are dealt with and not put off. In this way decisions to get on with something can be made quickly without the discussion and delay involved in going back each time to the PCC, subject of course to obtaining the necessary permissions. Obviously such a subcommittee will need to have agreed terms of reference together with the clear understanding that all contracts for work are with the PCC. Therefore it is advisable to limit both the budget and any work the subcommittee can put in hand to essential maintenance.

Essential items are the health and safety related matters, mechanical and electrical installation maintenance and most importantly keeping water out of the building – cleaning the gutters and downpipes and making sure the rainwater gets off the church roofs and away from the building as quickly as possible. Be realistic: £5,000 per year may be sensible. (How does this compare with what you are spending now?) Ingress of water in the wrong place is the most serious hazard to the fabric of a church building.

Health and safety for all users of the church building is an important matter and must be addressed. Protecting the volunteers and protecting others from what the volunteers may inadvertently do is essential, and is the responsibility of the PCC. In addition the PCC should consider preparing job descriptions for the volunteers.

Strategic review

Once the day-to-day management of the buildings is under control, the PCC building subcommittee should then conduct a Strategic Review of the building(s) for which they are responsible. We suggest you consider three interlinked components that between them determine whether your buildings serve the mission of the Church:

- **Condition**   The physical state of the premises to ensure safe and continuous operation while meeting the demands of the Building Regulations and other statutory requirements.
- **Suitability**   The quality of the premises to meet mission and ministry aspirations.
- **Sufficiency**   The quantity of and organization of spaces within the building, taking into account the requirements of existing and potential user-groups and the wider community.

This review will enable the PCC to consider the needs of all those who use the building(s) for whatever function, and to know whether the premises are suitable and the people's needs are satisfied. It will show where the building is 'chafing' against the activity within it, and therefore prompt you to consider how it might need to change to meet those needs better. If this Strategic Review then leads to some form of building project, you will have a great starting point from which to develop a project brief, and in time a Statement of Needs (see Chapter D6).

The proactive management of church buildings has considerable advantages over any reactive process, which results in the church community being constantly caught on the back foot and playing catch-up with regard to the building issues. Together, the Asset Management Plan (AMP) and the Strategic Review provide churches with a proactive management tool for their buildings and ultimately frees them to focus on their mission priorities.

B18

The Church-Carer's Calendar

Life is never boring with an old building

This chapter provides a month-by-month list of things to look for and perhaps to do; ideally these checks should be undertaken by more than one person, preferably a small works group or subcommittee as described in Chapter B17. This is all stuff within the scope of non-professionals. It is about looking and doing. The doing is limited to what volunteers can safely do; get help with the things you cannot do.

As we advised in Chapters B3 and B16, this checking doesn't have to be daily but should be done as frequently as you can and no less often than the periods suggested. The best time to check the rainwater goods (gutters, downpipes, gulleys etc.) is during or just after rain as this will help you spot any leaking sections or damp walls. Remember to record the various areas on a simple sketch plan and elevation, and keep this with the Log Book for future reference. This will make it easier to identify what you are looking for later.

We have begun the calendar in September as this is the time to begin to ensure your church is ready for the winter weather. Furthermore it is evident that many churches follow the academic year in the way they organize themselves. So here is the stuff to do for the benefit of your building from the start of the new term!

September

Coming back after the holidays, the priorities are the roof and the rainwater goods so you can be confident that the 'dry hat and boots' are in place.

Autumn

- Internally, look up for evidence of leaks – tell-tale staining of boards or at the wall plate or gable ends. You may need a torch and binoculars.

- Externally, from safe vantage points, check for slipped or missing slates and tiles, dislodged flashings and damaged lead work.
- Externally, look over all the rainwater goods for signs of damp especially below the gutter lines. Make sure all parts of the rainwater goods are clean and free of debris.
- Check that any air bricks or underfloor ventilators are in place to prevent unwelcome residents (rats, mice, hedgehogs or even foxes) and free from obstructions so the air can move freely.

October

Confident you have a dry hat and boots in place, have a look at the structure and prepare for colder weather. The clocks change and the nights draw in, so safe access to and from the building is more important.

- Check the masonry for signs of damage, erosion, signs of movement or failing pointing.
- Check that all the external pathways are free of hazards and that any external lighting is functioning.
- If the roof has snowboards, check they are in a good state of repair and in the correct position.
- Check the frost protection for water tanks and exposed water pipes.
- Continue to keep the rainwater goods clear of debris.

November

Cold, wet and windy weather is typical for this month and it might get worse, so make sure your church is ready.

- If your church has a flagpole make sure it is secure. Flagpoles mounted on tower roofs can all too easily be ignored, especially if access is difficult.
- Check over all the roof coverings again. Debris on the ground, in parapet or valley gutters (broken slates or tiles or lumps of mortar) are signs of problems.
- Continue to keep the rainwater goods clear of debris.

December

It's that time of year again and no doubt your building will be busy with carol services and nativity plays with lots of people who are unfamiliar with the building.

Winter

- Check that all the pathways, entrance porches and steps are safe and free from obstructions. Have procedures in place to deal with icy conditions and emergencies.
- Internally, make sure all the access routes are clear of obstructions, tidy away all the unused stuff, throw away the junk and make sure your building is looking its best.
- Check that the fire safety equipment has been serviced and is in place.
- Continue to keep the rainwater goods clear of debris.

January

Happy New Year! It's resolution time of year and possibly some winter weather will arrive.

- Check the dates for all the statutory inspections and specialist maintenance – gas installations, electrical safety, fire alarms, lifting equipment, organ tuning, spire inspection, lightning conductor and so on. If necessary, get them booked.
- Parapet and valley gutters without snowboards need to be cleared of snow to prevent the meltwater rising above the gutter-line and entering the building.
- Continue to keep the rainwater goods clear of debris.

February

The winter might continue for another couple of months but there is some spring preparation to do.

- Parapet and valley gutters without snowboards need to be cleared of snow to prevent the meltwater rising above the gutter-line and entering the building.
- Continue to keep the rainwater goods clear of debris.
- Check the condition of any ladders in the church, whether they are free or fixed.

- Make sure the tower, roofs and windows are bird-proof before nesting starts. Even 'vermin' birds are protected if they are nesting so prevention is better than cure. Do not disturb any bats.
- If the church has bells and a team of bell-ringers, ask the tower captain to ensure the bells and bell-frame are in good order and report to the PCC in time for the APCM.

Spring

March

The weather should be beginning to change but it can be both very wet and windy. Frost damage to stonework begins to become evident but it can crop up through the spring and summer months. It is still too early to begin repairs (apart from any emergencies), but it is time to prepare.

- Check for frost damage to gutters and downpipes. Look for cracks and leaks in the rainwater goods and note the damaged sections.
- Stone fragments and lumps of mortar or other debris on the ground around the building are signs of problems caused by frost. Don't ignore them.
- Check internally for signs of water ingress. If water is getting in, try to identify the cause.
- Continue to keep the rainwater goods clear of debris.

April

Spring hopefully has sprung, the weather should be calmer. By now it should be safe to inspect all the roofs.

- Look over the roofs for signs of damage (see the September advice). Don't forget to look at the flat roofs and any felt roof coverings. Note any damaged areas. Check the valley and parapet gutters for debris.
- Look at the lead flashings and mortar fillets to the junctions and chimneys.
- Continue to keep the rainwater goods clear of debris.

May

The weather should have warmed up sufficiently for the heating to be turned off.

- Check that all the ventilators are operational so that you can ventilate the church building as often as possible during the dry summer months.
- Lubricate door and window ironmongery.
- Clean out the rainwater gulleys at the base of all the downpipes. Clean out silt traps if they are fitted and check that the below-ground drainage is working effectively by pouring a bucket of water down each gulley.
- Remove all vegetation growing at the base of the walls and in any drainage channels.
- Once the heating is shut down arrange for the system to be checked and serviced.

June

Hopefully it will be warm and dry. Take advantage of the weather to do those things that need dry weather.

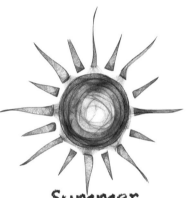

Summer

- Identify the metal parts that need repainting or oiling.
- Inspect all windows. With leaded windows, check for signs of bowing and cracks indicating movement and the lead cames, wire ties and horizontal glazing bars (ferramenta) for corrosion and decay.
- Check all timber in the underused, less accessible and hidden areas of the building, e.g. roof and floor voids, wall plates, under stairs and in cupboards. Look for signs of rot, decay, vermin infestation and insect damage.

July

It's just before the holiday season, so before things get overlooked, make sure someone has looked at this Church-Carer's Calendar and reported how they have got on to the PCC.

- Inspect all the visible timber. Look for signs of rot, cracks and decay. Identify all the parts that need redecoration.

- Check the lightning conductor test record. Ideally it should be tested every 1–2 years but at different times of the year when the soil conductivity may be different.
- Review the record for all the statutory inspections and specialist maintenance. Is everything on schedule?
- Just in case you forgot, continue to keep the rainwater goods clear of debris.

August

If you are up to date, take a well-earned break. It's all going to start again next month!

B19
Accessibility

How serious are we about providing a welcome to all those in our community? In principle we would all want to see the church as accessible to all, with no one excluded because of disability or for any other reason. However, our buildings often tell another story, since many of them do a very good job of keeping people out.

Accessibility is a multi-layered thing – attitudes play a major role but the physicality of our buildings provides perhaps the most obvious expression of those attitudes. If we have not done everything we can to improve access to our buildings, it is time (literally) to 'put our house in order'.

The first and most obvious thing to say is that accessibility is not just about wheelchairs; many of those with mobility issues are ambulant disabled (i.e. still walking, with the aid of sticks or frames). That said, wheelchairs determine some of the key dimensions in any new construction, such as door widths and the size of an accessible WC (see Chapter B13). However, alongside the needs of those in wheelchairs we should also be considering those with other disabilities, including the visually impaired and those with hearing loss.

But perhaps we should be thinking of accessibility more widely still – as accessibility into the worshipping community. What about those with learning disabilities? It is interesting to note how much of what we do in church demands good levels of literacy; that in itself excludes quite a number of people – more than we might imagine. Is it then any surprise that church appeals more to some social groups than others? Accessibility then is about 'church for the rest of us'.

(more than wheelchairs)

It's the law

The Equality Act came into force on 1 October 2010. This Act brought together over 116 separate pieces of legislation into one single Act. Combined together, they provide the legal framework to protect the rights of individuals and advance equality of opportunity for all.

The Equality Act simplifies, strengthens and harmonizes the legislation to provide the UK with a discrimination law that protects individuals from unfair treatment and promotes a fair and more equal society.

The previous Disability Discrimination Act 1995, which was incorporated into the Equality Act, provides the legislation that requires us to ensure our church buildings promote a fair and equal society accessible to all people.

The advice is out there

ChurchCare provide a really helpful advice sheet about making our buildings suitable for people with disabilities. The issue is much more than wheelchair access and there is a wealth of advice available from a variety of organizations to help church communities make the necessary alterations in historic buildings.

Lack of money is not an acceptable excuse to do nothing about investigating the issue and seeing what can be done if and when the funds are available.

So if you want to know where to start, look at the ChurchCare guidance note, 'Accessibility and Disabled People' on the ChurchCare website.[1]

Going on a journey

As with many things, the biggest limitation we face is our lack of imagination. If you're able-bodied it is a salutary experience to try to navigate a building you know well in a wheelchair, or simulating some other form of disability. Barriers present themselves that were invisible before, for example:

- The gravel path from the gate to the door.
- Those two or three steps up (or down) into the church; or perhaps there is level access into the building but it is via the 'tradesman's entrance' round the back.
- What about the door – is it wide enough for you to get through in your wheelchair? Even if it is, how much upper body strength do you need to open it (from your sitting position)?

- You've made it through the door – well done! Now what? Is there a choice of obvious places where you can go without other people having to move to make room? If the building is heavily pewed, are you forced to go right to the front?
- And then, as you look at the space, are there other lines of demarcation? What about those chancel steps – do they keep particular areas off-limits for someone like you? What theological implications lie beneath the surface there?

Reflect on this imaginative journey; for some it will have felt as though at every step the building has set out to humiliate you, forcing you to ask for help, to inconvenience others, to draw attention to yourself. Surely, with a little imagination, we can do better than this.

Your obligations

Clearly not all buildings, particularly historic ones, are able to provide level access to all areas without changes to the building that many, including those required to give permission, would find unacceptable. The law is therefore couched in terms that require building owners to do what is reasonable. The question is whether, hand on heart, you have really done what is reasonable, or have you stopped at what you choose to afford?

Other disabilities should be considered, including sight and hearing. Have you, for example, installed an induction loop (see Chapter B7)? Have you carried out a disability audit of the church; if not, you should either undertake one or commission one. John Penton's book *Widening the Eye of the Needle* is an excellent resource for this.[2]

Notes

1 See www.churchcare.co.uk/images/access_and_disabled_people.pdf.

2 John Penton, *Widening the Eye of the Needle: Access to Church Buildings for People with Disabilities*, 3rd edn, London: Church House Publishing, 2008.

B20
Health and Safety – General

Legislative requirements

Every PCC has a duty to ensure that employees and volunteers working on behalf of the church, and visitors to its property, are protected against unnecessary risk. This means we cannot ignore the rules and regulations that are there to protect people. In addition, as part of the Church we will recognize a Christian duty to our neighbours to ensure they are not placed in danger by what we ask them to do for us.

There is a lot of scepticism about 'health and safety gone mad', and some of that is justifiable. However, it is worth remembering that our health and safety legislation comes about because buildings, whether in their construction or maintenance, are responsible for a high proportion of workplace accidents and fatalities. While in general church buildings are considered to be low-risk environments, too many people have been killed or injured for us to ignore this.

Responsibility for the safety of persons in a church or churchyard lies with the incumbent and Parochial Church Council. Where a PCC has employees, duties are likely to arise under the Health and Safety at Work Act 1974 (HSWA). Regulations made under the Act prescribe certain duties, such as the production of a health and safety policy and a risk assessment, and the Health and Safety Executive (HSE) now considers that these regulations also apply for volunteers. If you have any doubt as to the applicability of health and safety law for your particular church, it would be sensible to get advice from the Diocesan Registrar.

Why should I care?

The point of health and safety is at root incredibly simple – it is thinking about what might go wrong before it happens, rather than after someone has been injured or killed. It is about care rather than carelessness. Since the Church is in the business of care, this stuff shouldn't be difficult for us. The fact that churches (and many other community organizations) so often struggle with this is partly because it is presented in bureaucratic language; but this is a symptom of a more fundamental mistake, which is that health and safety is seen as a legal issue as opposed to a pastoral one.

Should someone be injured or killed on church premises then the vague excuse that 'health and safety doesn't apply to us' will offer you no shred of comfort whatsoever. You therefore ignore this stuff at your peril …

General principles of prevention

When considering what precautions are needed, think about the following 'general principles of prevention':

- Avoid risks.
- Evaluate the risks that cannot be avoided.
- Combat the risks at source.
- Adapt the work to the individual, especially as regards the design of workplaces, the choice of work equipment and the choice of working and production methods, with a view, in particular, to alleviating monotonous work and work at a predetermined work-rate and to reducing their effect on health.
- Adapt to technical progress.
- Replace the dangerous with the non-dangerous or the less dangerous.
- Develop a coherent overall prevention policy that covers technology, organization of work, working conditions, social relationships and the influence of factors relating to the working environment.
- Give collective protective measures priority over individual protective measures.
- Give appropriate instructions to employees and volunteers.

That said, life should not principally be about avoiding risk; much talk in our culture presents risk as a dirty word, nowhere more so than in the weird world of health and safety. Yet the only person not taking risks is not alive (literally or figuratively). To be alive is to be a risk-taker – the issue is to know the good risks from the bad, and not to impose risks on others.

Help is at hand ...

The Ecclesiastical Insurance Group has produced some excellent guidance notes specifically addressing health and safety for churches. Every church should obtain this document and work through it, specifically the 'Self-assessment form' on pp. 4–13.[1]

Depending on tone of voice, 'What can possibly go wrong?' might be a statement of arrogant naivety preceding some disaster. But asked as a genuine question it is central to this process of anticipating risk. What follows provides prompts to help you apply that question to each of the areas in the Ecclesiastical Insurance Group self-assessment. This requires imagination and a missional mindset; that is, seeing the church (building) through the eyes of someone on the outside who is not familiar with it.

The numbering of the headings below follows that of the Ecclesiastical Insurance Group self-assessment, *and the two should be read together*. Note that we have concentrated on buildings-related issues since that is the purpose of this book; there are other areas that church communities will also need to consider.

1 Do you have a written health and safety policy?   If not, why not? Any organization with five or more employees needs a written health and safety policy (under the Health and Safety at Work Act 1974); not only that, your employees need to know about it. Note that the Health and Safety Executive now regards volunteers as employees, and persons who make use of volunteers as employers. So this requirement applies to all but the very smallest of churches.

2 Risk assessments   Do them. Record them. Think of it as an exercise in pre-emptive pastoral care.

3 Floors   Think about where someone might slip or trip. Look at unexpected changes of level and the edges of any carpets or rugs. Are floor gratings (if any) flush with their surrounds? What about broken tiles? Are there any areas that would be slippery if wet? What about stiletto heels (think baptismal parties, weddings etc.)?

4 Churchyard   As for inside, think about the places someone might slip, trip or fall. Any puddles will (of course) turn to ice when it freezes. Shaded areas may grow algae which, depending on the surface, can become very slippery when damp. Trees should be regularly inspected. Watch for any leaning gravestones – you will be responsible if the family cannot be traced. What about lighting?

5 Stairs   Are stairways adequately lit? What about handrails – a rope handrail is the minimum where something more solid is not possible. Where would someone most likely lose their footing? How far would they fall? Think about solitary working and public access, and don't forget other areas like basement boiler rooms.

6 Towers and other high-level areas   Towers present a range of risks: stairs (as above), parapets, trip-hazards galore. You need to think about these anyway, but all the more if you allow access to members of the public. How are you going to improve your idiot-proofing?

7 Falling from height   This applies externally and internally. Externally, think about roof access, parapets and so on; remember, you're clearing your gutters regularly (aren't you?). Internally, think about ladder access. How high are your light fittings (and have you changed to LED yet?)? Do you have a stair to a former rood screen? Do you need to prevent toddlers accessing a gallery stair?

8 Bell-ringers   The ringing room and bell-chamber present their own risks. You need to develop this section with the bell-ringers – after all, a single bell can be the weight of a small car. Think about where bell ropes are when not in use. Think about who else has access to the ringing room – they may not be familiar with the sensible dos and don'ts.

9 Hazardous substances   Once again, your likely status as an employer gives you various responsibilities, in this case under the COSSH (Control of Substances Hazardous to Health) Regulations 2002. Substances most likely to be found in churches are petrol, pesticides, insecticides, weedkillers, fertilizers and liquid petroleum gases. You also need to think about the sensible storage of more mundane cleaning materials. Beware pigeon droppings – seek specialist advice.

10 Asbestos   This is a serious issue. Breathing in asbestos fibres can kill people; we have had several friends in building trades who have died from asbestosis. Asbestos was a 'wonder material' with uses including insulation, lagging, fire protection, wall and roof linings, even in WC cisterns and some plastic floor tiles. It is often found in organ blower motor housings. Not all asbestos is equally dangerous; some can be safely left in place. The key thing is to get a survey done so that you know what, if anything, you are dealing with. This is a legal requirement. If you haven't already done this, you're breaking the law; organize it now.

11 Electrical safety   Question: How do you know your electrics are not about to burst into flames? Answer: Because you have had the installation inspected by a NICEIC registered electrician whose certificate is in the church Log Book. No? Then organize it now.

Anything you plug in, from kettles to computers to vacuum cleaners, will need a PAT (Portable Appliance) Test. Avoid trailing cables.

12 Public performances   Hopefully at some points in the year your building is full of people, many of them not part of the regular church congregation. If so, you need to think through (and write down …) how you will steward such occasions, including understanding what to do in case of a fire.

13 Lifting equipment (LOLER)   Lifting equipment could include means for raising heavy font covers, candelabra and sanctuary lamps. More obviously there may be passenger lifts and hoists. The Lifting Operations and Lifting Equipment Regulations 1998 require such items to be inspected by a competent person, such as an engineering insurance company surveyor.

14 Glazing   The creation of a mezzanine floor might bring people up to the level of a leaded window, through which they could fall if appropriate protection is not provided.

Large pieces of glass anywhere in a door and elsewhere at low level should be safety glass (i.e. laminated or toughened). This is now a requirement of the Building Regulations, but wasn't in the 1960s and 70s. Large pieces of glass also need clear manifestation (i.e. an opaque pattern of some kind) – otherwise they are surprisingly easy to walk into.

15 Plant and machinery (PUWER)   You need to ensure that all work equipment is suitable for its purpose and adequately maintained (under The Provision and Use of Work Equipment Regulations 1998).

This includes ladders, scaffolding towers, staging, boilers, lawnmowers, strimmers and so on. Training should be given in safe operation and appropriate PPE (personal protective equipment) provided. Don't you just love all these acronyms …?

16 Manual handling (MHOR)   The more ways your building is used, the more things will need to be moved around; often that involves manual handling. Anything from the stacking of chairs and tables to reconfiguring staging to moving pianos needs to be properly thought through.

Assessing how furniture will need to be handled is a requirement of The Manual Handling Operations Regulations 1992 (as amended). It is also a useful exercise in advance of purchasing new items (e.g. a space can be cleared quickly and safely if chairs can be stacked on trolleys, but only if you have chosen the right chair – see Chapter B6).

17 Food hygiene Making people ill through poor food hygiene, even if everyone recovers, is something you will never live down – there is something visceral (literally) about trusting that the food you receive in hospitality will not harm you. So it is important that churches get this right.

The requirements are more stringent for permanent facilities but are still important for occasional or temporary catering. The issue is to understand the sensible requirements for the scope of your church's catering activity, which could vary from an occasional biscuit to a full-on restaurant operation. You are best talking to the people responsible for policing food safety, the Environmental Health department of the local authority.[2]

18 Recording of accidents (RIDDOR) You need to keep a record of any accidents that happen. The Reporting of Injuries, Diseases and Dangerous Occurrences Regulations 1995 requires employers and people in control of premises to report certain types of injury, occupational ill health and dangerous occurrences to their enforcing authority. For places of public worship this is the local authority Environmental Health department.[3]

19 Child protection This is principally a people issue, and affects any church doing children's work.

However, if you are carrying out children's work alongside other community activities at the same time within your building then you will need to think through some further safeguarding issues. If a church is to engage with its community (e.g. with a café or lunch club) it needs to offer an open welcome without pre-qualification. That potentially includes the convicted paedophile; at the same time, the church has a duty to keep safe the children in its care.

Provided these different activities are located appropriately, this can usually be resolved by management procedures and/or technology, such as a keyfob system of electronic access control. Don't forget about outside play space. Think too about how the building would be evacuated in case of fire – specifically, who would need to escape through where and end up where. Hopefully you never have a fire, but you will still need to test your fire procedures when the building is in use.

20 Outdoor activities This could include such things as bouncy castles, fireworks and charity walks. And how would you screen a barbecue from general access? Abseiling down towers can be great fun for some – but it most definitely requires specialist advice.

21 H&S 'Monitor'   We endorse Ecclesiastical Insurance Group's suggestion that every church should appoint a member with specific responsibility for health and safety. Cherish and support that person.

22 Disability discrimination   You need to assess your building to ensure you are not discriminating against people with disabilities. Think about steps and levels, and whether this can be improved. Simulate disability by trying to navigate around the building in a borrowed wheelchair or in glasses that limit your vision. We guarantee you will see your building quite differently.[4] See Chapter B19 for more on this.

23 Fire-risk assessment   Do it. Record it. Check that you have a sensible provision of fire extinguishers, regularly serviced, and of the right type: as a general rule, water for general areas, CO_2 for electrical (e.g. organ chamber …), powder for oil or gas. Take advice.

Imagine trying to get out of the building if you couldn't see a thing (smoke takes many more lives than fire).[5]

But what about building projects …?

Just when you thought you had got to the end, there is a whole lot more in the next chapter about your particular responsibilities when undertaking building projects.

Notes

1 The Ecclesiastical Insurance Group guidance (*Guidance Notes: Church – Health and Safety*, Gloucester: Ecclesiastical Insurance Group, 2014) can be downloaded from www.ecclesiastical.com/churchmatters/churchguidance/index.aspx.

2 For guidance on the requirements of food hygiene legislation, see www.food.gov.uk.

3 The Health and Safety Executive have published *The HSE Accident Book*, which discharges your responsibility under the regulations to keep records of accidents to people at work – provided of course you use it! It is available from the HSE: https://books.hse.gov.uk/hse/public/home.jsf.

4 For more on disability audits, see John Penton, *Widening the Eye of the Needle: Access to Church Buildings for People with Disabilities*, London: Church House Publishing, 3rd edn, 2008. For more on your responsibilities under the Equality Act 2010, see www.churchcare.co.uk/images/access_and_disabled_people.pdf.

5 For more on fire safety, see www.gov.uk/government/collections/fire-safety-law-and-guidance-documents-for-business.

B21

Health and Safety for Building Projects

If you are thinking of doing some building work on your church buildings, you will need to think about CDM, which is all about health and safety during and after construction. There is no escape from it!

The reason why CDM is important stems from the fact that in the late 1980s the accident and death rates in the construction industry were far too high and out of all proportion to other trades, industries and activities. It was all too easy to get injured or killed on a building site and so the Construction (Design and Management) Regulations 1994 (subsequently strengthened in 2007) were introduced to reduce the risks to employees and construction workers by requiring the duty holders (clients, professionals and contractors) to:

'CDM' stands for:

 Clergy Discipline Measure

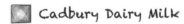 Cadbury Dairy Milk

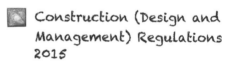 Construction (Design and Management) Regulations 2015

- improve planning and management of projects from the very start
- identify hazards early on so they can be eliminated or reduced at the design stage
- target effort where it can do the most good in terms of health and safety
- discourage unnecessary bureaucracy.

The aim of CDM is for health and safety to be treated as an integral part of the planning and execution of a construction project and not as an afterthought or bolt-on after the decisions have been made and the work is underway.

What does CDM mean for the church?

CDM regulations apply to the following types of building projects:

- New building construction.
- New services installation.
- Alterations, maintenance or renovations of a building or any of its services (but not including the maintenance of fixed plant, except where this is part of other construction work).
- Site clearance.
- Demolition.

So this means that any construction work in a church, whether the work be great or small, will engage the CDM regulations. Any PCC managing its own small project or carrying out its own repairs and alterations will be subject to these regulations and should be aware of the obligations that fall upon them as the *client*. If the project lasts for more than 30 working days (or more than 500 man-days of work will be needed) there are additional requirements, which fall on the client because the project becomes *notifiable*.

New CDM regulations came into force in April 2015 and apply to all building and construction projects, regardless of the size, duration and nature of the work.

The most significant change is that the former 'CDM Co-ordinator' role is replaced by a 'principal designer'. Where there is more than one contractor, the client must appoint a principal designer and principal contractor, and if the client fails to make either of these appointments, the client takes on those roles themselves.

The client now has specific duties:

1 Provide pre-construction information.
2 Ensure that a construction phase plan for the project is prepared before the construction phase begins.
3 Ensure that the principal designer prepares a health and safety file for the project.
4 Where a construction project must be notified, the client must submit a notice in writing to the relevant enforcing authority.

Who are the duty holders?

- The client.
- The principal designer.
- The (principal) contractor and other contractors.

Who is the client?

The short and accurate answer is: anyone who is having construction work carried out on their behalf. Any construction work carried out in a church is done on the instructions of a PCC. The PCC is therefore the client.

On any construction project, the client has one of the biggest influences over the way a project is run. Clients have substantial influence and contractual control; their decisions and approach determine critical aspects of the work. This is why churches must take CDM seriously.

The fact they are the client can be difficult for PCC members both to appreciate and to engage with. Some PCCs will try to find someone else to be the client – the architect, the vicar, the fundraiser, the diocese, the bishop – anyone but themselves! However, there is no escape; like it or not, *the PCC is the client.*

What the client needs to do – all projects

The CDM regulations state that the client must take reasonable steps to ensure that the following are addressed:

A competent team   The client must engage a principal designer, architects, designers, contractors and other team members who are competent (or who work under the supervision of a competent person).[1]

Adequate time   The client also has a responsibility to ensure those who are to be engaged are appointed early enough for the work they have to do; that is, there is no last-minute scrabbling around, which is how mistakes are made, risks overlooked and accidents happen.

Co-operation   The client must co-operate with others concerned in the project as is necessary to allow other duty holders to comply with their duties under the CDM regulations. For example, the area within which the building work is taking place becomes the responsibility of the contractor, so the church community will need the contractor's permission before entering.

Communication   The client must co-ordinate their own work with others involved with the project in order to ensure the safety of those carrying out the construction work and others who may be affected by it. Good communications and clear lines of authority are essential, otherwise volunteer church members and contractors can all too easily get in a mess. You need to think through the formal procedures that will be necessary if the work of the church will conflict or inhibit the work of the contractors. For example, you will need to think through what to do if the church building is needed for a funeral.

Construction phase plan   The client must ensure that the construction phase does not start until the contractor/principal contractor has prepared a suitable written construction phase plan.

Welfare facilities   The client must ensure arrangements are made (usually by the contractor) for suitable welfare facilities to be present for the start of the work, where the contractor's staff can take their breaks, drink their coffee and eat their lunch. While this is generally the contractor's responsibility, the client will end up paying for it, so agreement as to any allowable use of existing facilities is sensible. WCs, washing facilities and first-aid points are essential welfare facilities; during the winter, heating will be necessary.

Workplaces   While not a part of CDM (which deals with building construction and maintenance), any fixed workplaces that are to be constructed (e.g. a stonemason's yard or carpentry shop) will need to comply, in respect of their design and the materials used, with any requirements of the Workplace (Health, Safety and Welfare) Regulations 1992. This includes any office spaces or teaching and meeting rooms the client is to provide. Just because the building is listed and some compromise of building regulations is permissible, it doesn't mean workplaces can be unsafe or substandard.

What the client needs to do – more than one contractor

For projects with more than one contractor (for example a general builder and their subcontractor electrician), in addition to addressing the items above the client must also:

Appoint a **principal designer** to advise and assist with their duties and to co-ordinate the arrangements for health and safety during the planning phase. The principal designer's duties include identifying and controlling risks, assisting the client in the production of pre-construction information and the preparation of the health and safety file.

Appoint a **principal contractor** to plan, manage and co-ordinate the construction phase of the project; ideally this is early enough for them to work with the designer on issues relating to 'buildability', usability and maintainability, but that is not always possible, depending on how the work is tendered.

Make sure the **health and safety** file is prepared (by the principal designer), reviewed and updated (by the principal contractor) ready for handover at the end of the construction work. This must then be kept available for any future construction work or to pass on to a new owner (unlikely in the case of churches, but still very relevant given frequent change of office holders).

What the client needs to do – notifiable projects

For **notifiable** projects (those lasting more than 30 working days and having more than 20 workers working simultaneously at any point, or comprising more than 500 man-days of work), in addition to addressing the items above the client must also notify the Health and Safety Executive.

What the client (PCC) doesn't have to do

The client is not required or expected to undertake the following:

- Plan or manage construction projects themselves.
- Specify how work must be done (e.g. requiring a structure to be demolished by hand). Indeed they positively should not do so unless they have the expertise to assess the various options and risks involved. (They should, of course, point out particular risks they are aware of that would inform this decision.)
- Provide welfare facilities for those carrying out construction work (though they should co-operate with the contractor to assist with their arrangements).
- Check designs to make sure that Regulation 11 (which deals with the duties of designers) has been complied with. Note, however, that a client can become a designer if he or she 'prepares or modifies a design'.
- Visit the site (to supervise or check construction work standards).
- Employ third-party assurance advisors to monitor health and safety standards on site (though there may be benefits to the client in doing so).
- Subscribe to third-party competence assessment schemes (though there may be benefits from doing so).

Work undertaken by insurance companies

The one exception to the rule that the PCC is client is where an insurance company arranges for work to be carried out in a church under an insurance policy; in that case the insurance company would be the client, because they are instigating the work. If the insurer was acting through a loss adjuster who was engaging the contractors and the architect themselves, then the loss adjuster would be the client.

However, if the PCC arranges for the work and pays for it and is then reimbursed by the insurer, the PCC would be the client.

In conclusion

There is no need to panic!

Make sure you plan and consider the significance of health and safety and talk to the professionals who advise the PCC. Your church architect will be the person with whom to start the discussion.

Notes

1 The HSE has stated that:
'To be competent an organisation or individual must have:
- sufficient knowledge of the tasks to be undertaken and the risks involved
- the experience and ability to carry out their duties in relation to the project, to recognise their limitations and take appropriate action to prevent harm to those carrying out construction work, or those affected by the work.'

See www.hse.gov.uk/construction/cdm/faq/competence.htm; www.hse.gov.uk/construction/cdm/2015/summary.htm.

B22

Mr FixIt or Mr BodgeIt

Looking after an old church

If you have read most of Section B, 'Practicalities', you will be aware that looking after an old church takes a bit of thought and care.

Clergy, churchwardens and PCC members need to think carefully about kind offers of DIY help from members of the congregation or wider community. You wouldn't let a well-intentioned amateur loose on restoring an old master painting or a vintage car without checking they know what they're doing. The same principle applies here: quick fixes from the DIY shop are quite unsuitable for historic buildings, where DIY may stand for 'Destroy It Yourself'.

'But Mr BodgeIt is cheaper'

Mr BodgeIt may well be cheaper in the short term. His approach is often well intentioned and his work can be of a reasonable quality. However, Mr BodgeIt can let his desire to save the church money blind him to other considerations, and he is often lacking in understanding of what gives the building its particular character.

While most PCCs are now aware that any electrical work in a church, because it is a public building, must be carried out by a competent electrician, some are only too willing to let Mr BodgeIt run a trailing extension lead, which then becomes a 'permanent temporary' fixture, rather than spend the money having a proper job done by Mr FixIt. Eventually Mr BodgeIt might get round to replacing the trailing extension with some PVC cable in a nice plastic conduit smack across the front of the chancel step! Similarly both the PCC and fabric subcommittee are fully aware of the need for the building fabric to breathe but will allow Mr BodgeIt to paint over a wall of bubbling paint with a sealing compound that is 'Guaranteed to stop any more damp as that's what it says on the tin'. This is then followed up by some nice vinyl emulsion. Far better would be for Mr FixIt to first identify where the excess damp might be coming from and eradicate the cause, remove the existing bubbling paint and then redecorate using a lime-based material.

Timber

Mr BodgeIt is often keen to work with wood as it is easier and relatively straightforward. The current Mr BodgeIt comes from a long line of BodgeIts; some churches have had a BodgeIt in every generation since the Domesday Book. Recent generations, particularly Victorian-era BodgeIts, created all manner of internal storm porches, vestry areas and flower cupboards out of tongue and groove pine match-boarding; our contemporary Mr BodgeIt is just as keen to continue the tradition but uses MDF or chipboard instead. In recent years all manner of alterations have been made much easier for the enthusiastic amateur by cheap power tools and particle board.

Chipboard and MDF are modern timber particle board products that function well in dry atmospheres. However, unless they are painted, neither is particularly suitable in a building subject to damp (e.g. a traditional church). Chipboard can act like blotting paper, pulling the moisture out of the atmosphere and, in just a few years, dissolve into pulp. That said, if it is out of sight it may be better to install some basic domestic kitchen units in order to get some life (and therefore people) into the building, rather than waiting longer to do the 'proper job'. Just don't imagine it will be a long-term solution.

OPC:
Cementitious Hazard

Portland cement

As we have said already (see Chapter B3), the one material that should never be used on a church building, without professional supervision as to where, when and how, is (Ordinary) Portland Cement (OPC). This fantastic cement, which works brilliantly for modern building construction, does just the opposite for traditional buildings: it can ruin them, or at the very least cause all manner of problems to historic stone, brick and timber. Be vigilant – *never* let Mr BodgeIt on site with Portland cement.

Beware of domestication

Whether or not Mr (or indeed Mrs) BodgeIt is to blame, far too many church buildings are at risk of being domesticated by a DIY approach that it more suited to a private house. Churches are public buildings so the furnishings and fixtures (including light fittings, door furniture, electrical switches, sanitary equipment etc.) need to be sufficiently robust to stand up to rough and indifferent treatment; domestic fittings are rarely adequate. Furthermore the design of these elements needs to be in keeping with the sacred space and the quality of the architecture.

Floors can be expensive to repair and so it is all too easy for Mr BodgeIt to introduce too much carpet into a church as a quick, cheap and seemingly more comfortable solution to a deteriorating floor finish. The danger of too much carpet is that it can cheapen a church by making it more like a leisure centre or arts centre foyer than a place of worship.

Storage cupboards

(As Jane Austen might have said) it is a truth universally acknowledged that a church in possession of good storage must always be in want of more. Very few church buildings have sufficient storage space; curiously it is equally the case that far too many churches have storage cupboards that are in need of a radical clear-out. Because of the liturgical year it may not be possible to dispose of items that haven't been used for six months but it would be sensible to dispose of anything and everything that hasn't been used for two years.

Mr BodgeIt is a man of principle; when it comes to storage his principle is never to throw anything away because it might possibly come in useful. Sometimes the BodgeIt approach goes so far as never to put anything away. The church building ends up like an ecclesiastical jumble sale full of domestic items discarded from peoples' homes and dumped in the church. Well-intentioned gifts, unwanted furniture and cast-offs from parishioners' homes fill some churches, gathering dust along with the growing collection of the flower arrangers' old oasis, receptacles, pots, jam jars and so on. Favoured locations around the building include the west end, the side aisles, the corners, behind the organ and in the vestries. Curtains may be artfully contrived to hide these repositories, or where there are cupboards, why not consider booby-trapping them by cramming them full of junk that bursts out when the door is opened …?

The Mr BodgeIt approach is to make do and mend or to keep it because it might come in useful. He leaves a legacy of inappropriate repairs and improvements as well as filling 'his' church building with clutter, rendering it unworthy of the God we worship. You have been warned!

Section C   Principles

C1
Future Survival

Building withdrawal syndrome

The Church of England faces some significant challenges. One set of these can be summed up as 'Too many buildings, not enough people'.

If this is to be fixed, the Church has to become more missional. We need both to increase the number of people and to reduce the number of buildings. Both objectives are easy to state but more difficult to achieve. For instance, closing two of three church buildings, each with a congregation of 50, does not automatically result in a composite congregation of 150 people. So when it comes to pruning, should we be cutting buildings, congregations or paid staff? As discussed in Chapter A6, closing church buildings might reduce the costs to individual PCCs but simply shifts the problem on to the diocese.

Paradoxically, the same problem can arise with those Anglican churches that are growing fastest. Many of these come to see their traditional church building as too limiting for what they want to do; if such a church outgrows the facilities in its historic church building, the desired alterations and improvements can seem so difficult to achieve that out of sheer frustration the congregation can sometimes feel driven to abandon the building and relocate. Interestingly Liverpool Diocese which, during 2014, closed more church buildings than any other diocese, has in the same year started more new churches than any other diocese.

Buildings for mission and ministry

In our current situation, 'soldiering on as we are' is a recipe for a slow dribble to decline for many church communities. Unless we want to be in the business of decline management (we know that we're not) then a policy of 'No Change' is no kind of solution.

In Section A we touched on one legitimate parallel between the Church and the retail sector. Taking 'the retail view', we have a 'product' (the gospel) that is of life-changing relevance to the communities around us. The problem is that at present in many cases we are doing a fantastic job of presenting that 'product' in such a way that no one in their right mind would want to buy it. In retail terms, when 'customers' are no longer coming to your 'shop' you could respond by closing the business, perhaps blaming the market or perhaps because you have lost faith in your product. But if you still believe in the relevance of the 'product', the obvious response is to consider how you could present that same product differently. We are therefore not talking about changing the core of our 'business', the gospel, but about expressing it differently in such a way that the people around us see that it might possibly be something for them too.

Like it or not, those on the outside do not make tidy distinctions between the church building, the church community and the God we worship – if the building looks miserable, then the same is seamlessly true both of the worshipping community and also of God.

The need is to find the ways our buildings can help rather than hinder the missional work of making disciples. We need buildings that work for our mission and ministry in the twenty-first century. Before giving up on the building the church community should make an effort to make it sustainable, for example by exploring the possibilities to open up the building for community use. For the building to have a future we have to see it as an asset rather than a liability. The starting point of all successful mission and ministry is in the quality of the relationships among the people involved. Engagement, encounter, being alongside and dialogue feature in the gospel stories of Jesus' mission and ministry. There were times of didactic teaching and addressing large crowds but the stories of bringing people to a new place in their understanding of the nature of God and what it is to be human were commonly the result of a relationship that had been established between Jesus and the individuals involved.

'Sir, we wish to see Jesus' was a request made by some Greeks to Philip in John 12.21; and it is just as valid in our own time as it was when originally made. It is a request made by people on the outside to those on the inside.

Facilitating relationships

Consider these words in relation to your church building:

- Engagement.
- Encounter.
- Being alongside.
- Dialogue.

Identify to what extent your church building facilitates or inhibits these activities among people. Does it have the right sort of arrangement to facilitate the building of relationships?

What would need to change in order to improve the situation?

How much of that is dependent on changing the building and how much is dependent on changing patterns of behaviour?

Much of the remainder of this handbook aims to enable you to have church buildings that facilitate mission and ministry. That probably involves change – of ourselves and our attitudes, and/or of our buildings. For some that may be scary, and it is important to acknowledge that; but then again, to be alive is to change …

C2

Sacred Place, Holy Ground

A sense of place is part of being human – we are 'placed beings'. We interpret the world through the context of the places we experience. Our human experience is shaped by place.

When it comes to those deeper insights of who we are and the meaning of things, places can hold special relevance or significance. Particular places may carry a sense of the presence of God or perhaps more generally convey the spiritual dimension of life. Sacred places are those that communicate a sense of the *numinous*; that is, of those things that are beyond our understanding – they are therefore both challenging and attractive in a contemporary culture increasingly questioning of conventional certainties.

Across the UK the Church finds itself responsible for a high proportion of these sacred places, yet because we become familiar with these places it can be easy to miss their importance for others. This is a big subject and certainly sacred place is not the exclusive property or domain of the Church alone; but by the same token for some it will be the common ground from which to build a missional conversation. Philosophers, theologians (of all religions), poets, artists and psychologists have all written through the ages about the significance of place to people; for us to have an appreciation of places of worship as significant sacred places will therefore be a considerable help in the missional work of the Church. To develop this appreciation involves getting to grips with some of the relevant theology.

A Christian theology of place

John Inge (currently the Bishop of Worcester) has written a very useful book, *A Christian Theology of Place*.[1] It is not a light read but is worth persevering with. We suggest you don't skip the introduction as it provides the framework to comprehend the invaluable content of the following chapters.

At its core the book demonstrates the scriptural evidence for a three-way relationship between God, people and place. Holy places are those where a sacramental event (i.e. an encounter with the divine) takes place. As a consequence of this three-way relationship, holy places have been an integral part of the Christian tradition since early in the life of the Church. Waymarkers or shrines identify these holy places in the landscape and still act 'as memorials to the saving events of Christian history, a prophetic presence in the midst of secular society, and an eschatological sign of God's future'.[2] Pilgrimage is the dynamic expression and experience of this three-way relationship linking people, place and God.

There is, writes John Inge, a theologically justifiable case for treating all churches as shrines, for this is where 'sacramental encounter' takes place in the regular Eucharistic worship of the Christian community that develops around the place and becomes associated with it.[3] Holy places act as witnesses to the world; churches act as witnesses in the townscape and landscape of the UK.

With a renewed understanding of the importance of place in human experience it is possible to appreciate the need to work against the dehumanizing effects of the loss of a sense of place. Rapid transport, commuting long distances and globalization continue to erode people's rootedness and experience of place, to the extent that large numbers of people lose relationship with the places they inhabit and the places that mark the stories of themselves as individuals, communities, societies and nations. This 'marking' is essential in providing a sense of orientation and therefore of identity; without this there is a risk that people will no longer know who they are.

John Inge identifies a complex interaction that characterizes the manner in which people relate to places – both those they directly inhabit and those special to them in other ways. He recommends that attention should be given by the Christian community to 'place in general and not just holy places'. Such attention will both nourish the community and be a powerful prophetic action.

> Our study of the Christian scriptures and tradition has led us to the conclusion that a relational view of place emerges from them. I have argued that holy places are those that are associated with divine disclosure or what I have termed 'sacramental encounters' … The geographer Michael Godkin insists that 'the places in a person's world are more than entities which provide the physical stage for life's drama. Some are profound centres of meanings and symbols of experience. As such they lie at the core of human existence.'[4]

The next time you hear someone suggesting that the church building isn't important, John Inge's analysis will enable you to demonstrate that such a view is not only inappropriate to the witness and missional work of the Church but is harmful to the soul.

Churches as holy places and holy ground

All churches are in some sense markers of holy ground, both to the communities in which they are located and to the people who pass by. If John Inge is right (and we think he is) then we need to reawaken in the minds of church communities this understanding of church buildings as holy places. Such an appreciation of holy places is hugely important to understanding not only how people interact with church buildings but what it is to be human in the first place.

It is therefore worth reflecting on what makes a place holy and sacred, what it is that conveys the sense that a particular place or building is holy ground. As the poet R. S. Thomas wrote powerfully about an empty church in his poem 'In Church':

Is this where God hides
From my searching?[5]

And it is important for those of us who regularly use a church to have the humility to recognize that we're not the only ones who may appreciate its sacred character; our familiarity with it might even make us *less* able to see its importance.

Understand what you have

The challenge is to find a way to both respect the church as a holy place and also allow it to have a viable and sustainable purpose in contemporary society. Some would say that as soon as you begin to change a church building you will lose that sense of holiness. While it is certainly possible to change a building badly and so destroy what makes it special, we take the more optimistic view that change at its best can enhance a building's particular character.

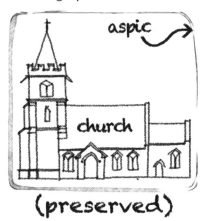

When it comes to church buildings some would say 'Mess with them at your peril'. We would respond with the counter warning: 'Preserve them in aspic at your peril.'

The issue is not whether to change but how to change well. The first step is to pay attention to what is there. Put aside what you might want to do with the building or how it currently frustrates you. Spend some time and effort to reach an understanding of what really is a 'precious inheritance'. Research its origins and seek to understand what made it holy. Understand how it was used by previous generations and how it is appreciated and used now.

Some church buildings are located on or adjacent to holy sites of the pre-Christian era; the Church in earlier times was very good at absorbing and redirecting existing sacred practices. The sense of sacredness for these church buildings therefore comes in part at least from their location, which is imbued with possibly thousands of years of holy activity.

By contrast, many more recent churches were often built as a result of pragmatic decision-making linked to available land or convenience to the resident parishioners; in such cases the sense of the sacred in these buildings is provided by the architecture and the internal arrangement of the building, and by more recent practice. Whatever the age of the building, the arrangement of the internal space can be a very powerful influence and hugely significant factor in communicating the sense of the sacred.

So before you do anything to a church building, get to know what you have and appreciate how it works to engender a sense of awe and holiness; to compromise this sense of the sacredness of the place would be to throw the baby out with the bath-water.

Notes

1 John Inge, *A Christian Theology of Place*, Farnham: Ashgate, 2002.
2 Inge, *Christian Theology of Place*, p. x.
3 Inge, *Christian Theology of Place*, p. x.
4 Inge, *Christian Theology of Place*, p. 124.
5 From R. S. Thomas, 'In Church', in *Collected Poems 1945–1990*, London: Phoenix, 1993.

C3
Working with Places of Worship

When it comes to looking after or making changes to a church building, understanding what you have is a fundamental principle – not only to grasp but to put into practice. You cannot redeem what you do not understand.

Know what you have

The PCC and those who look after the building and its site will be able to do their job  much better if they know what they are dealing with. Once you have properly understood what is special about your building (see Chapter C2 on sacred place and D2 on Statements of Significance), there are three practical essentials to put in place before you go any further (we deal with them more fully in Chapters A2, A6, A7 and B17).

Asset Management Plan (AMP)   Using either the current Quinquennial Report (if it has sufficient information) or a Building Condition Survey, the AMP will provide a forecast of the building's maintenance and repairs, with costs, for the next 25–30 years. See Chapter B17 for how to prepare an AMP.

Financial health check   The church needs to have accurate information about its finances and the income and expenditure trends. The PCC should have a financial strategy to meet its liabilities, balance the books and ensure long-term sustainability of both ministry and buildings.

Assets review   In addition to the church building, it is worth examining whether the best use is currently being made of any church property assets and identify ways to maximize their income-generating potential. This can be simply done by comparing the value of the capital asset with the income generated. If the property is generating less than 5 per cent of its capital value then it may not be earning its keep and could be storing up future repair problems. Another way is to put together an AMP for the property and compare its forecast average annual cost against its annual income. If there is a deficit you will need to take action and possibly get some help sooner than later.

Just to be clear, we are not suggesting that financial value alone is an adequate means of summing up the value of church buildings but it remains one important aspect. Just as there is more to a person than a body with a beating heart, so the value of a church building can never be reduced to a financial calculation. But by the same token it is one of the 'vital signs'; just as we know whether someone is alive or dead by taking their pulse, so an understanding of how money is flowing through a church building is a good indicator of its state of health. Every church therefore needs to think about ways their building could be used to generate some revenue and make a contribution to the cost of its upkeep (without of course destroying its special character).

Understand what you are dealing with

It can be very helpful for the church as a whole (i.e. not just the PCC or fabric sub-committee) to spend some time getting to know the building, its site and how they came into being and have evolved over the time that they have been in use. You may find this a weird suggestion, but experience has proved time after time that very few members of any congregation have much understanding of their place of worship. Experience has also demonstrated the same people are always hugely grateful when something about the building, its origins and its site is explained to them. They want to know but, like all of us, may be afraid to ask or to appear ignorant.

Getting to know what you have does not have to be a dry academic exercise. Use the building and the site as the prompt for the questions to be asked and the answers to be found. For example, the memorials, lists or photographs of previous clergy, a framed baptismal roll, the Log Book or particular architectural features can all be starting points with which to become more familiar with the story of the building. The churchyard is another valuable source of local history. Sometimes there will be so much history that you will need to choose one aspect rather than to attempt to research everyone buried there. For example, the era that has the most long-lived people, the periods of similar headstone shapes, who is buried on the north side.

Share the knowledge

The research may require a small team or at least a couple of people to do it. Their findings will need to be written up in a format and language that is accessible to members of the church community and can be retained for subsequent users. And don't be afraid to involve people from the wider community – this is precisely one aspect of the Church with which people without an overt Christian commitment are keen to engage. And besides, you might learn a lot.

It is really important to ensure the information is shared across the church community and not restricted to a small group who like the more academic or historical aspects of the building's history. Knowledge is power, so everyone needs to be in the know. The trick is to find a way to communicate the information to all the various generations and types of people in the church community. Closely typed sheets of A4 paper can be very offputting, so rather than expecting people to read pages of architectural notes or a detailed guide book, look for other ways to tell them about the building using the human stories associated with it. For example, an illustrated timeline along the interior walls of the church, a quiet day in the building using the stories as prayer stations, a *Time Team*-type presentation that unravels a curiosity or a work project that identifies, explains and then puts right a problem. If there is a really good inspiring story or even a human story of tragedy or scandal it may be possible to put this into a dramatic format. Just look at the cultural legacy inspired by the dreadful story of Thomas Becket.

Having done the work to understand how the building works and come to an appreciation of its cultural worth, it is likely that the PCC will be more willing to look after it properly and not do things that will cause damage or propose changes that might adversely affect its significance.

Remember the mission

It might not feel like it at times but church buildings should serve the work of the Church, which is to continue the mission given to the apostles, to continue the tasks they were sent out to do. The mission of the local church should be the driver of everything that it does, so it is essential for it to have agreed mission priorities.

For some people the word mission is a complete turn-off as it is associated in their minds with heavy-handed evangelism or a numbers game of increasing congregation sizes in order to generate revenue. But mission is much more than growing the church numerically. Mission is what the apostles were sent out to do, including service and witness. Mission is what we embody individually as disciples. It is the sense of mission (being sent out entrusted with tasks of ministry) that drives, energizes and directs the living out of our faith.

Buildings can all too easily inhibit the sense of being sent out with a task to do, precisely because of their solidity and immovability. And then of course there is the fear that they will swallow up all of your time, energy and money in order to keep them going. But buildings can serve to nurture and resource the prayer, praise and worship of the church (both as individuals and congregations) and of the wider community. Their very presence serves as a missional witness – which, of course, is why it is important they are kept open because if they are locked through the week we are positively preventing people hearing the gospel message. Locked churches reinforce the impression they are the private premises of a 'private members' club'.

Worthy of God

This is a serious matter.

All churches need to look after their buildings in a manner worthy of God. Run-down, unkempt neglected buildings are not worthy of God. Extravagant expenditure is not necessary, but ensuring the building is clean and tidy is absolutely essential.

As we know, money doesn't grow on trees, and there are few churches with sufficient funds that they can afford whatever they want and pay other people to provide it. It is important, therefore, to appreciate the precious inheritance for which the PCC is responsible. The rebuild costs of a stone-built church are considerable, so it sensible to look after the one you have and prevent large and unexpected repair bills by doing the regular preventative maintenance. Doing that maintenance is therefore all part of acting responsibly in a manner worthy of God; ignoring it is quite the opposite.

Working with church buildings, especially old ones, does take commitment and a willingness to engage with the building, understanding that it may have views of its own and that in time, if we listen well enough, we might even learn from it. Sadly some church communities don't seem to want to do this thinking for themselves but would prefer to have someone else tell them what to do.

Do it yourself

Changes to the building (of which more in the following chapters) need to be carefully considered and researched by the church community before any professional is instructed to act. Otherwise fees will be paid by the church for work they could have done themselves or for ideas and concepts that never see the light of day.

Some churches have spent five-figure sums (i.e. over £10,000 and in some cases over £50,000) on architects' drawings that never turned into reality precisely because of this reluctance to engage with their building in the first place. The plea, therefore, is to be clear about what work the church needs to do and what work it needs to pay someone else to do. There is a great deal an individual church needs to do for itself if it is to have a building that works for its community. If the building isn't working for your church, be prepared to spend time and effort to understand the issues; don't look for someone else to do this work for you.

C4
The Moment of Truth

We would urge you to get your church community to explore the similarities and areas of overlap between the Church and the retail sector. Such a view should not by now be a surprise to our readers (see Chapter C1) but the Church in general needs to think seriously about this concept before dismissing it out of hand.

It may not be a consumer product that we are selling but we are nevertheless in the business of attracting people to take an interest in something they don't yet know they want and need, in this case Christianity. As the Church we have a 'product' (the gospel) that we wish to promote, and we want to enable an encounter with the gospel in the life of the Church in the hope that these newcomers may make a long-term commitment to Christ. There are considerable similarities with what shops and businesses are seeking to achieve in promoting their goods and services to the general public. We have much to learn from the retail sector about how to promote what we are offering and how to attract and keep people's interest.

Church buildings as business premises

Extending this metaphor, the church building is the 'business premises' for the church community. In the various contexts of church life (parish, diocesan and national), our buildings and property serve as our 'shop windows' and they have an enormous effect on how what we are offering is perceived.

In the same way as with shop premises, our church premises can attract, serve and retain people or, conversely, put them off coming near let alone inside. Cold, dirty, closed, uncomfortable and unkempt church buildings are a significant barrier. They are a visible statement of a positive indifference to, or even the rejection of the prospective customer, and as we have noted elsewhere, the building is assumed to be speaking for the people inside it and the God it represents.

In some cases it is undeniably the building that is not 'fit for purpose'; but much more often it is the way we manage the building that results in its being a hindrance and barrier. If the building really is a significant barrier to the missional work of the Church then it may well be necessary to make changes to it and its management or even to relocate operations to more suitable premises. Many congregations move too quickly to that last option, and the thrust of this book is to encourage churches not to jump to that conclusion but instead to appreciate the building for what it does offer.

The Moment of Truth

Many non-church people have anxieties about and fear of church buildings, what goes on inside them and the people associated with them. For some people, churches are virtually alien territory and are viewed with apprehension.

Church members need to have an awareness of a retail principle called The Moment of Truth. This is the moment when all the advertising and promotional claims are measured against what the retailer actually delivers. The person doing the measuring is the customer. If the gap is too big between what is claimed and what is delivered, the customer may well be lost for ever.

The Moment of Truth applies to the Church as well – in its case it arrives when all the claims made in the name of Jesus Christ are measured against what the Church actually delivers. If the gap is too big then, similarly, this can result in the person never coming back. As Michael Riddell puts it:

> It is the form of the Church in the West which has become the biggest barrier to the gospel. The broad sweep of ecclesiastical life does not bear witness to the grace, passion, radicality, authority, tenderness, anger, excitement, involvement or acceptance of Jesus. Unfortunately for us, the medium has become the message. The popular image of Christianity is formed by encounter with the Church; and so Christianity is regarded as reactionary, oppressive, conservative, moralistic, hypocritical, boring, formal and judgemental.[1]

Both church members and church buildings have a big part to play in The Moment of Truth.

Note

1 Michael Riddell, *Threshold of the Future: Reforming the Church in the Post-Christian West*, London: SPCK, 1998, p. 39.

C5

Serving People – Four Modes of Operation

Buildings need people

Much of Britain's self-understanding comes from centuries of Christian faith, but many in Britain now have minimal knowledge of the Christian faith. The Christian story is no longer at the heart of the nation. Although people may identify themselves as 'Christian' in the national census, for the majority that does not involve belonging to a worshipping community, or any inclination that it should. Many people have no identifiable religious interest or expression. Among some young people there is little evidence of any belief in a transcendent dimension. During the twentieth century Sunday school attendance dropped from 55 per cent to 4 per cent of children, meaning that even the rudiments of the Christian story and of Christian experience are lacking in most young people.

Church of England Board of Mission, Mission-Shaped Church[1]

Buildings of any kind need people to survive, and this is particularly true of community buildings such as churches. Without people animating them they have no purpose, nor will they be maintained – and without that, of course, they will not survive.

If the Church has learnt one thing from the twentieth century it is that the inherited model of 'monocultural' single-function churches has failed. In place of this single-function model, this chapter proposes a four-dimensional model for church buildings, identifying four distinct modes of operation. You will note that none of the four describes the primary function of a parish church as a place of worship. This is because that is taken as read, as the unifying context that binds these four modes together.

Business, legal settlements, sociability and entertainment, in addition to worship brought people to the [medieval] church.

Katherine French, The People of the Parish[2]

Each building and context is of course different, and in no sense, therefore, are we proposing a one-size-fits-all solution. On the other hand, it is the case that the same themes recur again and again. This structure is therefore offered as a framework for further investigation, reflection and development. Think of these four modes as ingredients that you can choose to combine in an almost limitless variety of ways, to suit your particular circumstances; we invite you to take these ingredients and use them to bake your church's specific form of 'ministerial cake'.

Of course, for your building to function successfully and do its job it needs to serve you and your community and help you live out your particular corporate calling in your particular parish situation. You will therefore have to identify and agree what that calling is before you will know who the building is serving (or could be serving) and how this is being achieved.

Four modes of operation, theology and management

Church buildings as holy places need to operate in or facilitate four distinct modes which, in no particular order, are:

- Community meeting places.
- Teaching and learning places.
- Human creativity and artistic places.
- Aesthetic and threshold places.

As we have said, all four modes of operation are contained within and are complementary to the status of the building as a place of worship and its status as a sacred place and holy ground.

The balance of these four modes needs to be considered and adjusted to suit particular requirements, but care should be taken to avoid the overemphasis of one mode to the exclusion or detriment of the others. Thereafter the overall balance should be monitored, because you should expect the balance to continue to change as the needs of your community change.

1 Community meeting places

As we have said, church buildings need people in order to survive. This is hugely helped where parish churches are open (both in accessibility and in mindset) to operate holistically as community meeting spaces and places of assembly. This is the first and most obvious challenge to Victorian monoculturalism.

We should remember that if church buildings are not allowed to function in this holistic way they are failing to fulfil their original and primary purpose when our parish system, which dates from the Norman Conquest, came into being. The church-building programme of the Norman era either absorbed or replaced the associated holy sites of the Celtic and Anglo Saxon Church. In partnership with the Crown, ecclesiastical power increased and church buildings were enlarged or rebuilt to serve as the civic forums for both the Crown's and the Church's authority and the administration of the new social order. Church buildings built during the Norman period and after were sized to provide sufficient space for the people to assemble for the full range of communal purposes.

> The Norman combination of piety and power finds expression wherever they held control – from the lowlands of Scotland, in the border regions and throughout England. For they developed a strong sense of the village and town ruled by the feudal lord, who controls and runs an area in which the church is one of the main status symbols. This led to the building of some ten thousand parish churches that are still standing in Britain.
>
> *Martin Palmer*, Sacred Land[3]

In its conception the parish church building was at the heart of its community serving as the venue for most public activities. The churches were busy places full of the broad spectrum of human life because the whole of life was understood in religious terms; our distinction between sacred and secular would have been incomprehensible. In her significant book *The People of the Parish*, Katherine French shows that in the late 1300s (i.e. before the Reformation) the parish church was central to peoples' lives in medieval England, and that much of the activity in church buildings was what we would now term 'secular'. As well as meeting our expectation of the church as the basic forum for public worship, the medieval parish was 'a forum for community identity' (i.e. for the community as a whole).[4] For us to perpetuate the exclusion of communal activities from our churches is to collude in the secularist denial of the communal and social relevance of the Church.

Eamon Duffy describes this pre-Reformation holistic understanding of life as documented in one West Country parish: 'At Morebath, no rigid distinction was drawn between the community at prayer and the community as it went about its business.' It is also evident that the parish church is a building which is owned and precious to all the parishioners: 'For all the parish, the "worship" or honourable maintenance of their church was an aspect of their sense of worth and integrity as individuals and as a community.' Their church was a place in which they would habitually linger long after services because 'parish business was conducted there, bargains concluded, contracts signed and debts paid'.[5]

All too many church buildings are prevented from addressing contemporary community needs because they are 'closed'; that is, inaccessible for much of the week because of locked doors but also in terms of mindset. They are also 'constipated' by excessive amounts of furniture, insufficient circulation space and a lack of basic kitchen and WC facilities.

2 Teaching and learning places

With the excessive pewing of most Anglican churches during the Georgian (box, bespoke, not necessarily facing east) and Victorian (free, bench, catalogue range of designs, factory-made, facing east) periods, it became difficult for churches to operate as community meeting places. The emphasis on seating was to ensure the parish church could operate as a significant teaching and learning space for the residents of the parish.

In an age in which so much of the Christian story has been lost from the wider community, parish church buildings need to facilitate teaching and learning about the faith more than ever. However, this is not necessarily best achieved through traditional didactic methods of sitting up straight and facing the front.

Most parish church buildings include layered stories of change and development. The physical features, artefacts, alterations and changes in the buildings all have a human story behind the reasons they are there. If the buildings are to operate as teaching and learning spaces, the work of uncovering and interpreting what is there has to be done. The buildings need to work as places of discovery.

Parish church buildings are 'rich environments' that offer huge potential to facilitate interactive discussions, drama, group meetings, conferences, workshops and hands-on practical sessions. However, to make the most of these opportunities a single large place of assembly will probably be insufficient; a range of smaller more intimate and more easily heated spaces are necessary.

3 Human creativity and artistic places

Places of worship have a significant role in the celebration of human creativity and to serve as facilitators of artistic endeavour. For centuries the Church has funded, commissioned and enabled human enterprise and artistic creativity. Art therefore belongs in churches, so it shouldn't be seen as the preserve of the cathedrals. Not only should art be commissioned for parish churches, congregations need to be encouraged to explore ways their church buildings can be used to celebrate human creativity. For example, the Art Alive in Churches project began as a consortium of local authority arts officers and the Open Churches Officer at the Diocese of Norwich in 2008. The aims of the project were and still are:

- To promote rural and urban locations through their built heritage and local arts and crafts.
- To use the local church as a focal point with an artist or craftsperson in residence, demonstrating artistic skills associated with that church from the building of the church to the present day.
- To encourage an interest in art and craft skills, not always in common use, but which are essential for the restoration of heritage buildings and their artefacts.
- To encourage the use of the church in different ways and to encourage visitors into beautiful but often deprived areas.[6]

Such approaches bring life and energy to church space, moving them beyond that sense and feeling of a museum experience. People respond with enthusiasm when they discover a sense of life and vibrancy in a church because, sadly, it defies their expectation.

As a nation we are beginning to appreciate that human creativity is not restricted to the work of the designated 'Artist'. Churches can be used to showcase craft skills and celebrate local forms of human creativity. This includes the everyday necessities of food and drink.

Aesthetic and threshold places

Beauty, peace and a sense of wonder are some of the attributes of church buildings expected by the visiting public. Some people are moved by particular forms (architecture, design, detail, arrangement) but not by others. Some buildings are simple, some are complex, and there is no one form that will inspire everyone.

However, the best way of preventing this sense of wonder is through clutter and dirt. To be able to 'speak for themselves', church buildings need to be clean and well ordered, with minimum amounts of clutter and dirt. Attention to detail is essential for the aesthetic presentation of a building.

More significant but more difficult to pin down is how church buildings operate as 'threshold space'. The word 'threshold' is being used in a slightly different way from that in Chapter C7, but in both cases we are describing a boundary over which one crosses to enter a new or different place. Other terms we could use are 'liminal', 'thin' or 'encounter'.

> Moses, Moses … Remove the sandals from your feet, for the place on which you are standing is holy ground.
>
> *Exodus 3.4–5*

> Then Jacob woke from his sleep and said 'Surely the Lord is in this place – and I did not know it! … This is none other than the house of God, and this is the gate of heaven.
>
> *Genesis 28.16–17*

The journey to the new or different place was, in the medieval period, embodied in the practice of pilgrimage. The journey could be lengthy to foreign lands, such as from England to Jerusalem or to Santiago de Compostela; it could be within the country, for example to Canterbury or Walsingham, or it could simply be to the parish church which, through a staged process of thresholds of the lychgate, porch and nave, brought the pilgrim to the rood screen of the church.

The liminal, thin, encounter or threshold is the space between heaven and earth which, in the medieval church, was symbolized by the rood screen. Even though some rood screens, especially solid stone pulpitums, serve to separate the sacred space from everyday, the rood screen should not be thought of as a barrier or boundary. It demarcates the most significant threshold, where the part of the building associated with heaven (the chancel) is glimpsed from the earth (the nave).

The threshold place in a church building is usually focused at the east end but not always; sometimes it is deliberately contrived, sometimes it is the result of a layered history and happy accident. The amount of expenditure or the intricacy of decoration does not determine the 'success' of the threshold space. Both Kings College Chapel in Cambridge and the Methodist New Room in Bristol operate as threshold spaces – the latter more by the exclusion of anything secular, its simplicity and focus on the Word.

As with aesthetic spaces, a threshold space can be all too easily damaged or impaired by noise, activity or clutter.

[A]ttention to place by the Christian community will afford great nourishment and sustenance to it.

John Inge, A Theology of Place[7]

Re-ordering?

So whether you are thinking about re-ordering a church or finding a way for it to have a 'wow' factor, take some time to think through the need for it to operate in these four modes. What you inherited might be great and require no improvement but it will need monitoring. Many churches have lost their ability to invoke a sense of wonder because we have made them too domestic and too much like our front rooms or the auditoriums of a theatre. Human beings need to be able to gasp and wonder.

Notes

1 Church of England Board of Mission, *Mission-Shaped Church*, London: Church House Publishing, 2004, p. 11.

2 Katherine French, *The People of the Parish: Community Life in a Late Medieval English Diocese*, Philadelphia: University of Pennsylvania Press, 2001, p. 2.

3 Martin Palmer, *Sacred Land: Decoding Britain's Extraordinary Past Through its Towns, Villages and Countryside*, London: Piatkus, 2012, p. 70.

4 French, *People of the Parish*, p. 3.

5 Eamon Duffy, *The Voices of Morebath: Reformation and Rebellion in an English Village*, London: Yale University Press, 2001, pp. 5, 6, 81.

6 See www.artaliveinchurches.com/home.

7 John Inge, *A Christian Theology of Place*, Farnham: Ashgate, 2002, p. 137

C6
Conservation

Background to a troubled relationship

In merrily skipping through the missional landscape of their parish situation, churches may find themselves stumbling into what can seem like a pitched battle that is not of their making. As with a grumpy married couple, to understand why churches and conservation bodies often fail to get on, you have to go back to the passions that underlie their relationship; and to do that, it helps to understand how that relationship began.

This means becoming acquainted with the history of the modern conservation movement; it is this history that causes some 'engagements' with conservation to be played out in a particular (and destructive) way. In many ways today's battles are a continuation of yesterday's.

Lesson from history

Conservation must be understood as a by-product of modernity. There are two crucial aspects of modernity that make the relationship between modern conservation and the Church a particularly troubled one. The first is that modernity exalts the individual at the expense of the community whereas the Church since its beginning has provided a fundamental challenge to that ordering of priorities. The second is that modernity (and therefore conservation to the extent that it remains a subset of modernity) fundamentally misunderstands tradition; the Enlightenment was self-avowedly hostile to tradition, and particularly to what was seen as the dead hand of the Church.

Conservation is fundamentally a modern enterprise. While one could pick a number of 'birth dates' for conservation, in terms of any sort of organized and active programme of intervention to preserve historic buildings for future generations, backed up by legislation, the birth of conservation would be placed around 1790. Before the trauma of the French Revolution, interest in historic buildings was the preserve of antiquarians who rarely did more than draw the objects of their interest. Modern conservation emerged in the context of the post-revolutionary French state finding itself responsible for all manner of historic buildings that had been confiscated from the Church and other landowners.

Critical to this new understanding was seeing historic buildings as 'historic monuments', an idea made possible by the wrenching of those buildings from the cultural context that first gave them meaning. Close on the heels of this came the urgent need in the nineteenth century to define 'national identity', physical expressions of heritage such as historic buildings being obvious candidates for (ab)use in this way. These two developments combined to encourage the equation of heritage with preservation; the focus of heritage, and therefore of conservation, becomes the physical product itself rather than the people and processes that produced that product in the context of a living tradition.

In conservation terms this is the vexed question of whether the 'authenticity' of heritage lies in the physical product or in a dynamic cultural process. With greater recognition of 'intangible' heritage (as opposed to the tangible physical stuff), the world of heritage is changing. In Japan, for example, wooden temples and other historic structures can be completely rebuilt and yet retain their authenticity and sacredness. These concerns resulted in 'The Nara Document on Authenticity (1994)',[1] the first international conservation charter to incorporate non-Western understandings of authenticity.

In this respect our churchmanship is also relevant as different expressions of Church have very different understandings of 'tradition'. Evangelicalism has typically worn the vestiges of tradition more lightly (or reluctantly or not at all) than more Catholic understandings of Church. Our buildings, whether, for example, medieval, Georgian or Victorian, and however flawed or altered, are prime expressions of that tradition; which may explain why some of us are so reluctant to engage with our church buildings at all. The view of this book, written as it is from firmly within the Church, is that our tradition is very much alive. It is in recognition of the vitality of that tradition that we have the Ecclesiastical Exemption (see Chapter D8), a statutory recognition of the distinction between a mere historic monument and the 'living building' that a church in use is.

Madness in the method

Conservation methodology for England is set out in the Historic England *Conservation Principles, Policies and Guidance* document.[2] This 2008 document (which has lots of good stuff in it) builds on a series of international charters developed over the last

100 or so years. This system goes back to the Viennese art historian Alois Riegl, who produced the first such methodology in 1903 setting out competing classes of values. In its current form this methodology identifies four such classes of values: evidential, historical, aesthetic and communal.

> Significance [of a place]: 'The sum of the cultural and natural heritage values of a place, often set out in a statement of significance.'

> Conservation: 'The process of managing change to a significant place in its setting in ways that will best sustain its heritage values, while recognising opportunities to reveal or reinforce those values for present and future generations.'

> *Definitions from Historic England,* Conservation Principles[3]

The Historic England definition of conservation as the management of change has a lot to like about it; yet if conservation is the *management* of change then, like the Bank of England's inflation target, it is presumably just as wrong to undershoot by allowing too little change as to overshoot by allowing too much. If, however, one adopts the 'secular' approach of seeing historic buildings as principally historic monuments, as the methodology does (since it is derived from an art-historical understanding), then all change is loss and the 'management of change' is interpreted as the *minimization* or prevention of change. It is this understanding that often, but not always, predominates among conservation professionals such as local authority Conservation Officers and representatives of some national amenity societies.

There is another side to this coin, however. Modern conservation in the UK developed from a nineteenth-century argument between antiquarians with a historical interest in our built heritage on the one side, and the church 'restorers', both architects and church members, on the other. While acknowledging that the true picture is a good deal more nuanced, there is nevertheless truth in the caricature of Victorian 'restoration' as the destruction of the historical layering of our ancient churches in favour of a more stylistically unified aesthetic approach. In practice this might, for example, mean the removal of a number of windows dating from a variety of different periods and their replacement in a single favoured style; the ambition was to 'return' the building to a purer and more aesthetically coherent state which, it was freely acknowledged, might never have existed in reality.

The classic case of this so-called 'restoration' was St Albans Cathedral, which was heavily restored by the amateur Lord Grimthorpe. In his defence it should be said that the restoration works saved the building, but they did so at the cost of remaking it in Grimthorpe's own image (and it seems as his personal memorial). Decades of 'Disney-fication' of this sort drew the ire of William Morris and Philip Webb among others, leading to the setting up of the Society for the Protection of Ancient Buildings (SPAB) in 1877. Morris' polemical writing makes instructive reading, if only to confirm how central church buildings were to the development of conservation in Great Britain.

> If people really saw the true worth of our medieval churches they would realize how dangerous it is to introduce new work into old buildings. It is like putting new wine into old bottles, for both are destroyed.
>
> *William Morris*[4]

If one takes Morris' words in the founding SPAB *Manifesto* at face value,[5] it is difficult to avoid the conclusion that conservation is all about the *prevention* of change. For example, the *Manifesto* concludes with a plea 'to treat our ancient buildings as monuments of a bygone art, created by bygone manners, that modern art cannot meddle with without destroying'. For Morris, the 'living spirit' of which these buildings are an expression is now dead, and any change is loss. On this reading the 'Heritage lobby' and any future-facing expression of Church will find themselves in inevitable and unresolvable conflict.

In fact the thrust of Morris' argument is a (justifiable) reaction to the excesses of nineteenth-century historicism. Elsewhere in the *Manifesto* he says that up until the nineteenth century, 'every change, whatever history it destroyed, left history in the gap, and was alive with the spirit of the deeds done midst its fashioning'. If the thrust of Morris' argument is allied to an understanding that the tradition that formed these buildings is still alive and well, then there is scope for a much more creative and engaged approach to historic buildings. SPAB itself remains a fine organization in good health, with several recent initiatives that have done great service to the care of church buildings, such as Faith in Maintenance (FiM) and the recently introduced Maintenance Co-operatives Project.

Trinitarian cheese theory

In our view all of the above flows from a misunderstanding of what historic buildings are, and particularly in the context of this book, historic churches. We see three possible ways one can look at a historic church building, and in an effort to aid our reimagining we suggest each of these can be characterized by a different sort of cheese.

So, what is a church anyway? Is it:

- An art-historical monument? This essentially is the understanding behind classical conservation, as outlined above; the theory and sensibility is drawn from the discipline of art history. Seeing a church as a work of art is like sculpting a block of cheese (yes, people do sculpt things out of cheese – search online for 'cheese art'). However skilful, beautiful or impressive the result may be, as soon as I hack a slice off for my sandwich then I have destroyed its artistic integrity. All change is loss.

- A 'machine for worshipping in' (following the modernist architect Le Corbusier's characterization of a house as a 'machine for living in')? This is a reductively functional understanding of what a church should be, with no value attached to the historic fabric (or indeed to any other aspects of the tradition). Processed cheese might fit this category – in its way it is very impressive; it is 'fit for purpose', designed to melt in a burger bun at a particular temperature, but it is not cheese that we, at any rate, would choose to eat.
- A communal narrative? The cheese we suggest here is a round of Stilton (if you don't like blue cheese, then fill in with an alternative …). There is something fundamentally communal about a round of Stilton at Christmas, with everyone tucking in; so too narrative is essential to community and to tradition. Blue cheese owes its character to having matured over time; its imperfections, its cracked surface, its mouldiness even are all an essential part of that character.

There are two morals from this story. The first and most obvious one is: 'Blessed are the cheesemakers'!

The second moral is what we mean by **culture**, which is understood differently in each of the three categories above:

- The first (cheese as art) view understands culture to mean 'high culture' – a classical education, the Proms, the BBC and so on. And note that in the dominant contemporary understanding this is exactly the pigeonhole into which the Church of England is placed. This we could tentatively call a 'right wing' view.
- The second (processed cheese) view has little time for culture; here the concern is with efficiency and functionalism, and anything 'cultural' is an aesthetic non-essential produced as a by-product of technological progress. This we could term a 'left wing' view.
- The third (Stilton) view sees tradition as fundamentally generative, and predictably enough could be named the 'third way'; in this case 'culture' is seen as live, like yoghurt – you take some and from that you make some more, and of course the art of cheesemaking is not dissimilar.

So the second moral is really a restatement of the first, with the accent on the final two syllables: 'Blessed are the cheese*makers*.'

Conservation as narrative

Our view is that an art-historical understanding of conservation is potentially toxic, capable of destroying the very thing it wishes to protect. It sets church and conservation bodies up for conflict and alienates many communities from their buildings. Perhaps the greatest failing of contemporary conservation theory is that it has no account of, nor even concern with, how tomorrow's heritage can be created, because it has no understanding of change, of how to engage with a *living* building. For this a different cultural model is needed, and our view is that narrative offers just such a model. With narrative comes an orientation towards the future and therefore a positive horizon of expectation; seeing the church building as a multi-generational ongoing story locates us within 'our story' and provides hope both for the building itself and for the community that 'owns' it.

Competition

We wonder whether it is possible to build a chain of words from *church* to *change* via *cheese* (always six letters, changing one letter at a time, each step being a recognized English word). To the first person to do so we'll offer a free architectural consultation on their church anywhere in the UK – really … Answers submitted via the churchbuild. co.uk website.

Notes

1 See www.icomos.org/charters/nara-e.pdf.

2 Historic England, *Conservation Principles, Policies and Guidance*, London: English Heritage, 2008 – see http://historicengland.org.uk/images-books/publications/conservation-principles-sustainable-management-historic-environment/.

3 Historic England, *Conservation Principles*, pp. 71–2.

4 William Morris, quoted in Jane Fawcett (ed.), *The Future of the Past: Attitudes to Conservation 1174–1974*, London: Thames & Hudson, 1976, p. 108.

5 See www.spab.org.uk/what-is-spab-/the-manifesto.

C7

Open, Welcoming and Accepting

Any community building will necessarily be a place of threshold between the public and the private/communal. In the case of church buildings the issue of how thresholds are negotiated is central to their ability to act missionally. This chapter looks at thresholds, why they are important and what a building with low thresholds might look like in practice.

From centre to periphery

A medieval church would generally have stood at the centre of its community. The building 'advertised' itself in the landscape by means of its tower and perhaps spire; this was matched by a general understanding that, whatever the social politics involved, the church building was relevant to the community as a whole. The legacy of the nineteenth century is that many church buildings have in effect 'migrated' from this central location to the edge of their communities. In some cases this happened in terms of geography, perhaps where the centre of a village moved away from the church, leaving it stranded in splendid isolation. More often the church (both small 'c' as a building, but also large 'C' as an institution) has migrated to the periphery *in the minds of the community* and is seen now as nothing more than the 'private members' religious club'. We need to be careful: the building can reach the edge of the community and keep on going, falling over the edge into the oblivion of closure and eventual demolition. This book is written from the conviction that this process of marginalization is not inevitable and in principle is reversible; our aim is to help you move your church back towards the centre of your community.

Whether a building is or is not at the centre of its community in the way we describe is principally to do with the energy and life within it. Most of our church buildings were built in a context in which everyone in the community knew that what happened within the building was of relevance to them. In medieval times this was most likely justified, given that the Church was at the centre of Western culture and that the church building played host to a great variety of community activity.

That attractional model was still largely sustainable in the nineteenth century, even after the expulsion of whatever remained of the community activities into the newly constructed village halls and schools. However, the benefit of hindsight suggests that the Victorians were trading on the cultural capital of the past, and we are now reaping the consequences of this complacency. The attractional model no longer works, and for our buildings and worshipping communities to survive we desperately need to reimagine what our church buildings are and how we are going to work with them. If they are to survive, our buildings need to work harder than they have for the last couple of centuries.

Learning from retail

As we keep saying, there are strong similarities between the Church and the retail sector (see Chapters C1 and C4). Retailers have long been aware of the importance of physical thresholds for the very simple reason that a sense of approachability affects people's behaviour, including their purchasing behaviour. Shops traditionally make themselves approachable by using their shop window to display on the outside something of what you can expect to find inside – not only the product, but (where skilfully done) also something of the other supposed 'lifestyle benefits' you will attain by purchasing that product.

And when you do step through the door of a shop, what are you faced with? Successful retail space minimizes the initial threshold, and as you are drawn across that threshold you find yourself in a zone where you have lots of choice. You are free to choose what to look at and where to go, and you will not be asked to make a decision until you're ready. You certainly would not expect to feel judged as you enter, be handed a bundle of things you don't know what to do with or made to look stupid by failing some kind of test; retailers understand that any of these experiences would scare people away.

With that in mind, think again of the experience of entering a church for the first time. Most church buildings suffer from a sharp divide between inside and outside, which makes them buildings that demand 'pre-commitment' – you have to know in advance that you want to enter and what you will do there before you even approach them. This is increasingly countercultural and makes our buildings more suited to some sort of secret society. Is it any surprise that this is sometimes how the Church is seen, as the 'private members' religious club', with the built form echoing an implied theology that divides those inside from those outside, the saved from the unsaved? This is really unhelpful, not least because it does not reflect the means by which people typically come to faith. Most typically, coming to faith happens within community on the basis of relationship, people gradually being drawn from the outer edges into the centre, into active engagement with God. One such model of this is the Engel scale – for more on this see James Engel's *What's Gone Wrong With the Harvest*.[1]

Aside from the fact that in previous eras church buildings never needed to work to attract a crowd, we are also fighting against two interrelated legacies of the Victorian period. One was the decanting of community activities from the churches into the newly created village halls in the name of making the church more 'sacred'; in this way the wider community was excluded from what remains *their* building, except on *our* (religious/club membership) terms. The other was the cramming in of too many pews so that where a retail space might allow the easy flow of movement and un-hurried engagement in those initial spaces, the equivalent experience in a church is of a cramped space that conveys meanness, forces any welcomers to stand too close to you and creates an unnecessary and unwelcome feeling of pressure. For more on the specific issue of pews see Chapter B5 on seating.

In our view the healthiest model is seen in those buildings that combine a 'traditional' (i.e. community) understanding of Church with the low threshold of, for example, a café space that is easy and welcoming to come into. The time when the majority of people were willing to come into a building for 'the smell of God' is long gone. It is much more feasible to draw people in for something they can already imagine is rele-vant (e.g. for the smell of coffee, or for childcare or whatever). Having enjoyed their coffee or benefited from the childcare they may then find themselves in a place of community where we are able to share our stories in both directions, thereby earning the right to share the bigger story we believe we all need to hear and partake in.

If you look at church buildings within this frame of reference, what does a building that doesn't allow views in and appears closed say to those outside? Those wooden doors now appear defensive, as though we have some awful secret to hide, and the message seems to be 'Go away!' (or worse, 'F*** off!'). Whether or not it is our inten-tion, to the general culture such a building speaks volumes about God being dead; it says there is no life here, no sustenance, no affirmation, and feeds the common belief that God and the Church are bound to disapprove of anyone who does not live up to an imagined unattainable standard.

AIDA – singing for your supper

Let's return to what the Church can learn from retail and consider a church building as a form of advertising. Please note that we are not saying that our buildings are nothing more than a marketing tool! Rather, we are observing that the purpose of advertising is as a means for one subset of our society to communicate with the wider culture, drawing attention to what that organization offers, generally with the goal of some form of commercial gain. Are there not some legitimate parallels with a church building? In just the same way, a church building can be seen as a cultural expression on the part of a subset of society that identifies that subset and aims to communicate something of what that subset offers to the wider culture. The issue is not whether this communication is taking place – our buildings are talking all the time to those who pass by – but whether the message being 'broadcast' is an accurate reflection of the life within.

Aside from being a famous opera by Verdi, AIDA is also a marketing acronym first coined in 1903 by Elias St Elmo Lewis to analyse the process by which a consumer engages with print advertising. For Lewis, AIDA stands for:

- **Attention** Attract the customer's attention, generally by means of a provocative headline.
- **Interest** Engage the customer, not by talking about the features of what you offer but by demonstrating the benefits relevant to them; usually this is done by an attractive image that draws you in.
- **Desire** Demonstrate that the product or service is desirable and will meet their needs; this is done by providing some written information about the product or service.
- **Action** Enable the customer to take action or complete their purchase; 'contact us now', or 'sign up for a free trial' and so on.

Should the Church be reduced to nothing more than marketing? Of course not! Might the Church be able to learn something useful from the world of advertising? Perhaps. But how could this framework be applied to church buildings?

 **Attention** Many churches are built in prominent locations, and again many are high-status buildings that have stood in their communities for hundreds of years. If your church is a landmark of some kind then you are already attracting attention. Almost every church has a notice board – but do you use yours for any more than service times and a phone number? We are not just attracting attention, we are offering a greeting.

Interest   In a church context this is an open zone of engagement, where we offer **hospitality**. God's hospitality always was and remains deeply countercultural, but it is also very attractive even in our cynical age. Where appropriate, coffee does a great job in our culture of combining choice with hospitality. In other situations an appropriate expression of this hospitality might be a farmer's market, a village shop or a barbecue on the street/in the churchyard.

Desire   This is some form of arranged activity of relevance to the community. It might be childcare, healthcare outreach, debt counselling or a local history society. This is about **inclusion** in an event or a service that is hosted by the church. Or it might simply be making something of the heritage of the building; we often forget that the wider culture has a huge appetite for heritage (for more on this see Chapter C8). Clearly, managing a national collection of heritage attractions is not the primary purpose of the Church. But look at how the Apostle Paul used the altar dedicated 'to the unknown god' in Athens in Acts 17.23 to engage his hearers – he was using the cultural resources that lay at hand, and not just because they were there but because they were a place from which to build a conversation. Even the most humble church building provides us with similar resources for connecting with our communities – the only constraint is in our own imaginations.

Action   This is about drawing people into Christian community and commitment to God; it is about belonging and ultimately about **worship** of God.

Church anatomy

AIDA, or the church equivalent we have sketched out of Attention–Hospitality–Inclusion–Worship (which sadly lacks a snappy acronym), doesn't provide a blueprint for the physical layout of church buildings; however, we do believe it is a useful framework for analysing the missional character (or otherwise) of our buildings. Each of the four elements identified above can be described with a shape. Here are four examples of different ways these parts can be combined (and there are of course many others). Every situation is to some extent different but as a general principle, a building that works well missionally would display a balance between these four elements.

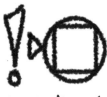

1. Medieval

This first is the medieval model. Generally the building is prominent in its location so does not struggle to attract attention. The **hospitality** element is small – generally the south or north porch, and a door – because in medieval times there was a general cultural understanding of the relevance of the Church. Most importantly there was no external division between the **inclusion** and **worship** elements; as discussed in Chapter C5, the rood screen functioned as a marker of this threshold within the building. In place of what we now think of as the split between these twin expressions of community, the medieval church represented a model of 'integrated community'.

2. Victorian

The second arrangement is more typically suburban or rural and implements the Victorian model with a separate hall alongside the church, or worse still on a separate site. This sort of arrangement expresses a dualistic theology of church separated from community – with a nod to both Augustine and Dickens, we could call this a 'tale of two cities' view. What is particularly toxic about this legacy arrangement is that with its lack of intermediate stages it attempts to hustle people from the initial **greeting** ('Church is for you – even if it appears dead and decaying') straight to **commitment** ('Give your life to God – and your money to the Church'). Whether or not this ever worked in 'the good old days' is irrelevant; our culture has changed hugely since the nineteenth century, and relying on such an approach now limits the Church's appeal to a rapidly shrinking subculture.

3. 'NM'-parallel

That said, if your church follows this pattern, there are always opportunities to improve matters; the third arrangement shows what could be called the 'new-medieval parallel' model. Where the 'two cities' are on the same site then it is often possible to use the space between to create a new gesture of welcome – that **hospitality** element. Whatever the physical expression, you need to implement an integrated theology of the two buildings working in partnership. In practical terms, success depends entirely on how the connections are made and particularly how much openness, flow and visibility there is between the major elements. Once again, this is a question of attention to thresholds – both the initial threshold into the building, which should be as 'porous' as possible, and the subsequent thresholds between the constituent parts.

The particular case where the 'two cities' are on separate sites of course offers no possibility of a physical connection. This detached arrangement demands that the church works really hard at making the connection between the two buildings in the community's minds; this will involve consideration of how each building is 'branded' within an overall identity for the church, and perhaps the deliberate moving of activities between the two buildings. The danger here is that all the energy migrates to what is often the better-placed, more attractive and more functional community building (**inclusion**), while the older church building (**worship**) is left to wither and die.

4. 'NM'-series

A final example shows a sequential arrangement – 'new-medieval series' – and is based on a recently completed project, St Philip's Church on Mill Road, in Cambridge (see also Chapter E2). This arrangement is more likely to apply where there is one principal public face (e.g. a deep plot with a narrow frontage in an urban setting, or perhaps a medieval church entered from the west end). In urban situations the **hospitality** element can often be provided by a café, as in the case of St Philip's. This is also the closest to the medieval model with the healthy blurring of boundaries between the two forms of community.

As we have said, each situation is different, and there cannot be a one-size-fits-all solution. However, we would argue that these principles can be adapted to apply to almost any parish church, and we hope you will enjoy thinking through how your church works at present and how the balance between the parts could perhaps be changed for the better.

The big picture

Our culture understands church attendance as a leisure choice – what one does on a Sunday morning instead of football, the car boot sale and so on. In the way we deal with our buildings we need to open up the idea that this building, the people associated with it, the strange activities going on inside it and possibly even the God we talk about might not be a leisure choice after all but instead might be *for everyone*. Inherent in this change of expectation is the upsetting of some deeply ingrained expectations of the building/people/God. We shouldn't be surprised, therefore, if people find changing our buildings surprising – unsettling even.

Notes

1 James F. Engel and Wilbert Norton, *What's Gone Wrong with the Harvest? A Communication Strategy for the Church and World Evangelization*, Grand Rapids, MI; Zondervan, 1975.

C8
Interpretation

As good children of modernity we struggle when it comes to understanding tradition. Enlightenment rationalism sought a new beginning; implicit in this was a faith in progress and a distrust of tradition. All over the Western world there is now much greater interest in heritage, very much including historic buildings; more than ever before it seems we are aware of the sense of rootlessness that comes with the Enlightenment project. Witness the National Trust, which is now the largest voluntary conservation organization in Europe and the only UK organization with a larger membership is the AA! Heritage is therefore increasingly big business.

The Church owns a great slice of Britain's heritage; of all the Grade 1 listed buildings in England, fully 45 per cent are churches that belong to the Church of England. Given the newfound interest in heritage, we have a huge opportunity to use our heritage to engage with the wider culture and explain something of the tradition we represent. Many people in the wider culture are interested and want to understand. So what stands in the way of this engagement?

Engagement

The first and most obvious issue is whether our buildings are open when visitors want to come into them. In principle the church building belongs to the *whole* community not just those who attend worship or serve on the PCC and so on. This calls for a fundamental realignment in our thinking.

Many churches of course worry about theft from or vandalism of the building, and in some situations this may well have followed bitter past experience. Yet if one asks those who insure our church buildings, such as the Ecclesiastical Insurance Group, they will tell you that the most secure building is one that is open every day, because as people begin to darken its doors once more the threat of vandalism *decreases*. A locked building is 'disowned', whereas an open building, if opened in the right way, will attract attention and care from the wider community. 'But what about the silver?' you may cry; to which the answering cry is 'But what about the community?' We know this is not easy, but the point is that there is potential loss on both sides of that equation. Essentially we have to ask whether our core business is curatorship or community engagement …

Once you have opened your church building, make sure you keep a visitor's book available for visitors to make their mark. This has been a long tradition, and also provides a useful record of public engagement when it comes to grant funding applications. It is also an important gesture of openness in a culture in which we increasingly expect to be able to 'have our say'.

Guide me …

Once visitors can get into your building there is then the need for some information to help them interpret the building. The traditional place to start is the church guide or handbook. Whether or not a church has one is a good indicator of whether or not the church community has engaged with its building. Preparing a guide requires some patient work but there is usually a good deal of information already available, for example in the Royal Commission on the Historical Monuments of England series (if your area is covered), the Victoria County Histories or the 'Pevsner' guides we have already noted in Chapter B1. It is always good practice to say where you have got your information, either in the text or by footnote, as these sources do not always turn out to be accurate.

The next level of research is into your parish records, which should have been archived somewhere, often in your County Archives. In any event, your County Archivist is a good person to talk to as they should be well placed to direct you to other sources of historic information and will be keen to encourage you. There is also the archive of the Incorporated Church Building Society, which was the chief grant-giving body for the building and restoration of Anglican churches throughout England and Wales, operating from 1818 to 1982. Most of the archive is kept at Lambeth Palace Library and includes architectural drawings and photographs where available, together with the attendant paperwork, which typically includes data on the population and character of the parish; some 700 plans are held by the Society of Antiquaries of London. The drawings are digitized (albeit at low resolution) and are viewable at www.churchplansonline.org (or at www.lambethpalacelibrary.org if www.churchplansonline.org is closed temporarily for development, often providing important clues as to changes carried out in the nineteenth century.

Price your guide sensibly to cover at least the costs of production plus a bit. Ideally produce them in small batches – they're unlikely to sell in great numbers and it is important that they don't look dog-eared; printing in smaller numbers also allows you to revise the text as other information comes to light. You may also want to distil some of the guide on to a single folded sheet of A4 paper, which is much more likely to be read and can signpost visitors to the main guide and other sources of information.

> Tradition is only democracy extended through time.
>
> *G. K. Chesterton*, Orthodoxy[1]

In terms of style it is important to understand your audience. Where a guide can perhaps assume some background knowledge, an introductory sheet should assume nothing. Many of the people who visit your church may well not know what baptism or communion are. For those not familiar with churches, things like altars and fonts may seem weird and will therefore need explanation. Writing for such an audience requires skill; but most of all, like all good writing it requires imagination. All the time we need to be looking for ways to make connections with what is known and familiar to our audience.

Beyond written material it is very helpful if you can have some visual material. If you have a framed photo of what the church was like 50 or 100 years ago, display it with a little commentary pointing out the changes. Get the material copied digitally (digital images of old photos can be greatly enhanced by someone with the necessary skills) and make sure the digital files are kept securely; you may also want to enlarge the image and use it as part of a display that traces the history of the building.

Narrative

At root, a church building is an expression of community narrative, the story of that community down the generations. Don't forget the people – it is the human stories that often provide visitors with the way of engaging with the story of your building. This should include the famous but if there are stories to be told of 'ordinary folk', that will be just as relevant.

Memorials can provide lots of food for thought. You may well have several gener-ations of the same family commemorated on gravestones, or indeed multiple names from the same family on a war memorial. Are there people with the same names still in the parish?

Digital media

While static information, in the form of printed material on display boards, may be entirely appropriate, current technology allows for a wider variety of interpretative material and for different means of engaging with your 'audience'. In terms of technology, for those comfortable with computers it is not difficult to create an animated slideshow with a commentary and music, and to have this playing on a TV screen.

Beyond that, it is possible to commission interpretative material, which is often best delivered to visitors in the form of a mobile device app – where this has been done, people often download the app before their visit and so come forearmed. The excellent organization Christianity and Culture at the University of York is one provider of this sort of material – they have created interpretation apps for a number of church buildings, including Coventry Cathedral and Holy Trinity Stratford (Shakespeare's church), which are free to download.

Further afield

When considering interpretative material, think about the wider area. If you are in an area that draws tourism it may be good to set up a walking trail between the various churches. This can be a good means of Christian witness in its own right. An A4 leaflet, if possible backed up by a website, briefly describing each of the buildings along the trail, is all that is needed. Talk to your local Tourist Information, who should be interested in helping you promote this.

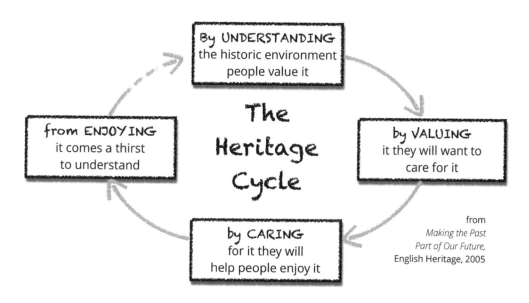

from
*Making the Past
Part of Our Future,*
English Heritage, 2005

Show us the money

The whole purpose of interpretative material is to engage with visitors and the wider community. This makes projects to create interpretative materials very attractive to grant funders, particularly the Heritage Lottery Fund, two of whose principal aims are to encourage people to engage with their heritage and to widen access and learning. You may very well find that you're able to access substantial funding to undertake the sort of work we describe.

Note

1 G. K. Chesterton, *Orthodoxy*, Mineola, NY: Dover, 2004, p. 39.

C9
God and Community

Struggling with the radical; anxious about change? If you are worried about introducing wider community activities into your church, here are a couple of things to put your mind at rest.

A biblical motif

> And again he said, 'To what shall I compare the kingdom of God? It is like leaven, which a woman took and hid in three measures of flour, till it was all leavened.
> *Luke 13.20–21 RSV; also Matthew 13.33*

Consider the parable. We happily interpret it as an example of God's transforming activity, with a straightforward moral that a little bit of God in something transforms it – makes it better, bigger, more effective and so on. However, there are other more significant messages in the parable that are not so obvious to us in the twenty-first century. We need to hear the parable with the ears and minds of those contemporary with Jesus.

Fundamental to the first hearers of the parable is an understanding of God and life that is defined by knowing what is holy and good. God is holy and good. The presence of God is not to be found in things considered unclean and corrupting, hence the emphasis in the Hebrew Bible on cleanliness and the need for ritual purity. The Kingdom of God was a common metaphor to the Jewish community at the time of Jesus, and would have been understood in this context of what was considered holy and good. The Kingdom of God is the fulfilment of the prophecies, the realization of God's righteousness and justice in human life, the way God works made manifest in the people of Israel.

The parable of the leaven directly challenges this understanding of the Kingdom of God. Jesus uses three key words that would have been considered unclean, taboo and suspect in the mind of the original hearer. *Leaven* was associated with death, rotting and corruption; *women* were unclean and of no account; and the act of *hiding* is subversive. All three symbols are negative and hardly, in the contemporary listeners' minds, to be associated with what is holy and good. The association with the Kingdom of God is underlined in the three meas-urers of flour which, while perhaps lost to us, would in the mind of the hearer be associated with a revelation of God: the three measurers of flour are used to make the bread when the angels visit Abraham to tell him he is to be the father of the nation.

Did you hear the one about the Yeast, the Woman and the Secret?

The challenge Jesus makes to the professional religious of his day is that the Kingdom of God is to be found in the mix of life, where (what we call) sacred and secular are jumbled up together, not in withdrawal from life. The parable is attacking the boundaries that separate holy from unholy and the conventional means of telling good from bad. The Kingdom of God it is not made visible in the human decisions of what is holy or unholy, clean or unclean, sacred or secular; nor is it limited to the morally righteous and the religiously faithful. The way God works is not by separation.

This is why the tax collectors, the publicans and all other sinners are invited to the party, and why our church buildings need to be open to all. Placing what is considered 'worldly' activity inside our churches challenges the distinctions we make between holy and unholy. It will not always be comfortable, or without its critics, but at least it looks like the Kingdom of God.

Consecration – adding to or setting apart?

Church buildings and some of the items within them are consecrated; that is, they are specifically dedicated, blessed and hallowed to the glory of God and for use for services of worship. Throughout the life of the Church and still today, solemn cere-monies of consecration involve anointing parts of the building and other items with holy water, oils and signs of the cross. It is a serious business and changes the status of the buildings and objects. Indeed in English law, consecrated church buildings have no 'book value' to be shown in the annual accounts of the PCC as a fixed asset, whereas the church hall or curate's house would be shown with a monetary value.

The concept and act of consecration – designating a physical object as sacred or holy – is found in virtually every human society of the world, whatever their faith or tradition. There is something in us as human beings that seeks to mark out those special places. In the pre-Christian society of the Greco-Roman world, consecration carried an additional understanding of being set apart so that the item consecrated could only be used for sacred activities.

Places of worship in the early Church, before the 'legalization' of Christianity in 325, were mostly private houses, barns, caves and catacombs where the persecuted disciples of Jesus could meet safely out of sight. In recognition of their sacred function these ordinary places were consecrated; but they did not cease to be used for their original function once consecrated. There were few if any specific churches acting as places of assembly for the Church. The few that were built were small shrines of witness on or near to the sites where Christians had been martyred.

So consecration for the early Church was an *adding to* rather than a *setting apart*. The consecration of a place in the early Church did not set that place apart as sacred to God and thus no longer to be used for everyday life. In the mix of sacred and secular the consecrated spaces used by the Church embodied the parable of the leaven. The early Christian understanding of consecration was that it is an action that acknowledges the dimension of the sacred that is extra and *in addition to* the ordinary purpose of the building or object. Places of worship for the early Christians did not have to be set apart from other uses.

The legalization of the Church by the emperor Constantine saw the building of new churches as Christians were no longer restricted to meeting in secret. These officially sanctioned and often state-funded church buildings were based on the design of the Roman basilica. However, the downside to the new government-sponsored Christianity was the imposition of the *set apart* interpretation of consecration. Very quickly following 325, the earlier understanding of consecration was lost to the life, practice and theology of the Church. By happy accident, the Norman Conquest enabled church buildings, in their function as instruments of state, to enjoy a few centuries of 'leavened' mixed use before an overbearing religiosity once again drove everyday life from the buildings.

With regard to church buildings, consecration should not prevent or stop the ordinary going on in the building. The correct Christian theology is one where sacred and secular are intermingled, not set apart from each other.

Section D   Process

D1
Making Changes

There is a growing consensus of opinion that recognizes that church buildings need to be allowed to change and adapt so as to meet the needs and expectations of contemporary culture and fulfil their missional role. In some cases there is also the (justifiable) recognition that if they do not change they will die. That does not mean, however, that you can change your church building as you wish – the change will need to be well thought through and, particularly in the case of historic buildings, you should expect to compromise.

Four drivers for change

If you are in the business of change it is important to be clear about the benefits you are hoping to achieve. When attempting to make church buildings that are fit for purpose for the twenty-first century it is helpful to think of the following four principal groups of benefits:

1   Comfort and facilities.
2   Flexibility and versatility.
3   Sustainability.
4   Openness and engagement.

The aim is to have buildings that are adapted to contemporary need without compromising their heritage value. Sometimes we will have to accept that what we want for the church building will be an unacceptable intervention into the historic fabric. However, this is not an excuse not to try. Experience demonstrates that for historic buildings, small is beautiful. Successful church projects do not have to be massive interventions and simple solutions can have significant benefits by providing the contemporary facilities without damaging the historic fabric.

A particular project will aim to achieve benefits within some or all of these groups. Examples of specific benefits might be:

Comfort and facilities

- To be welcoming, warm and comfortable, with some more intimate space for private prayer.
- To have legally compliant and decent WCs, appropriate kitchen/refreshment facilities and sufficient storage space.
- To have facilities for people of all ages, specifically babies, children and young people.

Flexibility and versatility

- To have sufficient space for people to meet throughout the week (not just before and after services), with the possibility of offering hospitality through the serving of refreshments.
- To have a worship space that is fit for purpose and meets the requirements of different worship styles and contemporary liturgies (e.g. allowing space for drama, choir, bands, worshipping in the round).
- To be adaptable for a wide range of uses and activities – not just worship.

Sustainability

- To benefit from modern technology.
- To be energy efficient and environmentally sensitive.
- To meet the statutory requirements of the Equality Act.
- To make the building straightforward to look after with minimum costs for maintenance and repairs.

Openness and engagement

- To be up to date, relevant and accessible to hearts and minds as well as bodies.
- To be understandable to people who do not know very much about Christianity or the Church.
- To be open seven days a week.
- To have a building that is connected to the wider community and does not appear to be just for the 'members'.
- To be welcoming from the outside through to the inside.
- To be less threatening, foreboding and hierarchical.
- To speak of today and tomorrow, not only of yesterday.

'Over my dead body ...'

Making changes to church buildings can at times be extremely hard
work. This is partly because we
often misunderstand our buildings
and partly because change of any
kind is always disruptive. But then
again change is an integral part of
being alive (both literally and fig-

uratively) and the Church is called to bring about societal change, so we shouldn't
be surprised by it. *Better Change in Church* by Rod Street and Nick Cuthbert is a really
helpful guide for dealing with change of all kinds in church situations; as the authors
say, 'Important changes are those that create discontinuity in peoples' lives. These stir
the emotions and generate anxiety.'[1]

Any proposals to change a church building can therefore evoke strong reactions
from people you might not have thought were interested or concerned. It is all too
easy for a church community, so convinced they are right and that they are doing
God's work, to be completely taken aback by objectors from outside the congregation
but for whom the building is nevertheless their parish church. It can be even more
frustrating if the heritage stakeholders object as well! Emotions may run high, and
positions become polarized.

In these circumstances, finding common ground and the willingness to compromise
can then become extremely difficult. It is wise, therefore, to do your best to avoid
these sorts of difficulty by preparing well and taking the time to build consensus. As
discussed in Chapter C3, before you do anything, get to know what you have; this
gives you credibility by demonstrating you understand what you are dealing with.
Just as important as knowing what you have is knowing what you need and why you
need it. These two aspects of making changes are embodied in the requirement for
the Statement of Significance and the Statement of Needs – for more on these, see
Chapters D2 and D6 respectively.

It also helps a great deal if you are supported by a professional advisor who properly
understands conservation as the management of change and whom you can trust to
argue your case well. They should also be able to help you in scheduling a time frame
for the process from start to finish (concept ideas to competed works), and which
includes sufficient time for consultation and the permissions process. This is important
to enable the PCC and congregation to appreciate the benefits of careful preparation.

Of course, not all changes to church buildings are contentious and nor do they
always elicit opposition. However, the PCC should endeavour to adopt good practice

and treat all proposals with the same degree of care. Identifying all the necessary steps is essential, along with knowing the implications if they are missed or something goes wrong.

Manage the process

If at all possible the church community needs to be in the driving seat of any proposed changes to the church building. There are other parties whose consent is required and at times their time frame and requirements for information or professional input may affect the process – but these should not rule it.

For the church to manage the process it is necessary for the congregation and those entrusted with the job to understand it and be fully acquainted with how it works

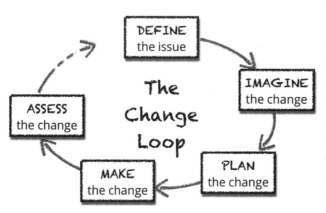

and its requirements. All too often the vicar, PCC or church community can find themselves feeling like the victims of a bureaucratic process that seems designed to frustrate their interests. Usually it is the case that the church in question was unaware of how the process works and are frustrated because they are not immediately getting the result they want! Part of the purpose of this book is to equip you with the knowledge you need to navigate the process intelligently. So do your homework and keep ahead of the process rather than react to it.

Change is a challenge in many situations, not just when it comes to church buildings, and there is much to be learnt from what has been written about change management in organizations. As a general rule, successful change is achieved in human organizations where everyone is kept informed and feels included.

Think about this in terms of the following essential items that will need to be dealt with at an early stage in order to ensure long-term sustainable success:

Capacity building of the congregation

The objective of capacity building is to provide the church community with the theological basis and historical information about the development and purposes of the church building(s), to agree the priorities for mission and to reach a common mind at the outset of the project.

Many congregations would value opportunities for learning and would appreciate the chance for some training, consultation and education to enable them to engage in the process of change. It is essential for the whole church to be invited and encouraged to participate at the beginning, even if at a later stage the PCC delegates some of the subsequent work to a subcommittee.

If these capacity-building events are run as workshops for as many church members as possible, this allows for issues and concerns to be voiced in a large forum and provides a common starting point so that no one can later claim ignorance of what is being proposed.

Essential to any church project is an agreed Mission Action Plan for the church community. So clarify what the church is doing and wants to do and agree the specific and contextually appropriate priorities for mission. You can use Robert Warren's *The Healthy Churches Handbook*[2] as a tool for this. Encourage as many of the congregation as possible to engage in the process. Be prepared to allow enough time to get through the process and to reflect on the outcomes.

If your church is considering re-ordering the interior arrangement then as many members as possible should become familiar with *Re-Pitching the Tent* by Richard Giles.[3] This book is justified in describing itself as 'the definitive guide to re-ordering church buildings for worship and mission'. It is just that, and while some of our church buildings might never be suitable to achieve all of the ideal objectives, at least you will know why and what is important. It is an essential book.

Looking outwards

It is absolutely essential to base any proposals for wider community use of the building on identified and agreed community needs. Funding bodies will all want to see the evidence of need derived from a thorough community consultation – more about this in Chapter D3.

Getting the process right and dealing with all the various issues in the best order can be quite daunting, especially if this is the first time your church has done something like this. Seek help within the wider Church at an early stage, but as a general rule be prepared to do the legwork yourselves rather than call in external consultants. Even if money were no object, the danger of using external consultants to do the research work and number crunching is that their findings are not 'owned' and valued by the whole church community because they have not had any involvement in the process.

The experience of others is very useful and among the range of advice available we would recommend *Crossing the Threshold*. Produced by Hereford Diocese and launched in 2009, this is a very useful toolkit with accompanying DVD.[4]

The Lottery Fund has good material on the processes of gathering the information and undertaking community consultations. So too will local community support organizations like Community First and local authority Community Development Officers.

All the organizations responsible for 'public' money will want evidence of the wider community's involvement in the project. The PCC will need to consider how non-church members are to be included in the process of taking the project forward.

Notes

1 Rod Street and Nick Cuthbert, *Better Change in Church: When Wholehearted Commitment Counts*, North Charleston, SC: CreateSpace, 2015, p. 10.

2 Robert Warren, *The Healthy Churches Handbook: A Process for Revitalizing Your Church*, London: Church House Publishing, 2004.

3 Richard Giles, *Re-Pitching the Tent: The Definitive Guide to Re-Ordering Church Buildings for Worship and Mission*, 3rd edn, London: Canterbury Press, 2004.

4 The *Crossing the Threshold* toolkit is available via the Diocese of Hereford website – see www.hereford.anglican.org/churchgoers/community_partnership_and_funding/about_us_and_latest_news/toolkit.aspx.

D2

How to Write a Statement of Significance

What is a Statement of Significance – and why is it, well, significant?

A Statement of Significance[1] is needed when making changes to a listed church (or an unlisted church in a Conservation Area); it provides a summary of the historic development and main features of the building and is read alongside the Statement of Needs (see Chapter D6). Typically, churches first hear of the requirement for a Statement of Significance when they are already considering changes to their building. Introduced at that stage it can often seem to be an imposed bureaucratic chore but it shouldn't be seen in this way because this document will help decide how the building can be changed without destroying its character. If approached in the right way, writing a Statement of Significance can in its own right be missional, connecting people both within and outside the church with the bigger story of Christian worship and service in that place. The Statement of Significance is certainly a serious document, but we firmly believe that producing it can also be fun!

The requirement for a Statement of Significance comes from the Faculty Jurisdiction process (see Chapter D8). The Chancellor of your diocese, acting on the advice of the Diocesan Advisory Committee (DAC), will need to be satisfied that any harm to the historic fabric of the building is both minimized and is outweighed by the benefits to the life of the church community. The aim is not to prevent change to historic buildings but to ensure that any change is well considered and properly thought through. There is an important premise here: **unless one understands the cultural worth of an object one should not carry out alterations that may adversely affect its significance.**

This is a very sensible starting point when contemplating responsible change to a historic building, but in practice churches often start from a (usually) legitimately felt need. In some cases a church may get a long way down the line with a design before considering the likely impact of the change on the special character of the building. It is much better to engage with this process *before* you have decided how you want to alter the building, and you should certainly avoid the temptation to 'reverse engineer' the Statement of Significance to suit the proposed changes you have in mind.

Our churches are 'multi-storied places', a weaving together of the lives of previous generations of our community of faith. A good Statement of Significance therefore begins with historical research, understanding how a building has changed and hopefully grasping the meaning of the different parts of the building. Above all we need to listen and learn from the preceding story – it may well help us define better questions for our current generation, which we then set about addressing. The point of the Statement is to uncover the 'grain' of the building so that, whether our interventions are bold or timid, we will be better able to work with it rather than against it.

What should go in?

Remember that the Statement of Significance is a summary, not necessarily the authoritative final word on the subject! A good Statement of Significance should be long enough to show you understand the important aspects of the building but short enough that people will want to read it – a document that is produced and then forgotten is next to useless. How long your Statement is will depend on the building – for a simple building it may just be a very few pages. The point is to identify the key elements and demonstrate that you have a grasp of their importance.

If you can't explain it simply, you don't understand it well enough.

Albert Einstein

ingredients

It is fine if your Statement of Significance is a work in progress. Think of it as a working document that is kept under review, to be revisited at regular intervals. It needs to be accessible to whoever wants to see it; in this way it can become an excellent source of information for anyone interested in the building and in turn can encourage good stewardship of the building. It could also form the starting point for a short guidebook – or an existing guidebook might form the basis of your Statement.

An outline of what the Statement should include

Grade of listing   (i.e. Grade 1, Grade 2*, Grade 2 or unlisted but in a Conservation Area – see Chapter A8) and the date of the listing. Include the List Description of the church.[2]

A plan of the church   Your church architect may be able to provide you with this, and/or there may be historic plans available online. If the church has grown by stages, the plan should if possible be shaded by date to show the ages of the various parts of the building.[3]

Historical   A section to explain the present built form of the church, starting from its earliest recorded origins. Include names of any significant benefactors, architects and craftsmen if known, and relevant dates.

Geographical   The significance of the building within the landscape of the area and parish, whether urban or rural. What contribution does the church make to the physical character and quality of its surroundings? Does it have landmark value on an eye-catching site? How does the church relate to its surroundings in terms of scale and architectural language?

Architectural   Set down what you know about when the various parts of the building were constructed and when notable additions were made to the interior, for instance the pews, the pulpit, organ or stained glass (if important). Some churches hold an important place in the development of ecclesiastical architecture – if you don't know, your DAC Secretary should know who to ask – and if so this should be stated. Look at the parts, but also think about the character of the whole, including the feel of the space. There's no need to go into details of furnishings and so on (i.e. movable items), unless they are of considerable significance. Comment briefly on the materials from which the church is made, and the current state of repair.

Environmental   Include details of your churchyard or whatever landscape setting there may be; is this significant in its own right? In a churchyard, identify your oldest graves, particularly if separately listed. Consider the age of any trees and whether any has a Tree Preservation Order (TPO) – your local authority Trees Officer will advise.

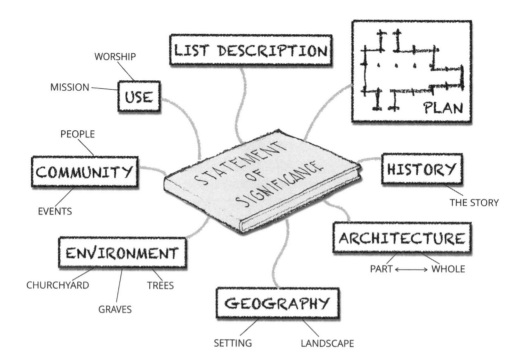

Community Who else sees the church as significant? How is this demonstrated? Understanding the significance of the church building in the wider community can be a useful ingredient of the parish consultation process – see Chapter D3.

Use A brief comment on how the heritage aspects above are used within the mission of the church.

Four ways not to do it, and one lifesaver

One difficulty for churches writing a Statement for the first time is never having seen one before. Here are four ways we have seen it done badly:

- **The back of a fag packet** Jot a few notes down on half a page and conclude that there is nothing of any significance – but only because no one could be bothered to look.
- **The Blue Peter** Here's one I prepared earlier! Simply copy out the relevant page from the 'Pevsner' guide or similar book – or worse, cut and paste from Wikipedia and season with one or two folk tales from a 1920s guidebook.
- **The Heath Robinson** Fill in a standard form with a few details; cut and paste from other documents.

- **The Rolls Royce**   Pay an external consultant a good deal of money to go away and produce this document for you.

While some of the above have advantages, none of them, including the last, makes for a good Statement. Why? Because fundamentally your Statement of Significance is a means for you as a church community to demonstrate that you understand your building. No one expects your understanding to be perfect but it is important to demonstrate that you have engaged with the relevant issues.

Thankfully there is a fifth possibility that has recently been developed – with the backing of Historic England – by the wonderful Christianity and Culture, which is based in York. This is a web-based tool that we call **The Business**. The tool has a number of advantages, providing a clear structure and lots of guidance. It also enables you to break the overall task down into manageable chunks, allowing different sections to be delegated to different people. It is highly recommended.[4]

Why should we care?

The Statement of Significance explains what matters about a building, why and to whom; it includes a description of the main features of the building and an explanation of their significance. If you come to consider alterations to your church, the Statement of Significance will be an invaluable base from which to start and will help provide a framework and reference for your Statement of Needs (see Chapter D6). Depending on the nature of any proposed alterations, you may need to expand your Statement of Significance on those aspects of the building that may be impacted by any proposed changes.

There are a number of benefits to engaging positively in this process:

- Better understanding of the way the church building is constructed, which means that the PCC is less likely to waste time and money doing unsuitable maintenance/repairs that are not cost-effective in the long term.
- Better understanding of the significance of the building, both as a whole and in its parts, which means that the PCC is less likely to waste time and money developing schemes likely to be rejected on historic conservation grounds.
- If responsibility for producing the Statement of Significance is shared, the process can be used to build relationships within the church and with outside groups, and thus encourage individuals to participate further in the life of the church.

- Increased awareness of the building's importance can result in the congregation and the community as a whole becoming more interested in and proud of its church building; this in turn can generate enthusiasm for maintaining the building …
- The Statement of Significance may reveal 'stories' that make the building more interesting to visitors and may potentially attract grant funding for conservation/ interpretation works. This is particularly relevant now that the Heritage Lottery Fund has become a major funder of church projects.
- The more a PCC knows about its church building and presents this information in lively and interesting ways to non-church people, the more you can make of it as a mission asset.

Conservation as the management of change

One considerable benefit of the Statement of Significance is that it can be used to guide and support change and development. A good Statement will give the PCC the facts needed to demonstrate that it, the PCC, is able to conserve the building (i.e. manage change and comply with the faculty process). Both the DAC and the amenity societies are much more likely to be persuaded of the case for change if they are confident the PCC members understand the cultural worth of what they have.

Any proposals to make changes to a church building can precipitate strong opposition from the most unexpected of people and places. Many objectors and detractors, determined to prevent change, will use all manner of emotive and specious arguments. Objectors often claim that the PCC does not understand the heritage significance of the building for which they are responsible or that the building has always been the way it is and therefore must not be altered. The Statement of Significance can help demonstrate that such claims and opposition are without substance.

A good Statement of Significance will also give the PCC the confidence to propose changes that are not detrimental to the heritage asset, will demonstrate to the interested bodies that they are properly informed and will collate the evidence that the church has previously been subject to any number of changes and alterations.

A team effort

Given the variety of skills needed to produce a Statement of Significance it is unlikely to be the work of one individual – the more contributors the merrier, provided you have someone with overall editorial control. One type of person you will need on your team is the 'ferret', who loves digging in the archives for the raw information; another is the 'interpreter', who can pull out the stories from the facts; a third is the 'compiler', who can stand back sufficiently to put the information together with an objective view.

In summary

- Keep it brief while being thorough.
- Share the authorship.
- Keep it available and 'live'.
- Enjoy the process!

Notes

1 Terminology: outside the Church, reference is often made to Conservation Statements, Conservation Reports or Conservation Assessments. These, along with Statements of Significance, now mean more or less the same thing. For Church Buildings Council (CBC) guidance, see www.churchcare.co.uk/churches/guidance-advice/statements-of-significance-need. The Prince's Regeneration Trust has produced a really useful 'How To' guide on writing Conservation Reports; this comes from a more general conservation position and is a great help in understanding the purpose and usefulness of the Statement of Significance – see www.princes-regeneration.org/publications/how-write-conservation-reports.

2 List Descriptions can be found at British Listed Buildings Online or from Historic England.

3 For historic plans, see Lambeth Palace Library, www.lambethpalacelibrary.org/content/about and their page about ICBS, which links to the ICBS archive, www.lambethpalacelibrary.org/search/node/ICBS.

4 Start your Statement of Significance here: www.statementsofsignificance.org.uk. For more comment on why this is so helpful, see www.churchbuildingprojects.co.uk/statements-of-significance-transformed.

D3
Public Engagement

Churches and the community

Whether William Temple actually said that 'The Church is the only society on earth that exists for the benefit of non-members' (there is apparently much debate), it encapsulates an important insight. Even where the local church has forgotten this calling there is a fundamental sense in which our church buildings remind us of it; for they belong to the communities in which they stand, and their very presence in the neighbourhoods where people live and work means they have an impact on people far beyond the worshipping congregation. The physical reality of the building therefore acts as a permanent statement of public engagement.

Jesus was able to relate to all parts of his community, from the despised to the exalted. In Jesus, God demonstrated his acceptance of people where they are; he doesn't demand they engage on his terms or jump through a series of hoops before they are worthy of his attention. Rather, he would be prepared to journey with them for miles in, supposedly, the wrong direction. How can we not take seriously both the context in which we find ourselves and the people among whom we live?

One of the huge strengths of the Anglican Church in particular is that its organization embodies this commitment to the local community. The parish system is geographical, each separate parish being supplied with a ministry interested in the people who live and work within it, their hopes and fears, needs and aspirations, joys and sorrows, whoever they are and whether or not they are members of the local church.

'Knowing our place'

The question, then, is at what points in the life of the church should you focus your attention outwards and listen to the views of your community. What about when you are re-evaluating your Mission Action Plan?[1]

What about when you want to bring new activities into your building? When it comes to seeking grants and funds from outside organizations it is particularly important to demonstrate you understand the context in which you are working and that there is wider community support for what you are proposing to do.

Our concern in this book is with buildings, and if you are proposing to do something with or to your church building it is essential to consult your community. This is a whole lot easier if you have done it before, so it is good to start small and make it a regular expression of your determination to face outwards, not just inwards. You might be tempted to delegate this to some external agency, but to do so would be to miss out on all those conversations and the positive benefits of taking an interest in other people – you need to own this process.

Whatever change you have in mind, it is essential that you 'know your place'. It will enable you to understand both the local context and the community's needs. This ensures that your project is a response to the needs and not a white elephant of pious aspiration!

The information is out there – find it and share it

A lot of basic information about your community is already available. Census data is collated by a range of organizations; your local authority and, if there is one, your local Council of Voluntary Services should have this information to hand. The government provides census, population, deprivation and all sorts of other statistical goodies at www.neighbourhood.statistics.gov.uk, and it's possible to create you own parish map and collate the statistics. Another good source of data is www.police.uk, which maps the crime in your local area – especially useful if you want a project to target youth disaffection, domestic violence or drug addiction. In the Church of England the key census information has been summarized into factsheets for every parish called the 'Parish Spotlight'. This will tell you some key figures for housing, income, ethnicity, age groups and poverty indicators. If you don't already have it, the Diocesan Office will be able to tell you how to get hold of this data.

Starting with the 2011 Localism Act the government is encouraging neighbourhood plans at parish or town level. Not all places have engaged with this process but it does enable communities to articulate their priorities for development, and where such 'local plans' do exist they have very relevant information.[2] Ideally you will have been involved in producing the plan; if there isn't one yet for your place, how about the church instigating it?

In every community there are people who see it from particular and very valuable angles because they are responsible for delivering services in the locality. These 'professionals' include the shopkeepers, postal-delivery personnel, rubbish collectors, head teachers, doctors, health visitors and local policing officers. Understanding their perceptions of the main issues facing the community can be really useful, particularly if you can then find ways that the church might help address those issues.

Whatever information you glean from these sources, you will need to supplement it with what you discover for yourselves as a church. This information and a growing understanding of 'knowing our place' can help you decide what are the key questions to ask the community or which aspects of the local context require further investigation. Don't forget to share what you find within the church, but make sure you present it in a lively way – perhaps by means of a quiz. In this way you can help to dispel misconceptions and enable the church community to find out things about their own parish that may surprise them.

'People mapping' your parish

This is an activity for the whole church, not just its leadership. Start by taking a large street-map of your parish, marking out the parish boundaries; if possible fade out the rest of the map.

This is the basic map from which you will need to develop the 'people mapping' further:

- Place coloured dots on the locations where church members live; if they live outside the parish, place their dot around the edge in the approximate direction they live.
- Mark the other places of worship and identify which denomination or faith.
- Mark the large institutions (big employers, shopping centres, schools, medical practices etc.) using larger coloured squares on the map.
- Are there locations of community interest or tension? Where do the community leaders operate from? What are the key places that give identity to the parish?

If you do this electronically, try to keep different classes of information on separate layers that you can turn on and off.

Then look at the information together and use it as a focus for prayer. Where does your church stand within its parish – centrally and in a prominent location or peripherally? Does the map show a particular concentration of churchgoers or an area where the church has no real contact? Where does the census data locate the areas of social or economic deprivation? Where are the shopping and services located that the parishioners use? How do adjacent areas affect the parish?

Walk the walk – don't just talk the talk

The mapping exercise may suggest possibilities for community engagement or perhaps ways the church could make a difference. But the information gathered by the map can only become missionally alive when experienced for real.

In the Anglican Church there has been a long tradition of 'beating the bounds' of the parish at Rogationtide, which involved walking around the parish boundaries in early May to pray for a good harvest. Beating the bounds can be adapted for today's Church as an exercise we have called the 'parish walk'. While the focus is no longer on food production, beating the bounds reminds us of the extent of 'our patch' and provides an opportunity to pray for the community. It is also an opportunity, in pairs or groups, to take a look at, for example, what sort of state the housing or the streets are in, whether it is easy to navigate the pavements with a wheelchair or where the young people gather in groups. Some of the information you discover may be entered on the map.

The parish walk can be both part of a practical survey, as you will see things you hadn't registered before, and the development of your church's worship and spirituality as it feeds your prayer. Like the desk-based survey and the parish-mapping exercise, the parish walk can help you clarify some of the questions you might ask when you move outside the church's membership and begin to consult the community.

What do you need to know?

The key to good consultation is to ask good questions – those that provide answers you need to inform your project. It may be sensible not to ask too many, nor to make them too specific too soon. Be prepared to conduct another more specific consultation at a later date if necessary.

If this is the first consultation your church has undertaken for ten or more years, you will need to be more general. You know what you need to know but you could consider using some of the following questions:

- What age group are you in?
- How long have you lived locally?
- What is the most significant change you have seen in the locality in that time?

- What is the best thing about living here?
- What is the most difficult aspect?
- What change would you most like to see in the next five to ten years?
- Have you ever been inside your particular church building and for what reason?
- What do you think your church community could do for you? For the wider area?
- What impression do you have of this particular church community?
- What (if anything) does this particular church community mean to you?
- What do you think of your church building or of other church buildings in the area?

Time to engage

If you are serious in what you are hoping to achieve, there is no escape from the need for the church (i.e. the people, not just the vicar or the PCC) to do the work of engaging with the community.

Believe it or not, it is at this point that many congregations seem to get scared. Some will try to find ways to get someone else to do the survey work while others will find excuses for not being involved. And the problem is the same, in that you both miss the party and miss out on being part of what God is doing. Recognizing how difficult it is emotionally for some congregations to engage with their community, here are some easier ways to do this.

Everyone knows someone

- Prepare the questions along with a brief explanation script of why the church is seeking this information.
- Distribute the questions and explanation to the congregation.
- Give the congregation members an achievable target to engage with people they know, but who are *not* members of their family. For example, they have three months to talk to five people. These could be their neighbours, friends at a social club and so on. It doesn't matter who they are just as long as they either live or work in the parish.

Community consultation drop-in

Running a consultation drop-in can be random but can offer those who live or work in the community a real chance to have a say in a way that is convenient. Choose a good community space, ideally a venue that a large number of people use or walk by regularly. Use local media to publicize the event and perhaps think of ways to make the entrance look particularly inviting to shoppers or passers-by. If possible, offer refreshments or some other incentive for taking part.

You then provide a range of display boards, for various topics, and a large stack of pencils and sticky notes. You will find it useful to have some simple instructions by each board to explain what that board is for. People then put their own ideas up on the board – make sure you allow the space and time for this to be anonymous – and at the end of the event you gather them in.

A street survey

Doing a simple questionnaire on the streets can be the hardest thing to find volunteers for, but can be a very valuable way of advertising your presence and getting a range of responses. Again it helps to use local media beforehand to advertise that your church will be carrying out this survey, and why. If the consultation relates to a specific project it can be a good way to draw attention to it. Surveys need manpower, and it is fine to supplement (but not replace) church members with volunteers from local schools (it might make a good school project) or from voluntary groups.

The survey team needs to approach people of all ages who live locally to find out their feelings and perceptions about the community. This can be done informally and without too much pressure, in pubs and shops, by consulting users of existing church facilities or even talking to the people who walk by the church building. The purpose of the survey is to build a story of the local experience and expectations. And make sure you engage with other denominations and faith groups; don't be afraid to consult with them, especially the laity.

Fitting it together – the church in the community

Having assembled the data, fitting it together is best done by a small project team of perhaps six people who, no doubt, will also engage in discussion and analysis and come to some preliminary conclusions as to the community needs, resources available to the church and the priorities for action. However, it is important to enable the whole church community to have an opportunity to discuss and respond to the results, and then to participate in the processes of setting the priorities, even if the PCC and/or the small project team provide much of the energy and drive for this process. This is best done through a workshop, facilitated by the project team, and with as many of the church community present as possible. By placing the information gathered from the community alongside the story of the church, another dimension is developed.

This 'community review' workshop should compare feelings and expectations with the picture painted by the hard data. Do not be afraid of negative comments – these can be the most insightful and valuable because of their honesty rather than their negativity. Then consider the following:

- Areas where there is a good match of expectations and reality.
- Areas with a clear mismatch of expectations and reality.
- Other areas between the first two.
- How far do the gathered facts fit in with the feelings and reactions of church members?
- What are the chief strengths and weaknesses of the present provision of ministers and buildings for the mission and ministry of the local church?
- What are the priorities for attention and possible development?

The workshop needs competent facilitation but should enable the church community to identify the priorities specific for your particular context. And don't forget to tell people how you are going to report the results of this community review, and then deliver on that promise while the process still has momentum.

Share the knowledge

The final step is to make the results of the process available to the wider community. This could be done with a one-off event such as an open day, when other items or activities of interest are also available, such as historic parish registers and artefacts, trips up the tower, a chance to ring the bells or play the organ, refreshments. Put the report on your website if you have one, with a prominent link from the home page, and in your parish magazine. And once again, try to get coverage in the local newspaper.

Notes

1 For more about Mission Action Planning, see Mike Chew and Mark Ireland, *How to Do Mission Action Planning: A Vision-Centred Approach*, London: SPCK, 2009.

2 For more on local plans see: www.gov.uk/government/publications/2010-to-2015-government-policy-planning-reform/2010-to-2015-government-policy-planning-reform.

D4

Consensus Building – Some Resources

This chapter looks at four examples of the sort of resources that can be of help to churches trying to build consensus when considering change to their buildings. These resources are designed to draw out some of the important issues that need to be discussed, and hopefully to identify a direction in which the community can move forward together. We're not saying these are perfect; they are intended simply to spark the imagination and provide different ways for people to engage better with their church buildings. The point of discussing them here is to illustrate the sort of materials other churches have found useful, to explain a little of the thinking behind them and to encourage you to think how you might develop resources of your own in response to the specific questions you face.

The first three of these resources were created by Archangel Architects, Nigel Walter's architectural practice, in response to a specific query or situation.[1] While initially intended for the use of their church clients, if you think they are relevant to your situation then you are very welcome to make use of them. This chapter describes the point of each resource and how they might be used; the resources themselves, each in pdf form, are available for download from the ChurchBuild website. (You may print them or circulate them electronically as you choose, but please do not use them without acknowledgement.) Any feedback you may have, or indeed ideas for new resources that could be developed, would be gratefully received.

Healthcheck

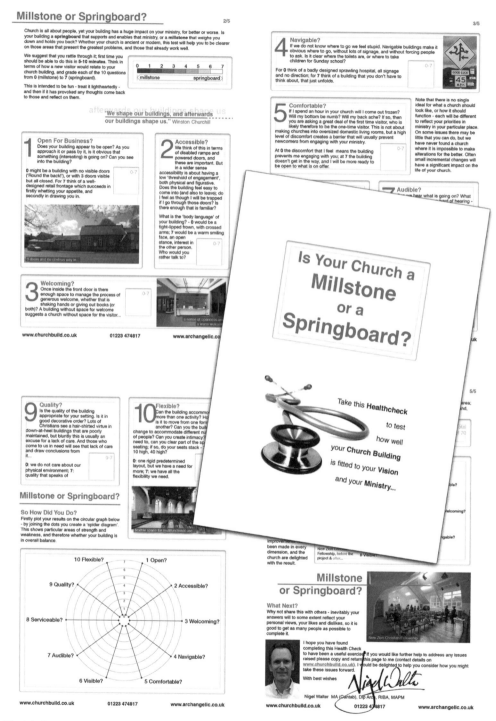

Healthcheck: See Appendix G1 for larger versions of each page.

Healthcheck

Is your church building a millstone around your neck or a springboard to ministry? This resource asks you to rate your existing building against ten criteria, modelled on the genre of the 'rate your boyfriend' magazine quiz. It is very simple, can be done in five minutes and is intended as a bit of fun to get people talking. Sadly familiarity breeds contempt; the aim of the Healthcheck is to encourage people to look afresh at a building they may have stopped seeing because it has become so familiar, and instead to see it as though encountering it for the first time. Doing the quiz gets you to evaluate the current state of the building, and by implication to consider how it might be changed for the better.

The Healthcheck comprises a cover plus four further sheets and can either be given to people to fill in on their own or completed as part of a group discussion. Each aspect is marked from 0 (bad) to 7 (good), which appeals to those of us who like numbers; those ratings can then be plotted on a spider diagram, which helps to identify areas of greater priority and also appeals to those who prefer to work with visual material. If you return to the exercise after your project is completed and compare the two sets of results, then the space between the two lines would indicate the benefit achieved.

Pizzamat

The Pizzamat is a collaborative doodling tool to facilitate a church's early-stage conversations. The metaphor here is the placemat that family-orientated restaurants provide to occupy children before the food arrives (and which can also be used collaboratively). This resource was developed in response to a church community who knew they needed to do something but didn't know where to begin. Its aim, therefore, is to help you get started with some strategic thinking before you embark on a building project.

You can think of the pizzamat as a 'play space', and the blank middle can be used for whatever you want: a list of problems to address or aims to achieve, a word cloud, a mind map – even a drawing! Essentially this resource is a blank piece of paper, because that is where any good idea begins its journey from idea to reality. However, many people are very afraid of 'making their mark' (on a blank piece of paper, on an old building, in life more generally …). This blank piece of paper is therefore bounded and defined; around the edge are a number of gently provocative questions that help to focus the sheet and the conversation, to give you something to respond to and therefore a way into the creative space in the middle.

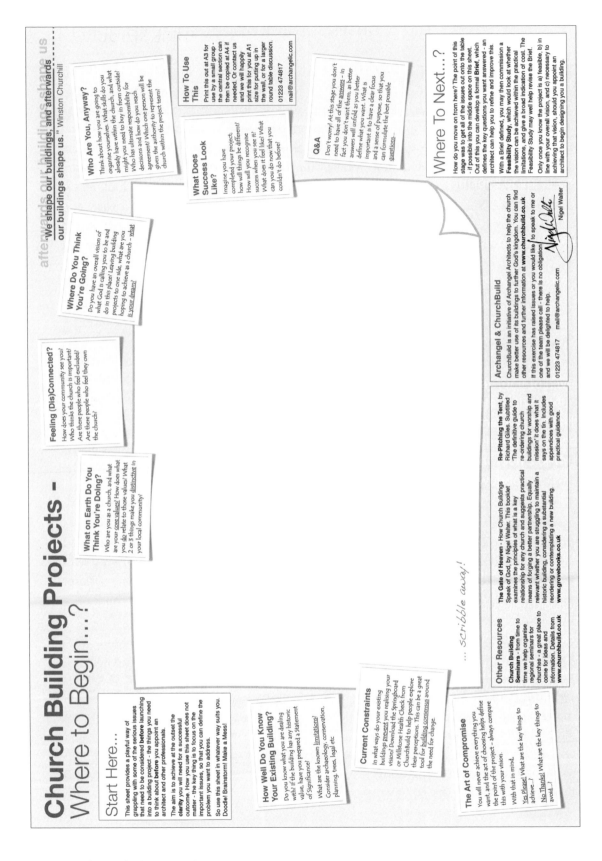

See Appendix G2 for larger version.

The pizzamat should be used in a group. If that group is small, say three to six people, you could print it out at size A3 and sit around it at a table and discuss as you doodle. If you are in groups of more than about six, you could print it out at A1 (send the file to a local copy shop) and put it up on the wall. You can then either have a facilitated discussion with someone acting as scribe or give people sticky notes to write on and then stick to the sheet. As with any such group activity, you will need someone to facilitate the discussion, framing it and drawing out its conclusions.

Church Buildings Audit

This is a set of three studies jointly developed with David Stancliffe, the former Bishop of Salisbury. Recognizable as more conventional study material, this is intended either for personal or group use. The studies could be used in a home group situation on three consecutive occasions, as the focus of a PCC away day or perhaps as the structure for a series of facilitated workshops.

The studies have a narrative structure, dealing respectively with past, present and future. The point of this format is that we need to think narratively; for the changes we make to our buildings in this generation to work well we need to understand the plot to date, how the story is developing in the current 'chapter' and to leave plot lines open for subsequent generations. So the studies encourage you to look in turn at the different phases of your church's narrative: its past history in that place, where it stands at present and its possible future.

The Church Building Audit is shown in full in Appendix G3; like the other resources discussed so far it is downloadable from www. churchbuildingprojects.co.uk/ downloads. It comprises eight

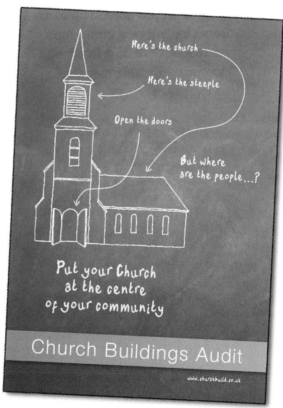

sides of A4 and it can therefore be printed double-sided on four A4 sheets (a cover with introduction plus the three studies) or in reduced form as an A5 booklet.

The crash course

In Appendix J of the indispensable *Re-pitching the Tent*, Richard Giles provides a six-week crash course on the design of liturgical space. Each of the six sessions is structured in three parts:

1   A preparation section with some passages of Scripture to read, around which the study is based.
2   The group session, with a series of questions to focus a discussion.
3   A practical task (e.g. visiting another church community).[2]

Notes

   1 The first three of these resources can be accessed from the ChurchBuild downloads page – www.churchbuildingprojects.co.uk/downloads.
   2 Richard Giles, *Re-Pitching the Tent: The Definitive Guide to Re-Ordering Your Church*, 3rd edn, Norwich: Canterbury Press, 2004, Appendix J.

D5
Needs Analysis

Developing your vision

Successful church building projects are a physical expression of a church's well-articulated vision and have a clear place within a broader missional strategy. In *Better Change in Church*, Rod Street and Nick Cuthbert encourage churches to distinguish their vision (their 'where') from their underlying purpose (their 'why'): 'if our "why" is clear it will drive everything we do.'[1] The starting point for any such project should therefore be a deep sense of what the church is for, of what 'business' you are in, which will hopefully be set out in the aims and objectives of your church's Mission Action Plan and perhaps mirrored in the community consultation discussed in Chapter D3. With these in place a review of your building should be able to identify a number of possible courses for action by the church.

The initial list may be wide-ranging and a bit of a muddle; the key thing is to identify what your church can do and then make every effort to do it well. You can use an Urgency/Importance matrix to determine which are the priorities for action.[2] Invariably this exercise will result in a number of projects with which the church will wish to engage, which will then raise issues about how suitable the building is for your needs.

The 'W' questions

Before embarking on a redesign of your buildings you need to be clear about what you want to achieve and why. Answering the 'W' questions will help you achieve this clarity. You may be considering a short-term one-off project with easily achieved outcomes, or it could be a much larger or much longer-term project. If your project is likely to involve re-ordering or a new building, the answers will yield some important information for the architect's brief.

Whatever the size of the project, it is worth asking and answering the W questions. It can be helpful to pull them together into a single loaded sentence – for example:

- Who will do what with whom; where, why, when and with what resources?
- Who does what with whom, where, why and when?
- How will it work; with whom will you do it; and what will be achieved and sustained in the long term?

Used by a group, these questions can provide a focus for arguing out what a particular project is about, what the benefits are and why you should bother. The result should therefore be a wider understanding and ownership of your plans, which is essential to the eventual success of your project.

Answering the W questions also provides you with the core information you need for most funding applications and gives you the basis of a written plan to support your activity. You may find that you cannot answer one of the questions. If that is the case, don't worry – you've simply identified part of the process that you need to explore further, and it's much better that this comes to light now than later in the process.

As individual words, here are the things to think about:

- **Who** are you and the people working with you? Who will benefit from your project?
- **What** are your aims? Provide a brief description of what you want to do.
- **Why** do you want to do your activity? What would the benefits be? Have you done any research or identified a specific need? Include professional reports and local community views.
- **Where** is your project to take place (e.g. in peoples' homes, in a community building)? State a locality or other geographical description.
- **When** do you want to carry out your project? Why now? Think about timescales, opening hours, contingency plans.
- **With** what resources will your project be carried out? How much money will you need? How will people find you? What resources will you use, including people, equipment, buildings and transport?
- **Work** out what success looks like. For example: How many people will you help? How will you support volunteers? What targets have you set? How will you monitor what is actually achieved?

Analysing your needs is crucial to making the case for change; if you are to convince others to support your cause you will have to present the evidence. Specifically, before granting a faculty, the Chancellor will need to see your well-argued case set out in your Statement of Needs; we give you some pointers on this in Chapter D6. Clear vision has little in common with idealistic waffle or hopeless aspiration. The need is to get real and nail the detail of what you want to do.

Notes

1 Rod Street and Nick Cuthbert, *Better Change in Church: When Wholehearted Commitment Counts*, North Charleston, SC: CreateSpace, 2015, pp. 72–3.

2 This matrix is a staple of business/life coaching and comes from Stephen Covey, *7 Habits of Highly Effective People: Powerful Lessons in Personal Change*, London: Simon & Schuster, 1989, 2004. The usual application of this is that one should spend as much time as possible in the top-right (important but not urgent) quadrant; our suggested use of it here is slightly different, and prior to that blessed state.

D6

How to Write a Statement of Needs

What is this – and when do I need one?

Along with a Statement of Significance, a Statement of Needs is a requirement of the Faculty Jurisdiction process for anyone wishing to make changes to a listed church building, or an unlisted church in a Conservation Area.[1] However, the process of producing one can be useful for any church considering a building project because it enables you to set out the thinking behind the proposed alterations, thus concentrating your mind on what is important and justifying the changes to others.

The danger with any project is that those who are driving it forward get so involved in the detail that they can sometimes forget that others (and there are usually lots

of other stakeholders) will not be as far advanced in their understanding of the thinking behind the proposals. A Statement of Needs serves the twin purposes of filling that information gap while at the same time inviting comment and other ideas. It also provides the **justification** for why you should be allowed to change your building. This is particularly important with a historic building, where the presumption is against change – you need to be able to explain why the proposed changes to the building are justified on the basis of the needs of the church community.

The Statement of Needs should be a specific application of your Mission Action Plan, and is an amplification of the needs-analysis process set out in Chapter D5. As with a Statement of Significance (see Chapter D2), the best approach is to be brief and to the point (no more than a few pages of A4) and to refer to other documents or appendices if necessary.

If yours is a historic building it is essential to work the Statement of Needs up in conjunction with your Statement of Significance. What you must not do is 'reverse engineer' the Statement of Significance from your Statement of Needs (e.g. saying that wall 'A' has no historic significance because it has already been decided you want to remove it).

A possible structure:

Your needs   A headline to describe briefly what you are trying to achieve. This might be in terms of:

- Facilities (e.g. 'an additional room to seat 25 with tea station; the room should have separate external access, and internal access to the WCs').
- Liturgy (e.g. 'a change to the pattern of worship or the use of the building').
- Building services (e.g. 'new heating and lighting').

The benefit   What tangible benefits(s) would you achieve? How would this change what you could do as a church, whether in terms of worship or mission? Fundamentally, why should anyone care?

The vision   Crucially, how does this fit with your overall vision for being the Church in your particular locality? If you cannot root your proposed change in a wider vision then you will not convince others to support your proposals.

The 'footprint'   How will this impact the church financially, particularly in terms of long-term running costs? An additional room may bring in some income from lettings but would also add to running costs (heating, lighting and maintenance). What impact will it have on environmental sustainability? Will it have an impact on staffing?

The timing   Why do this now? What trends if any do you see in patterns of attendance at the church? How might the proposals alter that? Always be aware that the rest of the community does not stand still while we in the church implement our vision.

The context   As a church, are you at the centre of your community or on the edge? Answer that both geographically and psychologically: How do people in the community think of the church building? Are there broader demographic changes planned in the locality, such as a new housing development? What other community facilities are there in the area to address community needs?

The history   Bear in mind that you are part of an unfolding narrative of God's people in your particular place. You are writing one single chapter of that larger story. How does this generation's chapter fit with the story so far? The story to date will be covered in more detail in your Statement of Significance; this is the opportunity to relate your perceived needs to that story, and (the exciting bit) to say where you think that story might go next.

The evidence   Who has been consulted in the process of refining this need, and how has this been recorded? If you hold an open day or other event it is always a good idea to invite written comments; this can be really useful in making your case for change, both in the early stages and further down the line, for example with various bodies (planners, DAC …).

The options   What alternatives have been considered? In the case of a historic building, how does the proposal fit with the more important aspects of the physical fabric of the building identified in the Statement of Significance?

Feeling 'Witi'?

If you struggle to articulate the basis of your needs, another method is to start with a result you might have in mind and work back to the beginning. Starting with your endpoint, ask the question, **Why is that important?** Repeat this perhaps four or five times.

An example of this might be wanting to add an extension to your church. The internal conversation might go like this:

- We want to add another room to the church. / Why is that important?
- The church lacks a social space. / Why is that important?
- There is nowhere for the children to meet separately during a service or for midweek meetings. / Why is that important?
- We feel called to offer God's hospitality and to be at the centre of our community; we believe the additional room will enable us to draw more people into the church community.

This exercise may feel artificial but if done in collaboration with others it may produce some really useful insights. It is important that you can account to all who ask you why you want to alter your building – having comprehensive answers will help you to meet legitimate concerns and build that all-important consensus required for any church project to succeed.

Summary

The key point is to think through what you are hoping to achieve and to root this in your vision for the life of the church. Often a Statement of Needs is prepared after a specific set of proposals has been drawn up and the design process is well advanced; but this is then an exercise in post-rationalization. As suggested above, a (draft) State-ment of Needs would form an excellent basis for a project brief and is therefore a great piece of thinking to have done *before* engaging an architect or other members of a design team. Even if you don't produce a finished document until the end, it is much better to wrestle with articulating your needs at the outset as part of the briefing process, and in conjunction with an understanding of the significance of the historic building.

Note

1 For Church Buildings Council (CBC) guidance for both documents, see www.churchcare. co.uk/churches/guidance-advice/statements-of-significance-need. Our approach to each is different but complementary.

D7
How to Organize Yourselves

As with many aspects of church life, undertaking a building project entails some substantial responsibilities and will make significant demands of you in terms of time and energy. Any project requires the client to make hundreds or even thousands of decisions, so it is important to have systems in place to ensure you are able to make those decisions in a timely and appropriate manner. Being a competent client is hugely important to the successful outcome of your project.

Delegation

The most important thing for a client body to understand, therefore, is the need for clear decision-making processes, and this will involve the delegation of responsibility from the PCC to a smaller group, which will report back to the PCC to an agreed timescale and format. It is essential that you avoid the situation where different people are issuing conflicting instructions to your architect and design team – that will cost you time, money and goodwill. Once you get into the design stages there should ideally be a single person, with a deputy, who has the authority to act as the single point of contact with the external team, and through whom all communications and decisions should be passed. This person should expect to be contactable during the working day – there will be a need to respond to queries as they arise. To represent the client well they need a sense of authority within the church community and a good ear for what people are feeling. They also need to have a thick skin – as anyone in leadership knows, it is never possible to please all of the people all of the time. This is therefore a demanding and important role; at the end of the project, don't forget to give this person a huge thank you.

Generally speaking it is better *not* to have the vicar perform this role, or perhaps to be on the steering group (see below) at all. This of course will depend on the nature of your project, on the capacity of individuals within the church and on the vicar's model of leadership. Two issues suggest that the vicar should be cautious before stepping up to such a central role, both of which relate to the reality that the project is likely to take several years to come to fruition. The first is that the life of the church does not stop during the lifetime of the project, and the vicar will therefore still be responsible for all the normal church-running activity. The second is the Anglican system of appointing incumbents, which doesn't allow for the handover of responsibility and knowledge, as you would expect, for example, between key post-holders in a business environment.

The steering group

There is also something important about empowering people within your church community. Behind your key individual, who will be the main point of contact, you would expect some form of building group or committee; finding the right people will be crucial to the success of the project. Typically this group might number between four and eight people (depending of course on the size of the project), which might include someone paid to be an 'employer's agent' once you have engaged an architect. Think about co-op-

tion: there are many useful skilled people out there who may be friends or family of parishioners who would be willing to volunteer their expertise. Also, if your project will house a partner organization then they should have at least one person on the steering group, and the same goes for the Friends' Group if they are doing the fundraising. Having your local councillor on board for a big project that needs planning permission can also be invaluable to help you through the processes of local authority consents.

These are some of the possible roles that need to be filled during a building project:

- **Chair person**   Co-ordinates the meetings and oversees the elements of the project. Reports to the church leadership.
- **Finance and fundraising**   Someone who will oversee the finances and fundraising and work alongside the church treasurer.
- **Communications**   A vital role to ensure that people within the church and the wider community are kept in regular contact with the project, from local dignitaries to church members, from the local media to local residents. It is helpful if this is someone who has experience of writing press releases and blogs, speaking at meetings, writing materials to present to the church family and so on.

- **Employers' agent**   On larger projects this would demand an average of a day a week to be given to the project – and during the construction phase this person will be the dedicated link with the architect, dealing with day-to-day matters. If you do not have someone with the skills to hand, the church may need to employ someone for a period to see the project through. They will need to have some knowledge of building processes.
- **Community**   A person who, for example, develops relations with the community, organizes community surveys, keeps an ear to the ground with regards planning permission objections, develops links to a residents' association where applicable.
- **Administrator**   Takes the minutes, puts together papers and spreadsheets where needed.

It is helpful to write down what is involved in each role, and the time expected to be taken for each person. That role description will help clarify what the expectations are and avoid confusion. Note that none of the roles (apart perhaps from employer's agent) is a technical one – if you appoint a good professional team it is not necessary to have any specific technical skills within the client body. If you do have such skills, these can be very helpful but you then need to be careful to define who is responsible for what – there's no point having a dog and barking yourself.

Encourage people to see their time on the group as a commitment of at least three years so that you get some continuity. Ensure people in the church know who is on your building group and give them a profile – that way members of the congregation know who to talk to about issues relating to the project.

D8
Ecclesiastical Exemption

Ignore this stuff at your peril

Whether an Anglican church building is listed or not, you need permission (a faculty) to make changes to it.

If your church building is listed, the Ecclesiastical Exemption (from local authority control) for consent to change a listed church is very helpful to the mission of the Church but it doesn't mean you can do what you like. A culture of 'We're doing what we want – it's our church building' has grown up in some churches but we still have a responsibility to change our historic buildings well, not just as we please. Following changes to the law in 2010 the processes for dealing with listed building consent for churches outside of local authority control are more formally prescribed; so you need to understand this stuff in order to avoid getting into trouble.

Ecclesiastical Exemption applies to the six major denominations. In the Church of England the rules are enshrined in a Measure, which has the same status as an Act of Parliament. Just as you would need listed building consent for any changes or improvements to a listed house, so you need permission to make changes or improvements to the fabric of a listed church building. In the case of churches the permission is called a faculty and the consent process by which permission is asked for and obtained is Faculty Jurisdiction. The legislation on faculties for church buildings is set out in the Care of Churches and Ecclesiastical Jurisdiction Measure 1991; the specific process is described in the Faculty Jurisdiction Rules 2013.[1]

(Note that for most building projects you will need other permissions as well. For changes to the outside of your building you will need planning permission, and for almost any project you will also need to satisfy the Building Regulations. Your architect will advise.)

A bit of history

Faculties have been around in England for a very long time, originating when the English Church got fed up with having to get permission from the Pope in Rome; so faculties predate Henry VIII. Over the centuries, obtaining a faculty ('permission to do something that normally would not be allowed') has sometimes been closely observed and at others totally ignored; rather like much of life, when it comes to faculties, some of us are less keen on rules and regulations than others!

The importance of the faculty process increased following the Second World War. Luftwaffe bombing, and the subsequent wave of post-war redevelopment, which some considered more destructive than the bombing, gave fresh impetus to the conservation powers that local authorities had been given in the 1930s to protect historic buildings. This resulted in the national scheme for 'listing' buildings and legislation to protect them from harmful changes that would affect their character. The legislation is not, and never was, intended to prevent changes or improvements, but any proposals to alter any aspect of a listed building needs permission, normally granted by the local authority; this permission is called listed building consent (LBC).

However, church leaders made the case that church buildings were primarily there to serve, support and enable the mission and ministry of the Church. It was claimed that it would be unreasonable to expect secular bodies to exercise control over buildings that are to serve that mission. Consequently churches and chapels were exempt from LBC and as part of this 'Ecclesiastical Exemption', the different denominations developed their own parallel system of controls and permissions. Some of these worked well, others did not.

Within the Church of England the ancient faculty provision was revised and adapted to act as the parallel LBC process for Anglican church buildings. However, the need for a faculty applies to all church buildings, whether or not they are listed, unless the bishop has made a specific exception for an unlisted place of worship.

Since 2010

In 2010 the Ecclesiastical Exemption was restricted to six denominations – The Church of England, The Church in Wales, The Roman Catholic Church, The Methodist Church, The United Reformed Church and those Baptist Churches where the Baptist Union is the trustee.

These six denominations operate acceptable systems of control for listed places of worship that are a parallel process to LBC. The Anglican Churches have Diocesan Advisory Committees (DACs), which advise the Diocesan Chancellor who makes the decisions; other denominations, dealing with far fewer listed buildings, each have a Listed Building Advisory Committee that makes the decisions.

There are of course also some listed places of worship that are outside the Ecclesiastical Exemption and therefore subject to local authority LBC. Unlisted places of worship may be subject to denominational consent and permissions as well as secular planning controls.

Faculty simplification

At the time of writing (2015), both the Measure and the Faculty Jurisdiction Rules are being amended under a scheme called Faculty Simplification. There are a number of items that, in future, may be implementable without a faculty. Some will be subject to consultation, others will not. The full schedule of items has not yet been finalized but there will probably be a limited range of 'permitted' items for listed buildings. It is likely there will be three classes of works to church buildings. List A items will not need a faculty or permission subject to certain restrictions and requirements; List B items will need permission and possibly consultation with the DAC; items not on lists A or B will require a faculty.[2]

When this system is implemented the necessary information will be available on www.churchcare.co.uk and from your Diocesan Registrar, DAC and your archdeacon. The latter will be the person responsible for issuing the permissions that do not require a faculty.

A faculty protects

'Faculty' has sadly become a word loaded with negative connotations, at least at parish level. This is unfortunate because it demonstrates that we have misunderstood the benefits of the faculty process, not least that getting permission via the appropriate channels and from the appropriate bodies provides protection. Faculties protect the following:

- The church's primary function as a place of worship.
- (Or at least discourage) the PCC from wasting money, time and effort.
- The parishioners who could be excluded from their church by fashion, mad ideas and theological bigotry.
- Clergy, churchwardens and PCC from accusations of negligence.
- The building, whether against inappropriate change or against unsuitable methods and materials for repairs.
- The historic environment for future generations.

Faculty

Refreshes
the parts other
permissions
cannot reach

All in all you would be mad to risk going without the protection a faculty provides.

Fundamentally the church building is not yours to do with as you please; rather it belongs to the whole community. As the 'parish church' for all those who live in the parish, it is right that the PCC act responsibly in both looking after the building and in developing it so that it serves the needs of the Church's mission in the twenty-first century. Having to ask permission to do stuff enables you to benefit from the wisdom and experience of others. One example of the potential for harm is the damage done to so many churches by Mr Bodgelt's enthusiasm for Portland cement mortar discussed in Chapter B22.

Step by step

The DAC is an essential part of the faculty process but is not the body that makes the decision. The DAC's role is to *advise* the Chancellor of the diocese, who is the person who makes the decision. The DAC does, however, act as some sort of gatekeeper; it is therefore important to understand what deadlines your DAC works to – many only meet every other month.

Once the DAC has considered your application it will advise the Chancellor with one of three responses: 'Recommended', 'No objection' or 'Not recommended'. In the same way as with LBC and planning permission, other parties are entitled to comment and, if they feel strongly enough, to object. A public notice needs to be displayed for 28 days, and in the case of listed buildings there are various other stakeholders (see below) whom you are obliged to notify of your proposals. These discussions, and the 28-day consultation period, may therefore generate a range of responses and perhaps some formal objections, all of which will be considered by the Chancellor along with the advice from the DAC.

Where there are major disagreements over a set of proposals, a Consistory Court may be convened to hear the arguments for and against before the Chancellor makes his or her judgement; the costs for this process are usually borne by the parish. Clearly this is best avoided by early consultation where at all possible, but if you find yourself going through this process you shouldn't be afraid of it.

It is recognized that DACs are not perfect, and the applicant is able to pursue their application even if the DAC has advised the Chancellor 'Not recommended'. The Chancellor may grant the faculty even if the DAC has advised 'Not recommended' and/or there are objections from other parties. You are also permitted to appeal to the Chancellor if you consider your application has not been properly considered by those advising him/her. If you disagree with the Chancellor's decision there is also an appeal process to the delightfully named Arches Court of Canterbury or the Chancery Court of York – but if you get that far you're *well* beyond the scope of this book and possibly the depth of your pockets.

St Alkmund

The best way to avoid a Consistory Court and get your faculty at the first time of asking is to prepare the ground well and to ensure you provide the best possible justification for your proposals. St Alkmund, Duffield was an Arches Court appeal decision in 2012 that helpfully sets out a decision-making process by which Chancellors are able to decide faculty applications. Consistory Court rulings since that date regularly refer to the St Alkmund process. Paragraph 87 of the judgement sets out a framework that involves answering the following five questions:

1 Would the proposals, if implemented, result in harm to the significance of the church as a building of special architectural or historic interest?
2 If the answer to question (1) is 'no', the ordinary presumption in faculty proceedings 'in favour of things as they stand' is applicable, and can be rebutted more or less readily, depending on the particular nature of the proposals ... Questions 3, 4 and 5 do not arise.
3 If the answer to question (1) is 'yes', how serious would the harm be?
4 How clear and convincing is the justification for carrying out the proposals?
5 Bearing in mind that there is a strong presumption against proposals which will adversely affect the special character of a listed building (see *St Luke, Maidstone* at p.8), will any resulting public benefit (including matters such as liturgical freedom, pastoral well-being, opportunities for mission, and putting the church to viable uses that are consistent with its role as a place of worship and mission) outweigh the harm? In answering question (5), the more serious the harm, the greater will be the level of benefit needed before the proposals should be permitted. This will particularly be the case if the harm is to a building which is listed Grade 1 or 2*, where serious harm should only exceptionally be allowed.[3]

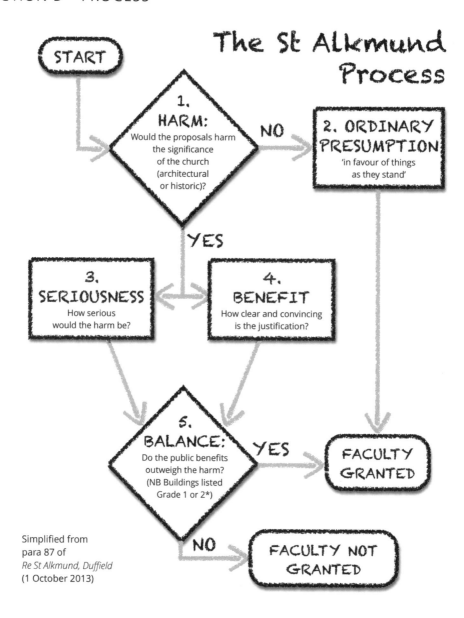

The St Alkmund Process

START

1.
HARM:
Would the proposals harm
the significance
of the church
(architectural
or historic)?

NO

2. ORDINARY
PRESUMPTION
'in favour of things
as they stand'

YES

3.
SERIOUSNESS
How serious
would the harm be?

4.
BENEFIT
How clear and convincing
is the justification?

5.
BALANCE:
Do the public benefits
outweigh the harm?
(NB Buildings listed
Grade 1 or 2*)

YES

FACULTY
GRANTED

NO

FACULTY NOT
GRANTED

Simplified from
para 87 of
Re St Alkmund, Duffield
(1 October 2013)

The context of the St Alkmund project was a lively church in Derbyshire wishing to move an ornate Victorian chancel screen to another location in their Grade 1 listed church building. The Chancellor had refused to grant a faculty but the Arches Court found that while there would be some harm to the building's special historic interest, there was nevertheless 'a strong and convincing case for change on the theological, visual and practical grounds' (paragraph 90), and a faculty was granted. The key point made in the St Alkmund judgement is that faculty decisions are a balance where any 'harm' is judged against the missional and other benefits. It is therefore really important for those proposing the works to demonstrate that they understand any harm, as expressed in the Statement of Significance (Chapter D2), and provide a convincing justification for the changes in the Statement of Needs (Chapter D6).

Statutory stakeholders

Obtaining a faculty does of course take time; if the application is well prepared, and the proposals are uncontentious and straightforward, it can take as little as three months. This should be planned in; the problems begin if you are playing catch-up and seeking permission late in the day to meet a deadline. Early informal consultation with the archdeacon and DAC is the most effective route to success, and having the willingness to work with the grain of the permissions process rather than against it helps enormously. Remember: neither the DAC, the Chancellor nor anyone else in this process is your enemy! In the case of listed buildings, the six national amenity societies also have the right to be consulted in the faculty process and to comment on the proposals. These amenity societies are special-interest groups with a specific area of concern; they have nothing to do with the government but you are obliged to give them the opportunity to comment. They also have a great deal of knowledge of their specialism, so can also be an invaluable resource. Your DAC can advise on the best approach to these consultations, but note that in most dioceses it is the parish as applicant that is expected to manage this process, not the diocese.

Some of these amenity societies deal with specific historical periods, evident from their names: the Georgian Group (1700–1840); the Victorian Society or 'Vic Soc' (1840–1914); the Twentieth Century Society or 'TCS' (1914 onwards) – yes, the Edwardian period was snapped up by the Vic Soc before the TCS came into being. Then there is the Society for the Protection of Ancient Buildings, which deals with pre-1700 buildings and has a more general concern for conservation theory and practice. The remaining two societies, the Ancient Monuments Society (AMS) and the Council for British Archaeology, are less likely to be involved with changes to church buildings, though the AMS may well comment on works to the outside of a church through the planning system.

Clearly many church buildings by their nature include work from a number of different periods, so the presumption should be that you consult with all of these societies, unless there is a clear reason not to.

There is one other stakeholder specific to churches who in some cases will also need to be consulted: the Church Buildings Council (CBC). The DAC is required to consult or refer particular types of cases to the CBC and so it is important to take advice from the DAC Secretary at an early stage. Referring specific items to the CBC is a requirement of the Faculty Jurisdiction Rules 2013 for listed churches, so you need to be prepared for this if you are proposing major changes. The CBC has published a helpful document setting out when to consult them, available from ChurchCare, but in principle they will want to be involved with proposals to buildings listed Grade 1 or 2*, and for Grade 2 buildings considering major liturgical re-orderings, new extensions and work affecting ancient trees, protected species or wildlife. Note that the CBC expects you to have made a start with preparing your Statements of Significance and Needs; this not only helps them understand what you are planning but gives you an opportunity for a dress rehearsal with someone more attuned to the needs of churches.[4]

In summary, then, if you are changing a listed building, you have an obligation to notify the '6+1' (national amenity societies plus the CBC) of your proposals and allow them to comment. As with the DAC, it is best to start this consultation early, before the scheme is too far developed. If your building is of interest to a number of these stakeholders, don't be surprised if their voices do not agree with one another. It can be helpful if you are able to get these competing voices together at the same time; that way they need to make their case to one another, avoiding you acting as postman between them.

Faculties made easy(ier)

As part of the Faculty Simplification, in 2015 the application process will be going online, diocese by diocese. The intention is to make the whole process easier and more transparent, and to enable individual churches to track the progress of their application through its various stages. Follow www.churchcare.co.uk for news on this.

Notes

1 Faculty Jurisdiction Rules 2013 – see www.legislation.gov.uk/uksi/2013/1916/contents/made.

2 Look out for the forthcoming book *Changing Churches: A Practical Guide to the Faculty System* by Charles Mynors, Chancellor of the Diocese of Worcester, due for publication by Bloomsbury in 2016. It will be a book that Diocesan Offices and DAC Secretaries will need to have to hand, so you should be able to consult a copy somewhere in your diocese.

3 See www.ecclesiasticallawassociation.org.uk/judgments/reordering/duffieldstalkmund2012appeal.pdf

4 On when to consult the CBC, see www.churchcare.co.uk/images/Churches/When_to_consult_the_CBC_Jan_2015.pdf

D9
They Think It's All Over ...

So you've decided to change your building; you've got all the permissions you needed; the money is raised; the building work is nearly complete. While the building project may feel like an impossibly long test of endurance, in reality it is only the preface to the story that begins unfolding as soon as the building work is complete. That story is all about people, and for that story to unfold healthily there are a number of things you need to have thought about beforehand. This chapter looks at some of the issues that may well arise during the first year of operation.

Plan the opening day a long way ahead

When anyone changes a building there is always a natural curiosity to see what is different, so with people 'queuing up outside', why not allow them in? Structuring this around a formal opening event is a great way to attract attention and build a sense of buzz. Invite local people within the community to your special day and perhaps gear your Sunday service to newcomers. An opening event is a golden opportunity to impact your community; it's your chance for a fresh beginning.

Plan the day or weekend carefully and think strategically about who to invite – think about who your key stakeholders are from outside the church, and don't forget that your church building belongs to the community too. Don't miss this opportunity to get some local press coverage to advertise all the new facilities; local newspapers are generally desperate for news, and it is nice to be able to make news for good positive reasons. At the very least send them a press release with photos and a contact name. And of course including food in the proceedings will always draw people in!

Having a 'headline act' such as the bishop or a civic leader also helps to formalize the event and bring in more people – a recognition that what has happened is worth taking note of. If your plans for a 'grand opening' do include a special guest, it is wise to set the official open day several months *after* you anticipate the building work will be finished. Even well-planned building work will throw up surprises and delays, often at the eleventh hour, and all the more so in the case of an existing and perhaps ancient building.

Managing and staffing the re-developed building

A re-developed building may require significantly more people to staff it. Will it need paid employees, in which case the church may for the first time become an employer. Even if the new facilities are run by volunteers, what training will they need? See also Chapter B20 for some legislative aspects of employment.

Well before your open day you will need to recruit, induct and train your staff and volunteers and allow time for them to get used to the building before any official opening. For example, if you have set up a café you will need to do a 'dress rehearsal' or two, perhaps with church members; there is so much to get used to that you cannot expect everything to run smoothly without this, and it is precisely in the first few days and weeks that you need to make a good impression. In your staff planning make sure you allow for time off, annual leave, sickness and statutory bank holidays in your rotas.

Plan regular reviews in the first year of operation as well as the normal annual appraisal reviews; good practice extends this process, albeit in a less formal way, to volunteers.

Develop an operating policy

Churches that let space to other community groups often worry about having to accommodate activities that may be incompatible with their own faith objectives. Normally for a charity that has been given charitable status on faith grounds this should not be a concern. There are specific exemptions that cover faith groups not having to rent their premises to certain groups who would be seen by the majority of their congregation as incompatible with their governing document. (Do you have a governing document? If you develop one, make sure it is well written and consistent with your aims.) If in doubt, take some legal advice *before* you have a problem to resolve.

A more open approach might be to view your building as a tool to use to build relationships with people beyond your congregation, and therefore to see it as a new opportunity. Either way, it's helpful to establish a written operating policy. This will cover group rentals, charges, use of the building in terms of alcohol sales, noise levels, opening and lock-up times (often these are stipulated as part of a planning approval, if one was needed, so check there), staffing levels and health and safety policy. Draft a policy and check with other churches to help you refine this.

Planning and monitoring the finances

A new building or extension is great but don't imagine that your enlarged building will cost the same to run as before (unless of course you have also invested in making it more energy efficient). Similarly a building that is unchanged but used for more days of the week will cost more to run. It is therefore really important to do at least a basic forecast of income and expenditure for the new building; this of course depends on your having a good understanding of the financial aspects of the existing arrangements.

Consider the income and expenditure of items such as a café, room-rental income, special events, insurance, any Council Tax (and your exemptions, which will usually range between 80 and 100 per cent), additional staff costs, utility bills, legal and accounting costs and, crucially for the long term, maintenance. Have a nominated person (perhaps in addition to your church treasurer) who can manage these additional finances. Train staff to manage budgets. If your building involves a significant business element, you may have cross-payments between a charitable company and a trading company to make, which may also be VAT registered; managing your bank accounts may be a significantly bigger task now than before the opening. Gear up ready for the extra work and don't be afraid to pay professionals to help with the workload; well-aimed financial advice may be able to save you significant amounts of money.

Keeping the vision

Hopefully before you first set out on your building project you took the time to set out in writing a statement of your vision of what you were hoping the changes would deliver. Keep this document in view, whether figuratively at the forefront of your mind or literally pasted up by your desk or wherever.

SECTION D   PROCESS

Buildings are surprisingly powerful things and it is not difficult for them to become ends in themselves. Part of your job, both when adjusting to a new building and thereafter, is to keep the vision in view and to prevent the 'tail' of the building from wagging the 'dog' of your wider purposes as a church. The building is there to serve the church's vision, not the other way round. While it is important to respect the building, when you become too precious about the new floors, walls or equipment, it may be time to return to the vision and ensure you are still on track. Remind yourselves regularly of the original vision, the point of it all.

D10
Friends' Groups

The benefits of a Friends' Group

The majority of the population want to see churches at the heart of their communities making a positive contribution to people's lives. Many people in our parishes have a feeling of goodwill towards the Church as an organization and even more positive feelings about their local church building. They want churches available for weddings, baptisms and funerals even though they themselves may not want to attend worship regularly or get involved with church life. Some of these issues are considered in Chapter A3.

This sense of goodwill is of considerable potential benefit if we can tap into this wider community support. It means we can encourage our local communities to share with us the burden of maintenance of the church buildings. It means we can ask for help.

Ideally each church should try and get to a position where the local community carries the burden of church maintenance, leaving the worshipping church community to pick up mission and ministry costs. A way to do this can be by means of a well-run Friends' Group (FG) that can raise funds by subscriptions, donations, legacies, Gift Aid and special events.

(Best Friends Forever?)

Setting up a Friends' Group

If the PCC is going to set up an FG, get the structure and governance right from the outset, otherwise an FG can be more trouble than it is worth. There is a good deal of guidance available, and some dioceses have an established procedure on how to go about the business with an agreed legal format, which should be followed. Whatever the situation, you will need to consult with the archdeacon and Diocesan Registrar to ensure that the FG is set up properly in compliance to both Charity Law and church legislation.[1]

Normally an FG is set up by resolution of the PCC and is therefore under PCC control and it works like any other PCC subcommittee. As well as avoiding possible conflicts between the PCC and the FG, setting it up in this way has the following advantages. It means that the FG:

- is under the authority of the PCC
- has charity status as a subcommittee of the PCC
- is tax efficient for donations and subscriptions through Gift Aid
- can use the Central Board of Finance (of the Church of England) investment fund
- requires no separate constitution
- can co-opt anyone to help run it
- can create its own list of members
- can only raise money for programmes and objects initiated by the PCC.

Sometimes the local politics or the size of the church building and the challenge it presents militate against such a subcommittee FG. If this is the case it is essential to take legal advice early in the process before too many ideas and proposals become fixed in people's minds.

A separate FG will need its own constitution setting out its relationship with the PCC and how any money raised is to be handled and what will happen if it is wound up. Furthermore instructing work on the church building can only be authorized by the PCC. It is not possible for an FG to decide what work needs to be done and to put it in hand. This has been a frustration to some FGs whose members have wanted to dictate to the PCC what work is permitted using the FG funds. This is why it is important to get the governance right and ensure that the tail does not wag the dog.

Think first, act second

When it comes to an FG the local church community need to think thorough why they want to set one up and what they hope to achieve. The following issues (some contradictory) require PCC thought and agreement:

The reason we would like to set up a Friends' Group might be because:
- It can enable a wider group of people to share the burden of maintaining our historic building.
- It can make sure that church buildings are in a reasonable condition to hand on to the next generation.
- The congregation on their own cannot afford to keep the building.

Many parishioners have a feeling of goodwill towards church buildings (especially historic ones) and so, while not wishing to support the Christian mission financially, they may be willing to contribute to their upkeep.
- What will we do for them in response to their support and goodwill?
- Will we respect their position and neither view them as second-class supporters nor try to recruit them to the congregation?
- How will we keep them informed and (hopefully) supportive when we are proposing changes?

Church buildings are places of worship; they exist primarily for 'the advancement of the Christian religion'. The object of a Friends' Group is to raise funds for the building to be spent by the PCC.
- Works that qualify for the funds raised by the Friends would be the maintenance, repair and improvement of the fabric of the buildings.
- What measures will the PCC put in place to ensure the funds are spent on the building and not used for other purposes?

Membership of the Friends would be open to anyone who wished to join and is prepared to support its objectives.
- How will we ensure and maintain open, trusting and co-operative relationships between the church community and the Friends?

The church will need to keep in touch with FG members and inform them of needs and progress. The PCC will do this by ensuring that the FG subcommittee organizes some or all of the following:

- A well-publicized and properly run Annual General Meeting.
- A regular FG newsletter in both digital and paper formats.
- An annual party with generous refreshments.
- An annual letter of thanks from the incumbent/churchwardens/chair of the FG with a subscription-renewal form.
- Social occasions and fundraising events.
- Site visits, talks and tours – especially to show them progress during works using FG funds.

Staying in the driving seat

The PCC first needs to agree to have an FG, and second needs to stay in the driving seat. Once the decision is made, designate two or three people to form a planning group to set it up. This group needs to deal with the following:

- Consult with the archdeacon and Diocesan Registrar (the ecclesiastical solicitor appointed for the diocese).
- Identify founding members of a committee to run the FG, which will include people from outside the church as well as within.
- Decide on whom to target as potential Friends.
- Decide how to approach them.
- Plan a series of events for the first year – to catch people's interest.
- Organize an open meeting to launch the scheme. Attendees could be invited to nominate people willing to be co-opted to serve on the FG Committee (the successor of the Planning Group), which would then run the scheme.

The PCC should review progress after the scheme has been in operation for one year and ensure it is reviewed at least every two to three years. A written report from the FG to the Annual Parochial Church Meeting (APCM) is an essential requirement of any PCC subcommittee or associated charity.

Give us your money (please)

If the FG is to have membership subscriptions the PCC will need to decide between various options:

- A set amount for annual membership, which would need to cover the costs of running the scheme.
- A higher set amount for annual membership, which would additionally include a percentage for funds.
- No fixed amount but suggested amounts, with an encouragement to Gift Aid these.

Don't forget that for an initial period, possibly the first 12 months, the PCC will need to budget to cover the costs of setting up the scheme and resource the first round of fundraising events.

Note

1 The National Churches Trust (NCT) provides a toolkit to guide you through the process and a model constitution to download – see http://nationalchurchestrust.org; www.nationalchurchestrust.org/friends-group-your-church. The Diocese of Canterbury offers another example – see www.canterburydiocese.org/stewardship/friendsschemes.

D11
Fundraising

Two types of money ...

Since any church needs to spend money, raising that money is an inescapable part of a healthy church's life.[1] However, at the outset it is important to make the distinction between fundraising for a specific purpose and the regular 'business as usual' giving of the church community in support of their baseline mission and ministry. Where that basic level of (sacrificial) giving is lacking, the life of that church will be fundamentally compromised and is probably unsustainable.

Money for church buildings could go into either of the two categories, either as business as usual (see the Asset Management Plan in Chapter B17) or as a one-off project. Furthermore many churches serve as wider community resources, and of these many are listed, making them heritage assets of significance to the nation. In these circumstances it is perfectly legitimate, and indeed healthy, to seek wider community support and make applications to heritage and community grant-making trusts in order to fund work on these buildings.

The Church Buildings Council, the National Churches Trust and the Prince's Regeneration Trust have a great deal of advice about raising funds for both repairs and 'one-off' projects for heritage buildings. There is a huge range of example projects on the Heritage Lottery Fund site, which will give you inspiration as to what can be achieved. However, the day-to-day maintenance of your church building is not eligible for grant aid as maintenance is considered to be the responsibility of the owners – 'If you can't look after it then you shouldn't keep it.' This approach, which is the line taken by government and informs the DCMS, Historic England and the Heritage Lottery Fund, can be a bit tricky for PCCs, who find themselves looking after a building on behalf of the parishioners. However, PCCs are not free to dispose of church buildings, which is why engaging with the local community and forming a Friends' Group (Chapter D10) is so important.

While we believe in a big and generous God (remember Jesus' comments about priorities in Luke 12.22–34), most of us find it difficult to ask for money. Henri Nouwen, in his booklet *A Spirituality of Fundraising*, helpfully defined fundraising as a form of Christian ministry. He went on to say:

> Fundraising is proclaiming what we believe in such a way that we offer other people an opportunity to participate with us in our vision and mission. Fundraising is precisely the opposite of begging … Rather, we are … inviting you to invest yourself … in this work to which God has called us.[2]

Fundraising

Fundraising is not for the faint-hearted and nor is it for those with a defeatist attitude – it does, after all, involve asking people to part with their money. It therefore requires a lot of hard work and determination, so if you are looking to raise funds for your church building you need to be passionate about the reasons why. You also need to do your research to understand the particular objectives, interests and requirements of the individuals and organizations you are asking for funds, so that you can tailor each application specifically to suit them. Look at their published information and identify the specific item(s) that will attract their attention and be of interest to the trustees. A scattergun approach using the same letter to a variety of funding bodies is almost guaranteed to fail. In fact it can do more harm than good; if you get it wrong the first time due to poor preparation it is very difficult to go back a second time.

The changes in the economy since the early part of the twenty-first century have created a very different climate in which to do fundraising. Low interest rates have resulted in many grant-making trusts having reduced income to give away. The lessons of the Lottery Millennium Projects mean (quite rightly) an increased emphasis on robust business plans to ensure the long-term sustainability of projects. Preserving old buildings just because they are there is no longer considered a sufficient reason to give money; the new requirement is 'increased access for all'. This doesn't just mean having the buildings unlocked, open and welcoming; it is about helping people understand and interpret the heritage asset, which we discussed in Chapter C8.

(A sense of) ownership

The consecrated church building is vested with the incumbent; the PCC have the duty in law to look after, maintain and repair it; as an Anglican church it is there for all the residents of the parish. In a very real sense a church building is 'public property' and morally belongs to the residents of the parish: 'It's their building just as much as ours.' Think through the implications of this statement – it is essential to invite, encourage and allow the wider community to be involved.

When it comes to the money every local church needs in order to function, a useful principle is for **the living church community to meet the costs of the living ministry while the wider community support the maintenance, repair and improvement of the building**. To quantify that second figure you need to have an Asset Management Plan (AMP) – see Chapter B17. Your greatest support can be from the local community if you make the time to engage with them. Friends' Groups, covered in Chapter D10, are an excellent means of formalizing that support. Many churches in England have been put back on a sound financial footing and in a good state of repair by simple initiatives to generate support from the parishioners. Generating the community interest and supportive response is missional work.

Fundraisers

Sometimes, however, you will need the help and guidance of an outside fundraising consultant. There are no shortcuts to fundraising, so if you are going to pay someone to help your church raise the money, you need to do your homework and get the right person for the job. The first two places to look for advice are the websites of the Institute of Fundraising and the Association of Fundraising Consultants.[3] Both are semi-commercial sites (i.e. funded by the individual fundraisers), but they also provide a wealth of advice and information in addition to the various fundraiser-members' contact details.

The Charity Commission has particular requirements where a PCC (or indeed any charity) engages a professional fundraiser. Check with the Diocesan Secretary and also have a look at the Charity Commission's downloadable 2011 publication *Charities and Fundraising (CC20)*, and particularly its Section G (or 7 in the HTML version) with regard to commercial partners, including professional fundraisers. Indeed the whole of *CC20* is important.[4]

Sacrificial giving?

In the world of professional fundraising there is a principle that you should get at least 33 per cent in the bank before going public with an appeal. Consequently the professional fundraisers go first to the very rich who can make big donations without affecting their lifestyle. Most fundraising strategies rely on the sacrificial giving of a few very wealthy people to kickstart the public stage of any fundraising campaign. This is why the cause has to be good and the case for support very convincing.

Church communities are often challenged to give generously, sometimes even sacrificially. While giving 10 per cent (a tithe) of your income is a biblically justifiable figure, the economic structures are very different from biblical times. For the church community, who are already funding the ministry, appeals for building repairs or improvements and re-ordering are an extra challenge. It is just as important for the cause to be a good one and the case for support to be very convincing.

Before asking the church or wider community for money, the PCC as trustees have a duty to ensure the assets for which they are responsible are generating revenue wherever possible. Revenue generation needs to be as much a part of the life of the church as breathing is to human life. We need to stop being scared or suspicious of money and realize that it is essential for the mission and ministry. Only with adequate funding will we ensure we have buildings with secure and viable futures that work for people.

Enabling development

'Enabling development' is a mechanism for realizing the development value of a piece of land for the purpose of investing the money in another building. An example might be the demolition and redevelopment of a church-hall site for, say, a health centre, and the use of some of the capital released by the sale to fund the creation of additional community facilities in the main church building. Another example might be the construction of housing on spare land around an existing twentieth-century church (which may have the land and often has no burials), and upgrading that building.

Historic England use the term 'enabling development' more tightly in a heritage context to describe development that would be unacceptable in planning terms but for the fact that it would bring heritage benefits sufficient to justify its being carried out, and which could not otherwise be achieved.[5]

For these arrangements to work there needs to be sufficient development value to make the deal worthwhile, and that of course very much depends on location. From a planning point of view, any heritage and other community benefits of the proposed development should outweigh the disbenefits of any departure from the local authority's agreed development plan or from national planning policies. Clearly the more sensitive the location, the more constraints there will be on new development.

Historic England has produced very thorough guidance on the sorts of situations in which, in the context of historic buildings, such development may or may not be appropriate. The guidance contains a useful digest of applications for enabling development that have reached a public inquiry.

This is an extract from Historic England's *Enabling Development and the Conservation of Significant Places*:

THE POLICY
Enabling development that would secure the future of a significant place, but contravene other planning policy objectives, should be unacceptable unless:
a) it will not materially harm the heritage values of the place or its setting
b) it avoids detrimental fragmentation of management of the place
c) it will secure the long-term future of the place and, where applicable, its continued use for a sympathetic purpose
d) it is necessary to resolve problems arising from the inherent needs of the place, rather than the circumstances of the present owner, or the purchase price paid
e) sufficient subsidy is not available from any other source
f) it is demonstrated that the amount of enabling development is the minimum necessary to secure the future of the place, and that its form minimises harm to other public interests
g) the public benefit of securing the future of the significant place through such enabling development decisively outweighs the disbenefits of breaching other public policies.

How to spend a windfall

Sometimes churches receive a significant windfall out of the blue, often in the form of a legacy. By definition such windfalls cannot be planned for, and in our view it is madness to use such monies to make up for the church's failure to cover its everyday operational costs. Churches operating in this way are unlikely to be viable (Chapter A7), and it isn't helpful in the long run to hide from your congregation the true costs of running their church's life.

Think instead about how you could use the windfall creatively, for example for pump-priming something the church wants to do. To this end your church will need to have a Mission Action Plan (MAP) and an Asset Management Plan (AMP) in order to know what the priorities for spending should be over and above the operational costs.

Having both an MAP and an AMP guards against such a windfall being spent on some crazy idea that happens to be the vicar's pet project.

One suggestion we would make is that whatever your PCC decides to do with the windfall for your local church, see if you can give an equivalent 10 per cent to the Church in need elsewhere. For example, if you are using the windfall to provide WCs and a kitchen, find a way to fund a church construction project, or indeed WCs, over-seas; or if your church is using the windfall for children's work in the UK, try to invest in an educational project in an area of the world where life is tough.

VAT

Along with your fundraising, make sure you understand the VAT status of your project – 20 per cent of the value of your project is a lot of money! You may well need special-ist advice, since VAT and buildings is a complex area, and one that the Chancellor of the Exchequer likes to tinker with. At the time of writing (2015) new church buildings, works to listed church buildings, independent annexes and disability-related works all offer good scope for limiting your VAT liability. However, given the shifting nature of the topic, we'll say no more here and suggest you look at the more up-to-date infor-mation on VAT and Church Buildings from the ChurchBuild Project Guide (web search for 'churchbuild VAT') and the Listed Places of Worship Grants Scheme which you will find at http://www.lpwscheme.org.uk/.[6]

Notes

1 This is not a fundraising handbook so we will limit ourselves to some general observations and try to direct you to other resources. One key resource is Maggie Durran, *The UK Church Fundraising Handbook: A Practical Manual and Directory of Sources*, 2nd edn, Norwich: Canter-bury Press, 2010.

2 Henri J. M. Nouwen, *A Spirituality of Fundraising*, Nashville, TN: Upper Room Books, 2010, pp. 16–17.

3 See www.institute-of-fundraising.org.uk and www.afc.org.uk.

4 See www.charitycommission.gov.uk/detailed-guidance/fundraising/charities-and-fundraising-cc20.

5 *Enabling Development and the Conservation of Significant Places*, London: English Heritage, 2008 – see https://content.historicengland.org.uk/images-books/publications/enabling-development-and-the-conservation-of-significant-places/enablingwebv220080915124334.pdf.

6 www.churchbuildingprojects.co.uk/how-to/6-finance/6-2-vat-and-church-buildings/.

Section E   Projects

E1
Practical Examples

Introduction

When it comes to church buildings, as with many areas of life it is very easy to assume that the way things are is the way they will always be; change is often seen as either too difficult or just too frightening. Undoubtedly some people are drawn to the Church precisely because they believe it will provide a haven from the unwelcome change experienced in other areas of life. As we argue elsewhere, the presumption against change is ahistorical, and the special status of church buildings is recognized in the separate legislation that governs their alteration (see Chapter D8). Christianity and Culture's DVD-ROM *The English Parish Church Through the Centuries* provides an excellent illustration of this in the form of interactive videos showing the development of a typical medieval church from both inside and out.[1]

Becoming familiar with examples of churches that have successfully negotiated the process of change can be hugely beneficial in lifting your horizon of expectation, demonstrating that 'different' is possible and that it could even be attractive to a broad cross section of people. If your church is considering a building project there is no substitute for visiting other churches that have successfully completed similar work.

Before and during a building project it can be very difficult to grasp the benefits of the proposed change, and another church's completed scheme can demonstrate some of those benefits. As well as looking at the bricks and mortar of the completed scheme it is just as important to listen if possible to the story behind a project. Try and get to talk to people who were involved in making the project happen; listen to the challenges and the joys; understand how well (or not) it is working now that it is finished. Ask what they would have done differently if they had their chance again.

The *danger* with examples is that one too easily assumes that what the neighbouring parish did will fit your church also. While there are obvious similarities between many church buildings, every one of them is different. It is invaluable to draw on the experience of others but you will need to find the right expression of that experience to fit your particular situation.

Finally, if one church struggled to get agreement with the Diocesan Advisory Committee (DAC) or found the amenity societies difficult, don't assume the same will apply to you. (Equally if everything went without a hitch, don't assume that will be your experience either.) People change, both in themselves and of course by personnel moving on to positions elsewhere. Even working with the same DAC, the tone of two meetings held in two similar churches can vary widely, depending on who is present, how the ideas are first presented and how the conversation develops.

This section of the book looks at five types of building project, using just a handful of examples in each chapter. These examples do not set out to provide exhaustive coverage of each type of work or even a representative sample of such projects in the UK. Instead these are simply offered as buildings of which we have direct experience, from grand schemes at one end of the spectrum to the relatively ordinary and therefore achievable at the other. With each chapter, therefore, the aim is to illustrate the typical issues that arise with that sort of work, and equip you with a series of questions to have at the back of your mind when you go and visit other buildings. Beside the examples, we give you a brief commentary and a list of what you might look for.

The point of including examples is to provoke your thinking – by deliberately offering a relatively narrow selection we are inviting you to go out and find your own examples to feed your imagination. We suggest you ask your DAC Secretary for suggested projects to visit in your diocese; you could of course ask that question of other nearby dioceses, which may perhaps offer some differences of approach.

General things to look for

- From the outside, what impression does the building give? Is it hospitable? Does it invite you in or does it make demands of you before allowing you to enter?
- If there were something compellingly interesting going on inside, would you be able to tell from the outside?
- Do you think this building works missionally? If not, how might it work better? Overall, do you feel welcomed and affirmed or disapproved of and judged?

Note

1 The DVD-ROM is available from www.christianityandculture.org.uk/products/epc.

E2
Re-orderings

Re-ordering projects are usually motivated by liturgical change or to free up the building for a wider range of uses; fundamentally, therefore, their aim is to do/be Church better. That might then translate into the adjustment of seating at the east end of the nave to allow for the use of a nave altar, or the addition of a kitchen or WCs (see also Chapter E5), with the removal of pews to reintroduce community use (Chapter E4).

The best sacred space has a simplicity to it. A huge amount can therefore be achieved by simply clearing away the clutter churches inevitably accrue. And that simplicity is deceptive – as with any form of minimalist design, it is very much harder to create something that looks effortlessly simple than to cobble something together with bits added to meet each additional need.

There is a parallel here with much of what we do in church worship. One of the essential skills of leading/reading/preaching is to be an enabler not a star attraction. Success here includes getting out of the way to enable that expression of Church to be focused on God rather than the individual. So too with the building. By getting out of the way, the best design proposals focus attention away from themselves and just seem to work effortlessly.

Aside from projects that re-order the building by adjusting the seating or focus of worship there are others that create new usable spaces within the existing envelope of the building.

Galleries

Many rural churches put in a WC and perhaps a small kitchen where the building previously had no such facilities; where the church has a tower at the west end, this can often be a good location for these facilities (for more on this, see Chapter E5). However, one change often leads to another. Where the bottom of a tower is altered in this way, then if the tower has bells that are still rung (rather than simply chimed), a new ringing floor will also need to be created. How access is provided to this requires careful thought. A proper staircase takes up a good deal of space and of course needs to be located far enough away from where the bell-ringers will need to stand. In some situations it may be better to create a staircase at the rear of the nave, leading up to a gallery that then gives access to the tower, provided of course that the tower arch is high enough to permit such access. Note also that it isn't just the people who have to get there; bells from time to time will need to be brought in and out, which usually means a trapdoor to suit the largest bell.

We're big fans of galleries because they also provide exciting opportunities for positioning a reader or some singers; and of course many medieval churches had galleries from where the musicians would play but which the Victorians systematically removed in favour of enlarged chancels for robed choirs. This, however, involves a bigger change to the character of the church as a whole, so the more listed the building is, the clearer you will need to be in justifying the benefits to be achieved.

Where a church also needs to create separate meeting rooms for children's' work and so on, this can sometimes be done by creating a larger gallery or mezzanine structure at the west end of the nave and/or aisles. The more such accommodation you create at first-floor level, the better the access you will need. It is not the case that as soon as you have any first-floor accommodation you will also need a lift, but not having a lift means you need to be prepared and able to move an activity to an equivalent space that someone with mobility difficulties can access. In practice, therefore, as soon as you have more than a single room at first-floor level you should allow for a lift. In most circumstances a simple platform lift (that does not require a motor room or a lift pit) is all that is required, but of course it still takes up some space, and will have maintenance costs associated with it.

The galleried schemes described above largely maintain the sense of space in the nave and can be relatively unobtrusive. The stage beyond this is the partial or full mezzanine floor – this involves putting a new first floor through part or all of the building. This has a more significant impact on the character of the building and therefore needs more justification where the building is listed (and all the more the higher the grade of listing). The upper spaces have the benefit of the remaining height of the building and what is often an attractive roof, but for the same reasons are much more difficult to subdivide; meanwhile the lower floor has a much lower ceiling and usually less, if any, natural light. Assuming a church use is retained, it usually works best to use the upper floor for the church space and the lower floor for the service spaces such as WCs, kitchens, smaller meeting rooms and storage. Essential to making an attractive building out of this sort of arrangement is allowing enough space and openness at the lower level for the process of arrival, and making it blindingly obvious how to get to the upper floor.

Things to look for – re-orderings

- What do you think was the motivation for the project? Do you think it delivered on that promise?
- How do the main spaces flow together?
- Is there a single unified floor finish or do different areas have different finishes?
- Is the seating fixed or movable? What benefit is achieved through that flexibility?
- Where is the heating? And does it feel warm?
- What about the lighting? What is the mixture of uplighting and downlighting, and where is it positioned. How much flexibility does the system have to vary the feel?
- How discreetly integrated is any technology such as audio or projection? Where is any audio controlled from?
- How well used is this place? What goes on there that couldn't take place before?

Examples

St Peter, Plymouth

This is a wonderful liturgical space, and the embodiment of a 're-pitched tent' inspired by Richard Giles. Themes of pilgrimage, liturgy and worship are at the heart of this re-ordering which, since St Peter's reopened in November 2007, has had a profound effect on both visitors and regular worshippers. The building contains some striking pieces of art, which add to the sense of significance and threshold experience.

Wyndham Square, Plymouth PL1 5EG.
www.plymouthstpeter.co.uk. Harris McMillan Architecture and Design, Exeter.
Photo: Girt Gailans.

St Barnabas, Cambridge

A previous re-ordering of this unlisted late-Victorian brick building had turned the church through 180° to face west, with entrance via the former chancel. The 2014 works included the removal of the remaining pews and the unifying of floor levels to allow greater flexibility of use, underfloor heating, a new glazed screen in the chancel arch and a full immersion baptistry.

Mill Road, Cambridge CB1 2BD.
www.stbs.org.uk. Archangel Architects, Cambridge.

St John, Downshire Hill

A Grade 1 listed church originally built in 1824. The re-ordering included retention of the existing box pews in a different format under the galleries to each side, leaving a clear central space where more flexible seating is provided. Even more impressively, a large hall, which opens into the re-landscaped garden, was created by digging out under the church.

Downshire Hill, London NW3 1NU.
www.sjdh.org.
MEB Design Ltd, Clerkenwell.
Photo: Des Hill.

St Michael & All Angels, Wilmington

A transformation of a dark and cluttered Grade 1 listed church of Saxon origin. A major re-ordering in 2012 resulted in replacement of pews with chairs, new underfloor heating and floor, new lighting and re-sited choir screen, to create much-improved flexibility, comfort, a sense of holy space and a welcoming atmosphere, and to encourage community use.

Church Hill, Wilmington, Kent DA2 7EH.
www.stmichaelswilmington.org.uk/
Malcolm and Linda Green.

E3
Extensions

'Traditional' church buildings, whether genuinely medieval or Victorian 'wannabe-medieval', have an established 'grammar' of forms. This grammar of course comes from the long history of these buildings being changed, most generations adding (and in some cases subtracting) from the building in response to changing needs.

When church buildings were altered to increase the accommodation, the typical means by which this was be done was by adding aisles to one or both sides of the nave (and in some cases second aisles beyond the first), or perhaps by adding transepts running perpendicular to the main orientation of the nave. Chancels and naves themselves might of course be extended in length. Entrances were enhanced by the addition of porches, and often took on a purpose of their own, for example as the place for conducting legal business. A narthex added to the west end of the nave was another means of creating space for additional functions.

When extending a traditional church building it is important to make an early choice between using this established formal grammar or creating a standalone building with its own distinct identity, which may or may not then be linked to the main church building. In our view the medieval model, offering a glorious mix of the church community with the wider community within a single space articulated into parts, is the best guiding principle. With this in mind, and while each situation of course varies, the basic advice is to achieve as much as you can *within* the existing building, and only then to consider extensions to the main volume; and then where an extension is appropriate, to keep it as closely integrated with the main building as possible. Why do we promote this 'new medievalism'? Because on the medieval model, the juxtaposition of multiple uses in the same space is hugely beneficial in locating the church community within its wider community.

Aside from finding an appropriate external form, the success of any extension to a church also depends on how well the new parts relate to the existing whole, and particularly how well spaces flow from one to the other. Where the individual parts of the building are and how they are connected is important – a church building has a 'grain' that needs to be respected. For example, to introduce one or more WCs into a church building will help it cater for a wider range of people and events, but to place them so that they are accessed from the front of the nave (or worse still, the chancel) will mean that they will be little used, at least during services.

Adding an extension to the side of an aisle may be appropriate for the external form of the building but will likely have implications for the natural light within the building. Sometimes this can be compensated for by dropping light down from generous roof-lights in the extension. Depending on the age and construction of the roof it may also be possible to introduce rooflights into the existing aisle roof; clearly this is not a part of the traditional 'grammar', but in the right situation can be used to powerful effect.

A narthex extension can not only provide valuable additional space, it also presents a great opportunity to give a church building a new face within its community. This is where you may get the chance to improve visibility into the building, the point of which, of course, is to allow some of the activity within the building to be visible to the wider community.

Things to look for – extension projects

- Viewed externally, how well does the extension fit with the whole? Can you tell old from new, and is that good or bad?
- What materials have been used? Are they in continuity or contrast with the existing building?
- Internally, how well does the extension integrate with the building as a whole? Is it obvious or is it hidden away?
- Did the form of the extension change the internal feel of the existing church (e.g. were light levels reduced by an extension covering over an existing window)?
- Does the extension 'have a life of its own' (i.e. is it usable independently)? Is that a good thing?
- How well used is it? What goes on there that couldn't take place before?

Examples

St Laurence, Alvechurch

The Ark is a striking 2004 extension on the north-west side of a Grade 2* building, largely rebuilt by William Butterfield in the 1860s. The extension does not attempt to copy the existing form but to complement it by making its own statement in a modern idiom. The poly-chromatic masonry echoes parts of the Butterfield work.

School Lane, Alvechurch, Worcestershire B48 7SB.
www.alvechurch-stlaurence.org. Graeme Beamish (Michael Reardon & Associates).

St Philip, Cambridge

A 2012 front extension to an unlisted building has given this church a new face, transforming its relationship with its community. Along with substantial work to the rest of the building, the front extension houses a café, introducing a welcoming threshold space. This project helped develop the church anatomy analysis in Chapter C7. The café is leased to the Papworth Trust, a social enter-prise that offers training to disabled and disadvantaged people.

Mill Road, Cambridge CB1 3AN.
www.stphilipschurch.org.uk.
Archangel Architects, Cambridge.

St Paul, Hammersmith

The current church, immediately to the north of the A4 flyover, dates from the 1880s and is listed Grade 2*. A west extension houses new facilities in a cloister around a central 'atrium', in the tradition of early Christian churches. As part of the project, the original building was cleaned, the better to reveal once again its polychromatic walls.

Queen Caroline Street, London W6 9PJ.
www.sph.org. Richard Griffiths Architects. Photo: Will Pryce.

St James, Norton juxta Kempsy

A discreet extension in a curvaceous and non-traditional form on the north side of this simple Grade 2* listed medieval building. The new building incorporates 'green' technologies with ground source heating, a sedum roof and timber-framed walls with sheep's wool insulation; it is available for both church and community activities.

Norton, Worcester WR5 2PX.
http://nortonchurch.org. Stainburn Taylor Architects.

St Mary and St Thomas of Canterbury, Wymondham
(Wymondham Abbey)

This Grade 1 listed Romanesque parish church is what is left of a much larger monastery, and includes at its east end a ruined 'monastic tower', which forms part of a scheduled ancient monument. Extensions to the north-east and south-east are modern in design and provide WCs, vestries, educational spaces and meeting rooms. The project, completed in 2015, received Heritage Lottery funding, and demonstrates how well deeply historic buildings can accommodate significant change.

Becketswell Road, Wymondham NR18 9PH.
www.wymondhamabbey.org.uk.
Freeland Rees Roberts Architects.

E4
Community Use

There are a growing number of examples of community uses being introduced into church buildings, and in this chapter we look at a few of these and at some of the attendant issues. The idea of using a disused church for a community use is hardly new; more recently, though, we have been seeing these sorts of activities in churches that are still also used for worship – examples include post offices and village shops, libraries, childcare, outreach healthcare and of course cafés. These are interesting projects because they raise a series of important questions, such as what a church building is, what it is good for, who it is for and ultimately what God is like.

The beauty of reintroducing community uses into church buildings is that it forces us to renegotiate that relationship between the local and church communities. As we discuss in Section C, the traditional model was that the church building hosted a mix of activities, some overtly church-related, others not at all. Juxtaposing such activities is therefore a contemporary expression of very old intuitions about the nature of community and the character of God.

The GNOME test

While the majority of people in the UK declare that they have a belief in a God of some kind, only a small minority actively identify themselves as Christian by attending church. The view of the great majority of people would, in one way or another, be that 'God is not for me', and even for those more open to God, sadly many conclude that the Church has nothing of relevance to say on the matter. There is a huge disconnect between what the Church offers to people outside the Christian community, and the perception of that offer.

Many churches of course have a long history of providing fantastic facilities for community groups, but in *separate* buildings; in such cases the church building will be doing little to challenge that disconnect. Even when it is open it is very easy for visitors

to come and go from the adjacent hall and steer well clear of the church building –
because the separateness of the two reinforces an underlying belief that 'God is not for
me'. Hence what we term the 'GNOME' test (God is NOt for ME): to what extent does
the building support a missional understanding that there should be no great divide
between the local community and the church community?

Propriety

The tight definition of what is appropriate in a church building, which is often un-
spoken, is a modern (i.e. Victorian) innovation. This arrangement suits our modern
culture very well because modernity doesn't know what to do with God; we therefore
put him into these convenient boxes called church buildings. With God suitably contained we can then choose not to visit or, if we want to join the 'God club', can set
aside a special time for that, leaving the rest of the week to get on with 'business as
usual'; either way, we avoid any need to encounter God in the rest of the week and
the daily round of life. Reintroducing community uses into church buildings unsettles
this cosy arrangement. It suggests, horror of horrors, that God might be interested in
all of us, not just the paid-up members of the God club. Given what else is at stake, it
shouldn't surprise us when proposals to put community uses back into churches elicit
strong reactions.

Things to look for – community use

- What local needs does this building aim to serve (aside from conventional church
  needs)? How does this congregation's situation relate to yours?
- Are church and community integrated or separated? Where within the building are
  the opportunities for interaction between these two expressions of community?
- Does the building pass the GNOME test?
- Does worship take place at the same time as community activities? If so, how?
- Does this building challenge your understanding of what Church is?

Examples

All Saints, Hereford

This influential project was described by English Heritage as the iconic example of a church redevelopment. Free-standing pods of contemporary design were inserted with minimum intervention in the historic fabric, and the re-ordered Grade 2* church reopened in 1997. Weekday church activities take place alongside the operation of the  café, which is run by a commercial partner; the project has repositioned the church in its community and saved the building from closure.

High Street, Hereford HR4 1AA.
www.cafeatallsaints.co.uk. Rod Robinson Associates.

St Paul Old Ford, Old Ford

After being closed for 13 years this Grade 2 listed church was transformed in 2004 with three storeys of community facilities, including a café in the entrance and a gym at roof level, enabling the church to minister to its multi-ethnic community in what is one of the most deprived areas in England.

St Stephen's Road, London E3 5JL.
www.stpauloldford.com.
Matthew Lloyd Architects.
Photo: Helen Binet.

SECTION E PROJECTS

St Peter, Wentworth

St Peter's is a Grade 2* listed twelfth- to fourteenth-century village church that was heavily restored in 1868, including rebuilding of the nave and south porch. A very simple 1992 scheme divided the chancel for worship from the nave as village hall, adding two WCs and a kitchenette. The division between the two 'rooms' is substantial, but folding doors at lower level provide views through, allowing the two spaces to be used together for larger services.

Main Street, Wentworth, Cambridgeshire CB6 3QG.
www.wentworthonline.org.uk. JE Mitchell.

St Leonard, Yarpole

In 2009 this remarkable community-inspired achievement created a village shop and post office within the Grade 2* listed church. A biomass boiler feeds the underfloor heating; the nave has been cleared of pews; above the shop is a gallery with café and kitchen. The project is particularly impressive for the consensus-building within the community.

Yarpole, Leominster,
Herefordshire HR6 0BD.
www.yarpole.com.
Robert Chitham and Marches Conservation.

E5
Kitchens and WCs

Adding these basic facilities to a building can allow it to be used in a much broader range of ways. We have dealt with a number of the practical issues with kitchens and WCs in Chapter B13, so look at the two chapters together.

Location, location, location

The key issue with both kitchens and WCs is where to put them. With kitchens that is a question of flow, of how people will get to collect whatever you are serving and then move away easily so as not to create a logjam. Do your best to avoid a feeling of the kitchen being stuffed in a corner. With WCs, as discussed in Chapter B13, there are specific cultural issues of not expecting users to draw attention to themselves.

How much is enough?

At the outset we may think that one WC will solve all our problems, but don't under-estimate how the use of the building will change in response to the new facilities. So if you're adding these facilities to your church with a view, for example, to being able to host a concert, plan for the numbers who might wish to use the facilities during the interval.

The three most frequently seen 'models' for WCs in churches are:

- 'The discreet': a subdivision of an existing space away from the nave, such as in the base of a west tower, in a side porch or perhaps by enclosing the space under a gallery.
- 'The out there': a free-standing 'pod' within the main space of the church; this works better when it stands in a side aisle rather than straying into the nave itself. If

space allows, the pod could be divided into two halves, with a WC on one side and a kitchenette on the other.

- 'The really out there': an extension to the building, which may of course include other facilities such as a meeting room.

A fourth option, not considered here, is to put a WC in a separate building in the churchyard; in some cases this might be the only option, but it is far from ideal.

Similar models to the first three apply for kitchens, the difference being that while WCs come in fairly standard sizes (the chief determiner being the number you have), kitchens come in all shapes and sizes. The simplest kitchens fit within a cupboard, possibly only the height of the base units. The next step from that is a cupboard plus a servery, which can be fixed (if you have the space) or possibly mobile. Then there are kitchens as rooms in their own right, starting from the glorified tea station and moving all the way up to the caterer's dream in stainless steel.

Lastly, don't forget the impact of any changes on other aspects of the building (e.g. putting facilities into a west tower in which the bells are still rung will necessitate a ringing floor above, complete with safe access – for more on galleries, see Chapter E2).

Things to look for – kitchens and WCs

- How discreetly have the facilities been incorporated in the building? Have they changed the feel of the church?
- Can you access the WC discreetly? If you needed to, could you use it during a service without drawing attention to yourself?
- When someone is in the WC, how much can you hear?
- Where is the kitchen and what level of catering was it designed for? Is there enough space, both behind the counter and in front?
- In putting these facilities in, how many holes were made in the building fabric? How are these spaces ventilated? Where do the drains run?

Examples

St Andrew, Bridge Sollars

This community-centre church is listed Grade 1. A new Tardis-like pod box in the north aisle contains a kitchen that 'unfolds' at the west end, a WC at the east end and the plant room between them. This is an ingenious solution, of the highest design quality, to an everyday need – a need that for a small and remote community can be a significant problem.

Bridge Sollars, Hereford HR4 7JH.
Communion Architects.
Photo: Chris Preece, Infinity Unlimited.

St Nicholas, Great Wilbraham

The scheme provides a kitchen and WC in the base of the west tower in this Grade 2* medieval church. A new ringing floor is created above, in this case with stair access from the back of the nave. The gallery provides both access to the ringing floor, and a space for creative liturgical use, the positioning of voices etc.

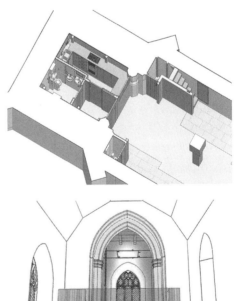

Church Street, Great Wilbraham,
Cambridgeshire CB21 5JQ.
www.fulbournandthewilbrahams.org
Archangel Architects, Cambridge.

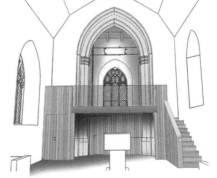

St Mary the Virgin, Orton Waterville

This has a pod of more traditional but elegant design at the west end of the north aisle. The pod includes a WC accessed from the north side (back), storage accessed from the east, and a kitchen that opens up to the south; the kitchen units can be closed away behind sliding doors, and a substantial but movable serving counter stands in front.

Church Drive, Orton Waterville, Cambridgeshire PE2 5HE.
PDG Architects.

St Mary Magdalene, Eardisley

An existing north door at the west end of the nave provided a possibility for a new extension to the medieval building to accommodate a kitchen and WCs. A close eye for detail and careful choice of materials makes the new work, completed in the 1990s, sit well with the original building. This is the opposite approach to St Laurence, Alvechurch, in Chapter E3; it scores well for fitting in, but less so for archaeological legibility.

Eardisley, Hereford HR3 6NW.
www.eardisleygroupcommunity.co.uk. Robin Salmon.

E6
New Churches

The Church in England has seen a number of waves of church building, often in response to liturgical or broader societal change. For example, many new churches were built in the nineteenth century because it was unthinkable that the parish system would not be extended to match the contemporary urban expansion. At the same time many churches were rebuilt or substantially 'restored', where a medieval building was judged no longer adequate to present-day needs, whether because of its condition, size or arrangement. Central to the funding of all this activity was the Incorporated Church Building Society, which was founded in 1818 and operated until 1982.

A similar mix of urban expansion and liturgical change combined to prompt another wave of church building in the 1960s. Alongside post-war reconstruction there was the building of the New Towns and the significant changes in patterns of church use that flowed from the Second Vatican Council. Before that, between the two world wars, there had again been substantial numbers of new churches built, once again in the context of urban expansion.

The present age looks quite different, with a general decline in church attendance (not forgetting, of course, specific pockets of growth). Nevertheless the established Churches generally find themselves with a surplus of buildings, or at least buildings deemed to be in the wrong place. An initial spate of church closures in the 1970s has now greatly abated, but the continuing reduction in usage of many church buildings is prompting a rethink within the Church (some would say long overdue) as to who the church building is for. This has resulted, particularly in more rural dioceses, in moves to reassert a pre-modern understanding and to 'return' the nave to wider community use; the setting up of Friends' Groups (see Chapter D10) is another expression of this.

In suburban and more urban areas where the church building is often of lesser architectural merit and/or where 'temporary' post-war buildings are reaching the end of their useful lives, some have been demolished and a new replacement built in the context of wider 'enabling development', often with a housing partner (more on this in Chapter D11). The narrow view of such enabling schemes is that the new development is no more than a means of releasing capital; where this is the case, such schemes usually lead to a zoned result, where the church becomes further side-lined in a new but inappropriate building of often poor design, often produced by an architect with little understanding of churches. The most successful enabling schemes produce a substantial 'missional dividend' by reconfiguring the church's relationship to its community. This often involves the inclusion of other community uses (such as healthcare, childcare) and the positive use of the enabling development to frame the church and set it in the centre of a new expression of community. All of this of course begs the more fundamental question of what we think a church building is in the first place – a theme woven through much of this book.

Theoretical groundings

The nineteenth-century church-building activity was stimulated and accompanied by the Ecclesiologists and the Oxford Movement. The twentieth century saw the influential New Churches Research Group, set up in 1957 by Peter Hammond and others; this group was active through the 1960s, providing an architectural response to the Liturgical Movement.[1] Among others this group included J. G. Davies, whose book *The Secular Use of Church Buildings* has continued relevance to the challenges faced by this generation;[2] Davies was central to the University of Birmingham's Institute for the Study of Worship and Religious Architecture, which was active in the 1970s and 80s.

What of today? Richard Giles first published his widely read *Re-pitching the Tent* in 1996; the book's original subtitle, *Re-ordering the Church Building for Worship and Mission in the New Millennium*, indicates both its date and its scope.[3]

The most common examples of new church buildings tend to be built by extra-denominational charismatic evangelical Churches such as the New Frontiers network. Where these Churches grow beyond the renting of space in schools and so on, and decide to build a home of their own, the chosen architectural language is usually self-consciously non-traditional. The approach could be described as 'low-Church functionalism', with a particular focus on catering for audiovisual display, which often pushes the worship space towards being a 'black box' performance space.

The twenty-first century also has its share of new areas of urban expansion. Where new church buildings are built by the established denominations this is often done on an ecumenical basis, and the buildings are almost invariably multifunctional.

Things to look for

- Is the building characterized more by functionalism or aestheticism?
- How has light been used to create spaces of different character?
- Is this a single-function building or does it host a variety of activities? If the latter, how well do those uses sit together?
- How well does the building relate to the community around it? Does it present itself as the 'private members' religious club' or does it permit a phased engagement with the wider community?
- Does the building use art either on the inside or the outside? If so, how well is it integrated into the building?

Examples

Cambourne Church

A visually striking but eco-nomical structure, this new ecumenical church for a new village between Cam-bridge and the A1 opened in 2009. The entrance space has a busy café at the front, with a multifunctional main hall behind and WCs and storage to the north. The main hall currently accom-modates 180, and it is hoped to expand this east-wards, together with a new chapel to the south.

Jeavons Lane, Cambourne, Cambridgeshire CB23 6AF.
www.cambournechurch.org.uk. BB+C Architects, Cambridge.

Miracle House, Wickford

New Life Church is the only church building on the large Wick housing estate, and deliberately looks 'un-churchy'. A double-height worship space is surrounded on two sides by meeting spaces, WCs, etc. As at Cambourne above, there is a busy entrance space for hospitality – in this case with overflow to the outside – and the ability to extend the building in future.

Silva Island Way, Wickford, Essex SS12 9NR.
www.miraclehouse.org.uk.
Archangel Architects, Cambridge.

St Edmund King & Martyr, Temple Hill

A modern church, built with the proceeds of adjacent enabling development, and with an NHS surgery and a Sure Start Children's Centre. The church itself is a lofty octagonal space, but perhaps over-glazed.

St Edmund's Road, Dartford DA1 5ND.
www.stedmundsdartford.co.uk.
Andrew Boakes Associates, Tonbridge.

Our Lady of Lourdes, Hungerford

A new Roman Catholic Church in a modern Arts and Crafts style, in red brick with dramatic red clay tile roofs, this was built along with adjacent enabling development housing. The building comprises a hall space with facilities, which acts  as a narthex to the church space, with minimalist glazing between.

Priory Rd, Hungerford, Berks RG17 0AF.
www.hungerford.org.uk/chain/churches/roman.htm. JBKS Architects.
Photo: David Stewart.

St Paul, Bow Common

 This may be old for a 'new' church, but worthy of inclusion because it is a very influential building. Built in 1960, it is now listed Grade 2*, and recently won the National Churches Trust UK's Best Modern Churches competition. A compact and tough-minded brickwork cube in a tough-minded area, the central altar is lit from above, with the columns and light fittings framing this holy place.

Burdett Road, London E3 4AR.
www.stpaulsbowcommon.org.uk. Maguire and Murray. Photo: John Salmon.

Notes

1 For more on the New Churches Research Group, see Peter Hammond (ed.), *Towards a Church Architecture*, London: Architectural Press, 1962.

2 J. G. Davies, *The Secular Use of Church Buildings*, London: SCM Press, 1968.

3 Richard Giles, *Re-pitching the Tent: The Definitive Guide to Reordering Your Church*, 3rd edn, Norwich: Canterbury Press, 2004.

Section F   And Finally ...

F1
Afterword – Our Heritage

We hope you have found this handbook helpful, whether you have read it from cover to cover or dipped into it in response to a particular query. It was written out of professional frustration in the hope of enabling church communities to match their buildings better to their mission.

Currently there is much talk about broadening access to heritage, but as yet no consensus as to what role the expert and the community respectively should play. This book was written because both of us found ourselves at conference after conference where a great deal was said by the professional participants about how to develop the use of church buildings, but with little engagement with the church communities themselves. In general, people at parish level still lack the confidence and capacity to make the changes and improvements they want and need.

Our conviction is that heritage is fundamentally something people do – it is a *process* rather than a *product*. Despite everyone's protestations to the contrary, all too often the individual inputs into the conservation process, doubtless all of them well meant, result in the 'defeat' of a set of proposals, and for the community an extinguishing of hope. We are not arguing for churches to be able to change their buildings (particularly their historic buildings) in any way they choose without constraint or proper consideration. Our point is that *both* of these approaches – 'no change' and 'any change' – result in the destruction of heritage; the second destroys heritage by destroying what makes the building worthy of care; the first by destroying the relationship between the building and those best placed to care for it. Instead of this false dichotomy of 'no change' versus 'any change', it is our simple belief that historic buildings should be allowed to 'change well'.

To that end, as we said at the outset, our aim has been to equip churches with a background knowledge of the principles and processes of buildings in order to allow them to fight their corner better. Where it concerns historic buildings, this book is therefore an argument for a form of grass-roots conservation. And in the case of all church buildings, our concern is with the empowerment of local communities to deal responsibly with their buildings themselves.

SECTION F   AND FINALLY ...

Winston Churchill once said: 'We shape our buildings, and afterwards our buildings shape us.'[1] This simple form of words combines two important insights: first, it signals the importance of our built heritage for our sense of identity as individuals and as communities; second, by implication it invites a creative engagement with those buildings. It is to furthering this understanding of the fundamentally mutual relationship between communities and their buildings, *to the benefit of both*, that this book is dedicated.

Note

1 From a 1943 debate following bomb damage to the Houses of Parliament.

F2
Organizations and Contacts

The Arthur Rank Centre, www.arthurrankcentre.org.uk

Bat Conservation Trust, www.bats.org.uk

Christianity and Culture, www.christianityandculture.org.uk, www.statementsofsignificance.org.uk

ChurchBuild, www.churchbuildingprojects.co.uk

Church Building and Heritage Review, www.churchbuilding.co.uk

The Church Buildings Council, www.churchcare.co.uk

The Churches Conservation Trust, www.visitchurches.org.uk

The Ecclesiastical and Surveyors Association, (EASA), www.easanet.co.uk

The Ecclesiological Society, www.ecclsoc.org

The Georgian Group, www.georgiangroup.org.uk

Historic England, www.historicengland.org.uk

Historic Religious Buildings Alliance, www.theheritagealliance.org.uk/hrba

The Incorporated Church Building Society archive, www.churchplansonline.org

Methodist Property Section, www.methodist.org.uk/ministers-and-office-holders/property

The National Churches Trust, www.nationalchurchestrust.org

Natural England, www.naturalengland.org.uk

The Prince's Regeneration Trust, www.princes-regeneration.org

The Representative Body of the Church in Wales, www.churchinwales.org.uk/structure/representative-body/property

The Society for the Protection of Ancient Buildings (SPAB), www.spab.org.uk

SPAB Faith in Maintenance, www.spabfim.org.uk

The 20th Century Society, www.c20society.org.uk

The Victorian Society, www.victoriansociety.org.uk

F3
Bibliography

Addleshaw, G. W. O. and Etchells, F., 1948, *The Architectural Setting of Anglican Worship: An inquiry into the Arrangements for Public Worship in the Church of England from the Reformation to the Present Day*, London: Faber & Faber.

Bartholomew, C. G., 2011, *Where Mortals Dwell: A Christian View of Place for Today*, Grand Rapids, MI: Baker Academic.

Binney, M. and Burman, P., 1977, *Change and Decay: The Future of our Churches*, London: Studio Vista.

Brook, P., 2008, *The Empty Space*, London: Penguin.

Brueggemann, Walter, 1993, *Texts Under Negotiation: The Bible and Postmodern Imagination*, Minneapolis, MN: Augsburg Fortress.

Cameron, J., 2007, *Building for the Gospel: A Handbook for the Visionary and the Terrified*, Belfast: 10Publishing.

Chesterton, G. K., *Orthodoxy*, Mineola, NY: Dover, 2004.

Chew, M. and Ireland, M., 2009, *How to do Mission Action Planning: A Vision-Centred Approach*, London: SPCK.

Child, M., 1976, *Discovering Church Architecture*, Aylesbury: Shire.

Church of England Board of Mission, 2009, *Mission-Shaped Church: Church Planting and Fresh Expressions of Church in a Changing Context*, 2nd edn, London: Church House Publishing.

Cooper, T. and Brown, S. (eds), 2011, *Pews, Benches and Chairs*, London: Ecclesiological Society.

Crofts, S., 2013, *The Good Maintenance Guide: A Practical Handbook to Help Volunteers Care for and Preserve our Historic Places of Worship*, 2nd edn, London: SPAB.

Cunningham, C., 1999, *Stones of Witness: Church Architecture and Function*, Stroud: Sutton.

Darby, D., 2012, *Compost Toilets: A Practical DIY Guide*, Winslow, Bucks: Low-Impact Living Initiative (LILI).

Davies, J. G., 1968, *The Secular Use of Church Buildings*, London: SCM Press.

Doig, A., 2008, *Liturgy and Architecture: From the Early Church to the Middle Ages*, Aldershot: Ashgate.

Duffy, Eamon, 2001, *The Voices of Morebath: Reformation and Rebellion in an English Village*, London: Yale University Press.

Duffy, Eamon, 2005, *The Stripping of the Altars: Traditional Religion in England 1400–1580*, 2nd edn, New Haven, CT and London: Yale University Press.

Durran, M., 2005, *Making Church Buildings Work: A Handbook for Managing and Developing Church Buildings for Mission and Ministry*, Norwich: Canterbury Press.

Durran, M., 2010, *The UK Church Fundraising Handbook: A Practical Manual and Directory of Sources*, 2nd edn, Norwich: Canterbury Press.

Dyas, D. (ed.), 2010, *The English Parish Church Through the Centuries*, York: Centre for the Study of Christianity and Culture [DVD-ROM].

Elders, J., 2004, *Revealing the Past, Informing the Future: A Guide to Archaeology for Parishes*, London: Church House Publishing.

Engel, J. F. and Norton, H. W. J. A., 1975, *What's Gone Wrong with the Harvest?: A Communication Strategy for the Church and World Evangelization*, Grand Rapids, MI: Zondervan.

Evans, Neil and Maiden, John G., 2012, *What can Churches Learn from their Past? The Parish History Audit*, Cambridge: Grove Books.

Fawcett, J. (ed.), 1976, *The Future of the Past: Attitudes to Conservation 1174–1974*, London: Thames & Hudson.

Fewins, C., 2005, *The Church Explorer's Handbook: A Guide to Looking at Churches and their Contents*, Norwich: Canterbury Press.

French, K. L., 2001, *The People of the Parish: Community Life in a Late Medieval English Diocese*, Philadelphia, PA: University of Pennsylvania Press.

Giles, R., 2004, *Re-Pitching the Tent: The Definitive Guide to Re-Ordering Church Buildings for Worship and Mission*, 3rd edn, Norwich: Canterbury Press.

Gorringe, T., 2002, *A Theology of the Built Environment: Justice, Empowerment, Redemption*, Cambridge: Cambridge University Press.

Hammond, P. (ed.), 1962, *Towards a Church Architecture*, London: Architectural Press.

Hill, M., 2007, *Ecclesiastical Law*, 3rd edn, Oxford: Oxford University Press.

Historic England, 2008, *Conservation Principles: Policies and Guidance for the Sustainable Management of the Historic Environment*, London: English Heritage.

Holmes, D., 2014, *Lighting for Places of Worship*, London: CIBSE.

Inge, J., 2003, *A Christian Theology of Place*, Aldershot: Ashgate.

Jeffery, G., 1989, *The Churchwarden's Year*, London: Church House Publishing.

Jeffery, G., 1992, *Handle with Prayer: A Church Cleaner's Notebook*, London: Church House Publishing.

Jenkins, S., 2000, *England's Thousand Best Churches*, London: Allen Lane.

SECTION F   AND FINALLY …

Kieckhefer, R., 2004, *Theology in Stone: Church Architecture from Byzantium to Berkeley*, Oxford: Oxford University Press.

Lewis, R., 1987, *The People, the Land and the Church*, Hereford: Hereford Diocesan Board.

McAlpine, W. R., 2011, *Sacred Space for the Missional Church: Engaging Culture through the Built Environment*, Eugene, OR: Wipf & Stock.

McCaig, I. and Ridout, B., 2012, *Practical Building Conservation: Timber*, Farnham: Ashgate.

McKay, W. B., 2005, *McKay's Building Construction*, Shaftesbury: Donhead.

Newsom, G. H. and Newsom, G. L., 1993, *Faculty Jurisdiction of the Church of England*, 2nd edn, London: Sweet & Maxwell.

Nouwen, H. J. M., 2010, *A Spirituality of Fundraising*, Nashville, TN: Upper Room Books.

Oxley, R., 2003, *Survey and Repair of Traditional Buildings: A Sustainable Approach*, Shaftesbury: Donhead.

Palmer, M., 2012, *Sacred Land: Decoding Britain's Extraordinary Past through its Towns, Villages and Countryside*, London: Piatkus.

Payne, B. A., 2014, *Churches for Communities: Adapting Oxfordshire's Churches for Wider Use*, Oxford: Oxfordshire Historic Churches Trust.

Penton, J., 2008, *Widening the Eye of the Needle: Access to Church Buildings for People with Disabilities*, 3rd edn, London: Church House Publishing.

Riddell, M., 1998, *Threshold of the Future: Reforming the Church in the Post-Christian West*, London: SPCK.

Stancliffe, D., 2008, *The Lion Companion to Church Architecture*, Oxford: Lion.

Street, Rod and Cuthbert, Nick, 2015, *Better Change in Church: When Wholehearted Commitment Counts*, North Charleston, SC: CreateSpace.

Strong, R., 2007, *A Little History of the English Country Church*, London: Jonathan Cape.

Taylor, R., 2007, *How to Read a Church: Pocket Guide*, London: Rider.

Wates, Nick, 2014, *The Community Planning Handbook: How People can Shape their Cities, Towns and Villages in any Part of the World*, 2nd edn, London: Routledge.

Walter, N., 2011, *The Gate of Heaven: How Church Buildings Speak of God*, Cambridge: Grove.

Walter, N., 2014, *Church Buildings for People: Reimagining Church Buildings as Nourishing Places*, Cambridge: Grove.

Walter, N., 2015, 'On Statements of Significance', Transactions of the Ecclesiastical Architects and Surveyors Association, volume 8, 2015.

Warren, R., 2012, *The Healthy Churches' Handbook: A Process for Revitalizing your Church*, London: Church House Publishing.

Yates, N., 2000, *Buildings, Faith and Worship: The Liturgical Arrangement of Anglican Churches 1600–1900*, rev. edn, Oxford: Oxford University Press.

Section G   Appendix

Is Your Church a
Millstone
or a
Springboard?

Take this **Healthcheck**

to test

how well

your **Church Building**

is fitted to your **Vision**

and your **Ministry...**

Millstone or Springboard?

Church is all about people, yet your building has a huge impact on your ministry, for better or worse. Is your building a **springboard** that supports and enables that ministry, or a **millstone** that weighs you down and holds you back? Whether your church is ancient or modern, this test will help you to be clearer on those areas that present the greatest problems, and those that already work well.

We suggest that you rattle through it; first time you should be able to do this in **5-10 minutes**. Think in terms of how a new visitor would relate to your church building, and grade each of the 10 questions from **0** (millstone) to **7** (springboard).

This is intended to be fun - treat it lightheartedly - and then if it has provoked any thoughts come back to those and reflect on them.

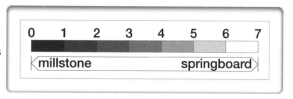

0	1	2	3	4	5	6	7

millstone   springboard

'We shape our buildings, and afterwards our buildings shape us.' Winston Churchill

1 Open For Business?

Does your building appear to be open? As you approach it or pass by it, is it obvious that something (interesting) is going on? Can you see into the building?

0 might be a building with no visible doors ('Round the back!'), or with 3 doors visible but all closed. For **7** think of a well-designed retail frontage which succeeds in firstly whetting your appetite, and secondly in drawing you in.

`0-7`

3 doors and no obvious way in...

2 Accessible?

We think of this in terms of disabled ramps and powered doors, and these are important. But in a wider sense accessibility is about having a low 'threshold of engagement', both physical and figurative. Does the building feel easy to come into (and also to leave); do I feel as though I will be trapped if I go through those doors? Is there enough that is familiar?

What is the 'body language' of your building? - **0** would be a tight-lipped frown, with crossed arms; **7** would be a warm smiling face, an open stance, interest in the other person. Who would you rather talk to?

`0-7`

3 Welcoming?

Once inside the front door is there enough space to manage the process of generous welcome, whether that is shaking hands or giving out books (or both)? A building without space for welcome suggests a church without space for the visitor...

`0-7`

a sense of openness and a warm welcome

4 Navigable?

If we do not know where to go we feel stupid. Navigable buildings make it obvious where to go, without lots of signage, and without forcing people to ask. Is it clear where the toilets are, or where to take children for Sunday school?

For **0** think of a badly designed sprawling hospital, all signage and no direction; for **7** think of a building that you don't have to think about, that just unfolds.

0-7

5 Comfortable?

If I spend an hour in your church will I come out frozen? Will my bottom be numb? Will my back ache? If so, then you are asking a great deal of the first time visitor, who is likely therefore to be the one-time visitor. This is not about making churches into oversized domestic living rooms, but a high level of discomfort creates a barrier that will usually prevent newcomers from engaging with your ministry.

At **0** the discomfort that I feel means the building prevents me engaging with you; at **7** the building doesn't get in the way, and I will be more ready to be open to what is on offer.

0-7

Note that there is no single ideal for what a church should look like, or how it should function - each will be different to reflect your priorities in ministry in your particular place. On some issues there may be little that you can do, but we have never found a church where it is impossible to make alterations for the better. Often small incremental changes will have a significant impact on the life of your church.

6 Visible?

Can I see what is going on? Are the sightlines clear - how many seats are unable to see the speaker or reader? Is the space light enough, both in terms of natural light and artificial light? Is there too much light - do we have a problem with glare? Can we adjust the levels of light to create different moods?

0-7

0: 'What's going on? - I've lost interest; **7**: I can see all that I need to.

7 Audible?

Can we hear what is going on? What about those who are hard of hearing - do you have a hearing loop that works? If you use a traditional organ, where is it located? If you have a sound system, is this optimised for your various needs - there are very different requirements for the spoken word, for singing, for a band.

0-7

0: 'What was that?' **7**: Loud and clear!

8 Serviceable?

Is there adequate provision of WCs & would you want to use them? Is the kitchen up to the tasks you expect of it - this could be catering for 150 hot meals on a weekday, or more modestly providing teas an coffees after a Sunday service. Do you have enough storage, is it usable, and is it in right places? Like it or not, inadequate provision of services will limit the usefulness of your building, and thus the life within it.
0: unserviced; **7**: ample provision.

0-7

9 Quality?

Is the quality of the building appropriate for your setting. Is it in good decorative order? Lots of Christians see a hair-shirted virtue in down-at-heel buildings that are poorly maintained, but bluntly this is usually an excuse for a lack of care. And those who come to us in need will see that lack of care and draw conclusions from it...

0: we do not care about our physical environment; **7**: quality that speaks of

0-7

10 Flexible?

Can the building accommodate more than one activity? How easy is it to move from one format to another? Can you the building change to accommodate different numbers of people? Can you create intimacy? If you need to, can you clear part of the space of seating; if so, do your seats stack - 2 high, 10 high, 40 high?

0: one rigid predetermined layout, but we have a need for more; **7**: we have all the flexibility we need.

0-7

flexible space for multifunctional use...

Millstone or Springboard?

So How Did You Do?

Firstly plot your results on the circular graph below - by joining the dots you create a 'spider diagram'. This shows particular areas of strength and weakness, and therefore whether your building is in overall balance.

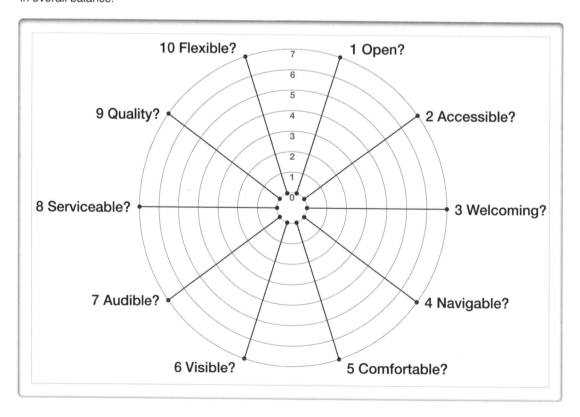

Looking at the individual areas, scores of 5-7 mean the building is already functioning well in that area; there may be room for improvement but there are probably more pressing needs. On the other hand, 0-2s mean you have significant, perhaps urgent, issues in that area.

Secondly, add the individual scores and enter the total in the box; this gives you an average for the building as a whole. Above 45 and your building will be a good fit for your ministry - you have a **Springboard**; below 25 and your building will be a significant constraint on the life of the church - you have a **Millstone**.

Total
out of 70

A Worked Example:

Here is a 'spider diagram' for a recently completed church project. The dark red line shows the church's assessment of their strengths and weaknesses beforehand; the green line shows their scores after the alterations. Improvements have been made in every dimension, and the church are delighted with the result.

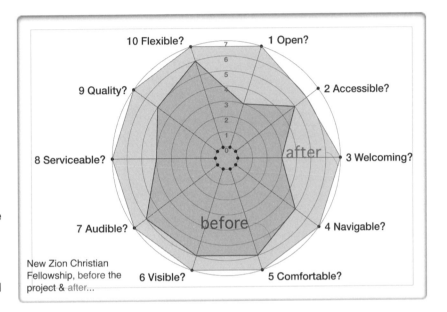

New Zion Christian Fellowship, before the project & after...

Millstone or Springboard?

What Next?

Why not share this with others - inevitably your answers will to some extent reflect your personal views, your likes and dislikes, so it is good to get as many people as possible to complete it.

New Zion Christian Fellowship

I hope you have found completing this Health Check to have been a useful exercise. If you would like further help to address any issues raised please copy and return this page to me (contact details on **www.churchbuild.co.uk**). I would be delighted to help you consider how you might take these issues forward.

With best wishes

Nigel Walter MA (Cantab), Dip Arch, RIBA, MAPM

www.churchbuild.co.uk   01223 474817   **www.archangelic.co.uk**

Church Building Projects - Where to Begin...?

Start Here...

This sheet provides a playful way of grappling with some of the serious issues that need to be considered **before** launching into a building project - the things you need to think about **before** you appoint an architect and other professionals.

The aim is to achieve at the outset the **clarity** you will need for a successful outcome. How you use this sheet does not matter - the key thing is to focus on the important issues, so that you can define the problem you want to address.

So use this sheet in whatever way suits you. Doodle! Brainstorm! Make a Mess!

What on Earth Do You Think You're Doing?

Who are you as a church, and what are your core values? How does what you do relate to those values? What 2 or 3 things make you distinctive in your local community?

How Well Do You Know Your Existing Building?

Do you know what you are dealing with? If the building has any historic value, have you prepared a Statement of Significance?

What are the known limitations? Consider archaeology, conservation, planning, trees, legal etc

Current Constraints

In what ways do your existing buildings prevent you realising your vision? Download the Springboard or Millstone Health Check from ChurchBuild to help people explore their perceptions. This can be a great tool for building consensus around the need for change.

The Art of Compromise

You will never achieve everything you want, and the act of choosing helps define the point of the project - always compare this with your vision.

With that in mind,

Yes Please! What are the key things to achieve...?

No Thanks! What are the key things to avoid...?

... scribble away!

Other Resources

Church Building Seminars - from time to time we help organise regional seminars for churches - a great place to come for ideas and information. Details from **www.churchbuild.co.uk**

The Gate of Heaven - How Church Buildings Speak of God, by Nigel Walter. This booklet examines the principles of what is a key relationship for any church and suggests practical means of forging a better partnership. Equally relevant whether you are struggling to maintain a historic building, considering a substantial reordering or contemplating a new building. **www.grovebooks.co.uk**

'We shape our buildings, and afterwards our buildings shape us." Winston Churchill

Feeling (Dis)Connected?

How does your community see you?
Who thinks the church is important?
Are there people who feel excluded?
Are there people who feel they own
the church?

Where Do You Think You're Going?

Do you have an overall vision of
what God is calling you to be and
do in this place? Leaving building
projects to one side, what are you
hoping to achieve as a church – what
is your dream?

Who Are You, Anyway?

Think about how you are going to
organise yourselves. What skills do you
already have within the church, and what
might you need to buy in from outside?
Who has ultimate responsibility for
decisions and how do you reach
agreement? Which one person will be
given the authority to represent the
church within the project team?

What Does Success Look Like?

Imagine you have
completed your project;
how will things be different?
How will you recognise
success when you see it?
What does it feel like? What
can you do now that you
couldn't do before?

How To Use This

Print this out at A3 for
use by a small group -
the central section can
then be copied at A4 if
needed. Or contact us
and we will happily
print this for you at A1
size for putting up in
the wall, or for a larger
round table discussion.

01223 474817

mail@archangelic.com

Q&A

Don't worry! At this stage you don't
need to have all of the answers – in
fact you don't want them, as better
answers will unfold as you better
define what you want. What is
important is to have a clear focus
and a sense of purpose, so that you
can formulate the best possible
questions...

Where To Next...?

How do you move on from here? The point of this
stage was to get all of the issues out onto the table
- if possible into the middle space on this sheet.
Out of this you can develop a formal **Brief**, which
defines the key questions you want answered - an
architect can help you to refine and improve this.

With a Brief defined, you may then commission a
Feasibility Study, which would look at whether
the vision can be achieved within the practical
limitations, and give a broad indication of cost. The
Feasibility Study may well help revise the Brief.

Only once you know the project is a) feasible, b) in
line with your overall vision, and c) necessary to
achieving that vision, should you appoint an
architect to begin designing you a building.

Re-Pitching the Tent, by
Richard Giles. Subtitled
'The definitive guide to
re-ordering church
buildings for worship and
mission' it does what it
says on the tin. Includes
appendices with good
practical guidance.

Archangel & ChurchBuild

ChurchBuild is an initiative of Archangel Architects to help the church
make better use of its buildings to further God's kingdom. You can find
other resources and further information at **www.churchbuild.co.uk**

If this exercise has raised issues or you would like to speak to me or
one of the team please call - there is no obligation
and we will be delighted to help.

01223 474817   mail@archangelic.com

Nigel Walter

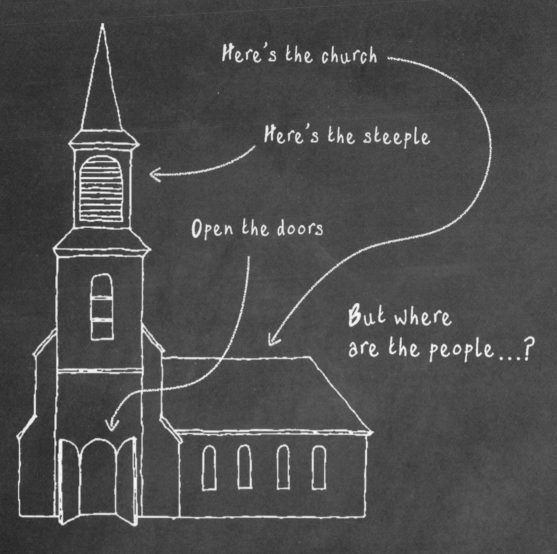

Church Buildings Audit

Welcome to the Church Buildings Audit

Churches are increasingly rethinking their worship and the buildings in which that worship takes place. New patterns of worship make us increasingly aware of the conflict between what the building proclaims both in its external appearance and its internal arrangement, and what the worshipping community believe and wish to express; sadly, many of our churches are suitable only for Victorian worship.

If a church discussing these issues is to move beyond an expression of personal 'likes' and 'dislikes', then it is important to have a tried and tested process for making good decisions. That process needs to balance changing uses with continuity of purpose, and to provide criteria for the development and re-ordering of churches that look beyond the merely utilitarian questions of function to what a church building really is.

That's what this audit aims to provide. We have written this material for use in small groups, with each session providing sufficient material for an evening of discussion, but you may find other means of using it, perhaps in other settings - we would be keen to hear. The issues you will discuss are serious and important, but we hope the process of discussing them will be exciting and enjoyable - please make that process fun!

We have created this resource to be used, and are very happy for it to be copied and circulated, provided the content is not altered and the authors are credited. We would be pleased to receive feedback on its usefulness and any suggestions you may have for improving it.

We hope this Audit will be of relevance to a wide range of churches across the denominations. Where we have had to choose, the terminology used is from the Church of England (eg 'PCC'); if you are from another tradition we hope you will not feel excluded and will be able to do the necessary translation.

David Stancliffe is the former Bishop of Salisbury and the author of *The Lion Companion to Church Architecture* (2008); in the early 1990s he oversaw the reordering of Portsmouth Cathedral.

Nigel Walter is an architect based in Cambridge with a specialism in the church sector. He is the author of *The Gate of Heaven - how church buildings speak of God* (Grove Books, 2011) and blogs at churchbuild.co.uk.

The authors can be contacted via mail@archangelic.com

Structure of the Audit:

1. Where have you come from?

   a) Talkative buildings
   b) How would you describe your building's character?
   c) Engaging with your story

2. Where are you now?

   a) How does the worshipping community express its faith today?
   b) How does the wider community see the church?
   c) How do you believe the church should be used?

3. Where are you heading?

   a) Dreaming the future...
   b) Three key principles for delivering change
   c) Conclusion

1. Where have you come from?

a) Talkative buildings

Your church building is talking all the time, but what is it actually saying?

1. About its history?

2. About the community for which it was built and those communities that have made adaptations since?

3. About the purpose for which it was built and the reasons for any change?

What is your Church saying?

4. About its purpose today - how do you use it now?

5. Is it cared for? And therefore will I be cared for?

What does that teach us about the relationship between

- God (theology)?
- worship (liturgy)?
- the community (social history)?

Does the building suggest that God is absent, worship irrelevant and the community excluded? Or does it speak instead of relevance and the integration of God, worship and community?

b) How would you describe your building's character?

1. **What are the general characteristics of the building** - large, small, cold, homely, spacious, light, cluttered, dark, tidy ... ? What are the shapes of the 'rooms'? What spaces and levels? Can you see what is going on?

2. **Furniture and fittings** - do they help or hinder? Are they in the right place? Could some be discarded or used elsewhere? Which should be retained?

3. **Lighting and acoustics** - are the lights in the right place? Can they be used to highlight a particular part of the service or building? Can the units be controlled flexibly and independently? Can you hear clearly? For the spoken word, and for music?

4. **Heating and access** - Can you get into the building and move about in it safely, or is it just an auditorium? Is it adequately warm? Does the heating restrict movement or clutter the space?

c) Engaging with your story

We understand the world in terms of story. But have you ever stopped to think about your community's story? Has the building always been like this (very unlikely) or has it changed over the years? Who has been associated with the building in the past, what do we know about their lives, and how does that relate to the Christian story?

Resources:

- *What Can Churches Learn from their Past* by Neil Evans and John Maiden (Grove Books, Pastoral series, P131)
- *The Lion Companion to Church Architecture* by David Stancliffe (Lion, 2008)

God invites us to be a part of his story in our particular place. Understanding that narrative is really important - it enriches the present by uncovering our past and opening up our future. Church buildings are a physical representation of that narrative, and like that narrative, they help to form our character and root us within our tradition.

Remember, tradition needn't be dry and boring! Tradition can help us understand where we've come from and what God is calling us to be. Tradition can be radical!

Get help! There may be other people interested in your building who would be keen to help, such as a local history society. www.churchplansonline.org might have drawings, if the church was changed by the Victorians. And you could try the county archive.

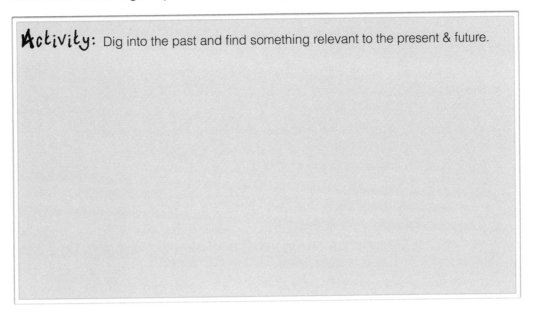

Activity: Dig into the past and find something relevant to the present & future.

2. Where are you now?

Religious Club   Community Life

a) How does the worshipping community express its faith today?

'Any person or body carrying out functions of care and conservation under this Measure or under any other enactment or rule of law relating to churches shall have due regard to the role of a church as a local centre of worship and mission.' Care of Churches Measure (1991)

1. How does the PCC understand its 'worship and mission?

2. What models of being the church do you resonate with?

   - The house of God
   - The house of the People of God
   - The gate of heaven
   - The Body of Christ
   - The People of God
   - A Temple of the Spirit
   - A sign of the Kingdom
   - Pilgrims on the Paschal Journey
   - Something else...

3. Has the PCC considered how their preferred model(s) of the church can be proclaimed and expressed in its worship?

4. What should the church be proclaiming about its nature and mission by its liturgy and the arrangement of furniture and fittings, with special regard to:

   - Corporate worship and the Eucharist
   - Proclamation of and reflection on the Word of God?
   - The relationship of the members of the community to one another?

- Personal commitment and initiation, especially the sacraments of Baptism and Confirmation?
- Personal growth and the spiritual life?
- The church's ministry in relation to the community?

b) How does the wider community see the church?

Where is the centre of your community?

Is the church seen to be at the centre, or on the outer edges? Have you asked the community what they think?

To outsiders, does the church demand that you belong before you're 'allowed' to enter?

Or is the church so active in its community that it makes the place tick?

c) How do you believe the church should be used?

1. Liturgical
   a) Sunday worship, of a variety of kinds
   b) Weekday worship
   c) the Pastoral Offices, eg weddings, funerals
   d) Special services and events
   e) Personal prayer (how is it to be kept open?)

2. Educational
   a) Workshops, lectures and discussion groups
   b) Drama and music - plays and concerts
   c) Art displays and exhibitions
   d) A place to discover local history

Resources:

- *The Gate of Heaven - how church buildings speak of God* by Nigel Walter (Grove Books, Spirituality Series, S118)
- *The Community Planning Event Manual* by Nick Wates (Earthscan, 2008)

3. Community
   a) as a community gathering space, Parish hall or meeting room
   b) as a Day Centre, for a Lunch Club or other social activity
   c) for a Library, reading room, Post Office, cashpoint or charity shop
   d) for casual visitors - what tourist / cycling / rambling routes are you on?

Activity: Put down your honest thoughts about the status quo. What would it take for this to improve?

3. Where are you heading?

a) Dreaming the future...

1. Bearing in mind all that you have discussed together, in what ways is the present building a help or hindrance to your worship and the Church's mission in the community?

2. Think of consulting the Diocesan Advisory Committee or similar body about your worship or building. Consider arranging a Study Day or a visit to another church.

3. Make a large plan of the church, showing all the attached buildings like vestries and halls, removing all the furnishings and fittings, so that you can see what the spaces are and how they interrelate. Think of a large service with lots of visitors, and a small weekday service, and think about the different ways the space would be used:

- How are people welcomed? Are visitors 'ambushed' with information, or can they find their own way?
- Is the action visible? Can the congregation move, or use different parts of the church at different stages? Where will they sit, for which part(s) of the service, and on what? Check lighting as well as sightlines.
- How is the music led, and accompanied, and by whom and on what?
- Where will the children be, and for which parts of the service?
- How easy is the building to navigate? Can the visitor find the toilet, or the meeting room?
- Consider other Sunday activities - socialising, teaching, study or prayer groups, the ministry of healing - in relationship to what you have put on the plan.

b) Three key principles for delivering change:

- **Narrative**: Understand your (plural) story.
- **Vision**: Understand what you believe God is calling you to be; why should I believe in (and give to) this?
- **Delegation**: Get organised - Who is going to be responsible for what?

c) Conclusion

Only when you have thought through these issues will you be in a position to begin to brief your architect. This process should result in lots of discussion and ideas, but it is helpful if you can summarise your main conclusions in written form - brief bullet points is probably best. By following this process we believe you will make wiser and creative decisions and arrive at an overall plan that is an expression of your ministry, rather than responding to individual issues in an incoherent and piecemeal fashion. Once you have that overall plan, you can then choose how it is to be implemented.

Resources:

- *Re-Pitching the Tent - The definitive guide to re-ordering church buildings for worship and mission* by Richard Giles (Canterbury, 2007)
- **Prayer**...

Some architectural/liturgical principles to guide you

1. Churches are different from our homes - avoid the soft furnishings, potted plants etc
2. All design, including movable fittings, altar ornaments, vestments, etc should be related to the overall plan of the building and its architectural character.
3. Churches are not furniture stores, and should be kept uncluttered; try to dispose of at least as much furniture as you might add (following the appropriate processes).
4. Architectural, liturgical and social needs should be allowed to interact, eg the position of the Font and Altar, but then priorities must be chosen and the reasons made explicit.
5. Churches are often made up of different interconnecting 'rooms'. Use different spaces for distinct functions: lighting can create spaces as can changes in floor texture.
6. Aim for as much open space as possible, flexibility as regards seating and emphasis on the fixed points of key liturgical and mission significance, eg Font, Bible and Altar.

Activity: Dream your future as described above, and then summarise your main conclusions in bullet points...

...'and here are the people!'

Index

access, maintenance 54, 65, 108, 109, 135, 155

accessibility 118, (B19) 149–51, 158n, 282

accreditation, conservation 10

AIDA 202–3

Alkmund, St. 257–9

Alvechurch, St Laurence 288

amenity societies 44, 195, 228, 259, 260, 280

amplification 80–1

annual accounts 19, 20, 34, 140, 212

archaeology 91, 112–3, 120

archdeacon 15–6, 43, 71–2, 268

architect 10, 115, 135, 140, 250

art 190, 301

art history 194–8

asbestos 155

aspic 176

asset management plan 28, 33, (B17) 137–42, 178, 270

audiovisual (AV) (B7) 80–4, 300

Austen, Jane 167

baptistries (B6) 76–9

bats 110, (B14) 123–7, 131

bells 54, 146, 155, 236, 282, 296

benefice 16–7, 44

bishop 40–1, 43, 262

Bodgelt, Mr 24, (B22) 165–7, 256

Bow Common, St Paul 303

breathability 57, 58, 66, 68, 92

brickwork 59

Bridge Sollars, St Andrew 297

Brierley, Peter 37, 38

Brueggemann, Walter 46

buildings at risk (A5) 21–5

business planning 263, 271

cables 83, 107, (B12) 111–16, 156

cake, ministerial 187

Calendar, Church Carer's (B18) 143–8

Cambourne Church 301

Cambridge, St Barnabas 284

Cambridge, St Philip 205, 288

Canon Law 17–19, 20n, 78

Canterbury, St Martin 52

capacity building 221

carpets 68, 89, 167

CDM (Construction (Design and Management) Regulations) (B29) 159–64

cement 54, 58, 61–2, 68, 166

chairs 70, 72–5, 156

Chancellors 44n, 256–8

change 24–5, 36, 75, 176, 195–8, (D1) 217–22, 228, 246, 279

change loop 220

charity status 14, 31, 262, 266

cheese theory 196–7, 198

Chesterton, G. K. 208
Christianity and Culture 209, 227, 279
church anatomy 203–5
Church Building Projects
  (Pizzamat) 239–41, (G2) 320–1
Church Buildings Audit 241–2,
  (G3) 322–9
Church Buildings Council (CBC) 10,
  124–5, 229n, 259–60; see also
  ChurchCare
Church Property Register 7, 20
ChurchCare 10, 91, 110n, 123, 150,
  255, 260; see also Church Buildings
  Council
Churchill, Winston 308
churchwardens 13, 14, 40, 165, 255
churchyards 12–14, 91, 112–13, 115,
  154, 225
clergy (A4) 15–20, 38, 41–3, 255
client (B21) 159–64, (D7) 250–2
closing churches xi, 38, 171
coffee 119, 201, 203
cold (B8) 85–91, 93
community buildings 4, 69, 83, 199,
  205
community consultation 221–2, 226,
  233–5, 243, 248
community use 29, 122, 172, 221,
  (E4) 291–4, 299
compost 122
condensation 66–7, 92–3, 101
consecration 41, 78, 212–13
conservation 10, 23–5, (C6) 193–6, 228
Consistory Court 44n, 256, 257
construction (B2) 55–9, 61, 66, 71
contractor 104–5, 114, 125, (B21) 159–
  64
COSSH (Control of Substances
  Hazardous to Health) Regulations 155
Covey, Stephen 245

Crossing the Threshold 222

Dad's Army 6, 128, 130
damp 64, (B4) 66–8, 89, 122
Davies, J. G. 300
deathwatch beetle 128–9
decay 22–3, (B15) 128–31, 132
defects 23, 133
delamination 56–7
denominations, other 38, 253–5
dentistry 137
Diocesan Advisory Committee (DAC) 43,
  223, 254–5, 256–7
Diocesan Registrar 12, 152, 255, 266,
  268
Diocesan Secretary 8, 272
diocese 37, 40, 43, 44n, 171
Disability Discrimination Act, see Equality
  Act
DIY 105, 133–4, 165, 167, 181–2
domestication 121, 167, 192
downpipes 62, 64
Downshire Hill, St John 284
drains 63, 78, 91, 116, 119–20, 122
dry rot 65, 130, 131
Dudley, St Thomas 87
Duffy, Eamon 189
Durran, Maggie 275n

Eardisley, St Mary Magdalene 298
ecclesiastical exemption 194, (D8) 253–
  60
Ecclesiastical Insurance Group 154,
  158n, 206
Ecclesiologists 88, 293
Einstein, Albert 29, 224
electricity 91, 100, 101, 104, 155
enabling development 273–4, 299–300
Engel, James 201
English Heritage, see Historic England

environment 95–6, 99, 100, 109, 218, 225, 247

Environment Agency 116, 120

environmental health 119, 157

Equality Act 80, 150, 158n, 218

extensions 260, (E3) 286–90

faculties 3, 17, 43, 115, (D8) 253–60

Faculty Jurisdiction Rules 253, 255, 260

Faith in Maintenance 132, 134, 196

fellowship 32

finance 33–5, 178. 251, 263

fire 145, 156, 157, 158

fonts (B6) 76–9

foundations 57

French, Katherine 187, 188

Friends' Groups 30, (D10) 265–9, 272, 299

fundraising 251, (D11) 270–5

galleries 155, 281–2, 295

gas 91, 99, 100, 104

gates 8, 98

Giles, Richard xii, 221, 242, 300

glebe 17, 41, 43

GNOME test 291–2

God club 288; see also private members' religious club

grants 28, 37, 231

Great Wilbraham, St Nicholas 297

Grimthorpe, Lord 195

gulleys, rainwater 57, 63

gutters 60, 62, 64–5, 155

gypsum plaster 57, 68, 89

hall, village/church 4–5, 200–1, 204

Hammersmith , St Paul 289

Hammond, Peter 300, 304n

hat and boots, dry (B3) 60–5, 129

health and safety 141, (B20) 152–8, (B21) 159–164, 263

Healthcheck 238–9, (G1) 315–19

heat loss 94, 100

heat pumps 98, 100, 101

heating 67–8, (B8) 85–91, (B10) 97–102, 283

Hereford, All Saints 293

heritage 43–4, 194–6, (C8) 206–10, 228, (F1) 307–8

heritage cycle 209

Heritage Lottery Fund (HLF) 10, 28, 138, 210, 228, 270

Hexham habits 87

hirers 8

Historic England 39, 52, 194–5, 274

history 179, 196, 248

holiness 78, (C2) 174–7, 187, 191, (C9) 211–13

HSE (Health and Safety Executive) 152, 158n, 164n

Hungerford, Our Lady of Lourdes 303

ICBS (Incorporated Church Building Society) 71, 207, 229

imagination 46–7

impact assessment 113, 114

induction 13, 15, 18

induction loop 83, 151

Inge, John 174–6, 192

Integrated pest management (IPM) 131

interpretation (C8) 206–10, 228

inventory, see Church Property Register

Kemp, Eric 18

KISS 83, 89, 97, 101, 107

kitchens (B13) 117–22, 189, (E5) 295–8

koinonia, see fellowship

lavatories, see WCs

Le Corbusier 197

leases 8

leaven (C9) 211–13
LED lighting 106, 107–8, 155
legal status 17, 40
leisure choice 5, 205
lighting (B11) 103–10, 247, 283
lime 58, 61, 134
lime plaster/render 56, 58, 68, 85, 89, 95, 114
listed buildings 27, 37, 39, 52, 225, 253–5
living churches/buildings 33, 194, 198
Log Book 7, 19, 20, 136, 179
LOLER (Lifting Operations and Lifting Equipment Regulations) 156

maintenance 28, 108–9, (B16) 132–6, 141, (B18) 143–8
maintenance plans 138
making changes (D1) 217–22
McCaig and Ridout 130
Measure 17, 19, 253
MHOR (Manual Handling Operations Regulations) 156
minster model 3, 44
Miracle House, *see* Wickford, Miracle House
Mission Action Plan 221, 230, 236n, 243, 246, 274
Mission-Shaped Church 186
moisture 55, 57, 58, (B4) 66–8, 129, 130
Moment of Truth (C4) 183–5
money 31–2, 165, 269, (D11) 270–5
Morris, William 132, 195–6
Multimedia (B7) 80–4

Nara Document on Authenticity 194
narrative 14, 197–8, 208, 241, 248
National Churches Trust (NCT) 269n, 270

National Trust 3, 206
Natural England 125–7, 131
needs analysis (D5) 243–5
neglect 23–4, 132–3
neighbours 8, 234
new churches (E6) 299–304
New Churches Research Group 304n
new medievalism 6, 46, 204–5, 284
Normans 3, 41, 52–3, 188, 213
Norton juxta Kempsy, St James 289
Nouwen, Henri 271
numbers, church in (A8) 36–9

oil 98, 99, 100, 104, 158
Old Ford, St Paul Old Ford 293
Ordinary Portland cement (OPC), *see* cement
Orton Waterville, St Mary the Virgin 298

paint 68, 100 165–6
Palmer, Martin 188
parish map 231
parish share xi, 29, 32, 33–5
parish system 3, 40–4, 188, 230
Parochial Church Council (PCC) 13, 18–19, 31, 44, 112, 152, 266–9
parsonages and vicarages 16, 17, 41
PAT (Portable Appliance Test) 156
Penton, John 151, 158n
Pevsner guides 52, 207, 226
pews 69–72, 75, 87, 189, 201, 281
pipes 102, (B11) 111–16
Pizzamat (Church Building Projects) 239–41, (G2) 320–1
Plymouth, St Peter 283
pointing 54, 58, 61, 63
Prince's Regeneration Trust 229n, 270
private members' religious club 4–5, 14, 181, 199, 201, 301
property records 7, 19, 140

PUWER (Provision and Use of Work Equipment Regulations) 156

quinquennial inspection (QI) 10, 34, 137
quinquennial inspection report (QIR) 20, 33, 38, 136, 137, 178

rainwater goods (B3) 60, 62–5, 140
re-ordering 52, 192, 221, 260, (E2) 281–5
redecorating 100, 126
relative humidity 67
renewables 88, 101
repairs 19, 23, 37, 132–3, 140, 272
retail 3, 46, 172, 183–4, 200–2
Riddell, Michael 184
RIDDOR (Reporting of Injuries, Diseases and Dangerous Occurrences Regulations) 157
Riegl, Alois 194
Roman cement 61
roofs 60, 62, 64, 85, 92–3, 126, 287

St Albans Cathedral 195
St Alkmund judgement 257–8
St Elmo Lewis, Elias 202
sandwiches (B2) 55–9
seating (B5) 69–75, 189, 281
security 29, 46
sewerage, see drains
'Shrinking the Footprint' 94, 109
Society for the Protection of Ancient Buildings (SPAB) 10, 65, 96, 132, 134, 136, 195–6
sponges 67
staffing 162, 247, 262–3
stakeholders 25, 27, 259–60
Statement of Needs 142, 219, 223, (D6) 246–9, 259

Statement of Significance 115, 195, 219, (D2) 223–9, 246–7, 248, 259
statistics (A8) 36–9, 231
steering group (D7) 250–2
stonework 52, 53, 55–6, 61, 115
Street and Cuthbert 219, 243
surplus and profit 9
sustainability (of church) 34–5, 138, 178
Synod 17, 19, 40

Taylor, Richard 52
Temple, William 230
Temple Hill, St Edmund King and Martyr 302
Terrier, see Church Property Register
theology xiii, (C2) 174–7, 187, 204, 213
Thomas, R. S. 176
timber 71, 121, (B15) 128–31, 166
tourists 79, 209
traditional construction 51, 54, 57, 61, 66
traffic lights 34
trench arch drain 120, 122n

underfloor heating 94, 99, 100, 102
users (of church buildings) 9, 89, 141, 235

VAT 263, 275
vesting 12–14, 17, 19, 272
viability (A7) 31–5, 257, 273, 274
Victorians 46, 65, 70, 95, 134, 200, 282
vision 236n, 243, 247, 249, 263–4, 271
visitors 81, 152, (C6) 206–10, 228, 291

wall plate 121, 143, 147
Warren, Robert 35, 221
water 56–7, 60–5, 66, 76–7
water ingress 56–7, 60–1, 64, 65, 141; see also damp

WCs 115, (B13) 117–22, 189, (E5) 295–8
welcome xi–xiv, 26, 70, 73, 157, (C7) 199–205
Wentworth, St Peter 294
wheelchairs 118, 150, 158, 233
Wickford, Miracle House 302
Wilmington, St Michael & All Angels 285
windfalls 274–5
withdrawal 5, 171, 212

Withington, St Michael and All Angels 88
'Witi' (Why is that important?) 248–9
woodworm 71, 128–30
World Heritage Sites 37
worship 46, 81, 104, 175, 186–7, 203
Wortham, St Mary 75
Wymondham Abbey 290

Yarpole, St Leonard 294